THE
UNITED CHURCH
OF CHRIST

The

United Church

of Christ

Its Origins, Organization, and
Role in the World Today

BY

DOUGLAS HORTON

THOMAS NELSON & SONS
Edinburgh   NEW YORK   Toronto

TO THE GLORY OF GOD
AND IN GRATITUDE TO THE MEN AND WOMEN
WHOSE FORESIGHT, CONSECRATION, AND PATIENCE
MADE POSSIBLE THE UNITED CHURCH OF CHRIST

CONTENTS

I	An Introduction	11
II	Constitution	13
III	Fundamental Characteristics of the United Church	42
IV	The Sacraments	88
V	Unity and Diversity	98
VI	Naming a Church	108
VII	General Organization	112
VIII	The Office Bearers	113
IX	The Importance of the Congregation	117
X	The Ministers of the United Church	138
XI	State and County Groups	168
XII	The National Body	177
XIII	The Arms of the Church	193
XIV	The Board for World Ministries	196
XV	The Board for Homeland Ministries	226
XVI	Christian Social Action	254
XVII	A Church of Laymen and Laywomen	261
XVIII	The Past is Prelude	272
XIX	And So, Good Reader . . .	278
	BIBLIOGRAPHY	281
	INDEX	283

THE
UNITED CHURCH
OF CHRIST

AN INTRODUCTION

IN ORDER TO EXPLAIN WHY I AM A UNITED CHURCHMAN, it is necessary for me first to introduce my readers to the United Church of Christ. This I do with unstinted pleasure, with the hope that the introduction itself will serve to make the explanation for me, indicating the features of that church which draw me to it.

As you will note, when I speak of myself as a United Churchman I mean that I am a member of the United Church of Christ, an American communion which came into corporate being in 1957. The name had been chosen in 1943. There are several other united churches. The best known under that name is the United Church of Canada; the Church of South India is a church which unites several communions; and there are others. The National Council of the Churches of Christ in the U.S.A. has a General Department of United Church Men and a General Department of United Church Women. When I designate myself a United Churchman, I mean simply that I am a member of the United Church of Christ in the United States.

Asking myself how best to introduce you to the United Church, I have concluded that there can be no better way than to lay before you its written Constitution and comment upon it paragraph by paragraph. This will provide against my leaving lacunae in my narrative, for the Constitution, though brief, is inclusive. This will also tend (I dimly hope) to hold me in restraint when I come to describe the parts of the church which are my particular enthusiasms, and so will lend balance and proportion to the book.

That Constitution, when seen in the right light, is a most engaging document: colors appear, as in an opal, that are not necessarily evident as it lies casually in your hand. The colors here are brought out by light from the long history of the Christian Church: the Constitution sets forth in concrete form general principles wrought out by the past and here organized into an instrument for the future. I remember a description of Petrarch poring in ecstasy over a manuscript of Homer, his emotions welling up from his sense of living in two worlds, the spacious world of classical Greece and the then-dawning world of the Renaissance between which the manuscript served as a bridge. The Constitution of the United Church of Christ is something like that: it reflects a Christianity (to borrow an idea from St. Augustine) that is as old as creation, but it points a way for the United Church of Christ to take today as it moves into the broadening future. It therefore has in it the lights of excitement that invariably accompany an encounter between old and new. It is seasoned wisdom in a courageous mood.

CHAPTER II

CONSTITUTION

CONSTITUTION—THE VERY TITLE OF THE DOCUMENT BRINGS US
into the midst of historical tension. The United Church of
Christ arises from the forging together of two Christian traditions, the Congregational Christian and the Evangelical and
Reformed. The former derives from England and the English
way of looking at things, the latter from the Continent of
Europe and Continental ways—and England and the Continent have each had their own way of looking at a constitution.

It was almost to be expected that churches with an English
ancestry would be found living without a written constitution
—and that was indeed the case of the Congregational Christian group. As is well known, there is no single document to
which an English barrister may refer as the English "constitution," as American lawyers arguing before the Supreme Court
of the United States may, and do constantly, refer to the
American Constitution. If there is any constitution to be
spoken of in England, it is the entire ensemble of common
law, statute law, and conventional usage.

So it was with the Congregational Christian fellowship. To
be sure there was a constitution for its General Council, which
was (and is) the national body composed of delegates from
the Conferences, which were (and are) the state bodies.

Each one of these Conferences had its constitution, too; so did the smaller bodies, roughly coterminous with counties, called "Associations"; and so did every one of the fifty-five hundred churches. There were plenty of constitutions but there was no Constitution—no single instrument setting forth the fundamental principles of the common life and ratified by all. The constitutions were linked with each other: that of the General Council referred to the Conferences, those of the Conferences to the Associations, those of the Associations to the churches, and vice versa. This reciprocal reference supplied the connection which held the parts together, but there was no one master paper to govern all. The constitutions therefore afforded the protection rather of chain mail than of one-piece armor.

It had not always been so. The first ecclesiastical constitution to see the light in America had been the creation of Congregational Churches: the Cambridge Platform, which took shape as a result of debates at the Cambridge Synod of 1646 to 1648, had governed the destinies of Congregationalism for generations. John Wise half a century after its adoption had hailed it as a bulwark of Christian liberties, and as late as the first years of the nineteenth century it supplied precedent in Massachusetts and Connecticut. But with the separation of church and state in those two states, the break between Trinitarians and Unitarians, and the growing distrust of the Deacon's One Hoss Shay, as Holmes named the rigid Calvinism of the eighteenth century, it lost its power, and no attempt was made to supplant it with a more modern document. Habit, buttressed by state ecclesiastical law, could take the place of a written constitution for the church. Certain things were done, others not done: orderly procedures provided an unwritten constitution, which was quite as effective, under the circumstances, as a written one. The churches settled back on their ample traditions of procedure and muddled through in typically English fashion, with satisfaction to themselves and not without success, until the mid-twentieth century.

In the Evangelical and Reformed Church the situation was different. The members of this church had had their origins in the old countries of Europe, where there had been little more need for comprehensive constitutions of national churches than there had been in Massachusetts and Connecticut; but when they settled in America, where the thirteen original colonies themselves had united under a written constitution, they found it natural to utilize for their own church government the same type of instrument that set forth their freedoms and responsibilities under the national government. By the end of the eighteenth century, thanks largely to the leading examples of the United States and the French Republic, constitutions had become associated with liberty and the outlook toward the future. More than that, the two bodies that had united to become the Evangelical and Reformed Church—the Evangelical Synod and the Reformed Church of the United States—had been so nearly the same size that neither could automatically fall in with the precedent of the other. A Plan of Union, which was itself a provisional constitution, had formally united them, and in it there had been promise of a full-scale constitution, the formulation of which had become the first task of that united church.

The Congregational Christian Churches also represented the joining of two bodies—the Congregational Churches and the "Christian" Church—but the former were so much larger than the latter that all that was needed for the union was a temporary set of articles of agreement, after mutual assent to which the two groups fell readily into step under the unwritten constitution of the larger one.

A society under a written constitution does not differ from one without such an instrument as much as might be popularly supposed. As already suggested, there were (and are) written elements in the governmental framework of the

Congregational Churches, as there are written laws and codifications of law in England, though no over-all written constitution exists in either. This is the case in any literate society that owns no single constitution. But the opposite is true: in any society which utilizes a single written constitution there are unwritten laws and other written laws that are not incorporated in the document. The Constitution of the United States, for example, points beyond itself to our common law: it mentions "treason" and "trial by jury," for instance, without defining either. For the definition it is necessary to consult precedent outside. And so it is with any written constitution: all that it can do is to gather together the basic principles under which the common life is to be lived; it cannot cover the whole of that life. Societies governed completely by written constitutions and those societies completely without the elements of written constitutions do not exist in the civilized world: the two systems overlap.

One of the problems at the time of negotiating for the union which became the United Church of Christ, however, was to devise a scheme whereby a denomination used to no over-all constitution whatever could join forces with one to which a written constitution seemed the veritable backbone of orderly procedure. That the problem was not as formidable as might have been expected was due not only to the general consideration just mentioned but specifically to the fact that the Evangelical and Reformed brethren on the one hand were well aware of the dangers of that kind of "constitutionalism" which elevates written law to the position of an idol, and the Congregational Christians, on the other hand, were already beginning to feel bad effects from the looseness of their association. What was finally done was to set forth a constitution in writing (in the Evangelical and Reformed mode) but to make it lithe and supple enough for all (even Congregational Christians used only to unwritten custom). It is that Constitution, now duly ratified by both parties, which serves as a guide for us in this book.

The Constitution of the United Church of Christ begins with a

PREAMBLE

The United Church of Christ, formed June 25, 1957, by the union of the Evangelical and Reformed Church and The General Council of the Congregational Christian Churches of the United States. . . .

Comment upon this first clause of the Preamble might in itself be expanded to the dimensions of a book, but let me make only three observations: first, a somewhat extended comment on the union negotiations which brought the United Church of Christ into being; second, a brief reference to an interesting legal feature; and third, a word as to the recent history of the branches of the church which formed the new communion.

The Promise and Pitfalls of Church Union Negotiations

"Formed June 25, 1957," is the phrase used in the Constitution. It refers to the assembly which was held in Cleveland, Ohio. This meeting will live long in the memory of those who were present. The air was electric with a sense of great event, for all knew that there had never been a meeting just like it in the history of the Christian Church in this country. Representatives not merely of two parts of a single church family—Congregationalists and Congregationalists, for instance, Presbyterians and Presbyterians, or Episcopalians and Episcopalians—but of two different church families, people of Congregational and people of Presbyterial background, the one stemming ancestrally from Great Britain, the other from the Continent, about a million and a quarter of the former, about three quarters of a million of the latter, on that occasion declared themselves members of one communion.

The numbers involved in the conjoining of the Congregational Christian and the Evangelical and Reformed bodies are comparable to the population of the original thirteen colonies which by union became the United States of America. If to the two million communicant members of the two uniting groups were added the baptized but noncommunicant children and the adult members of the parishes not members of the churches, the grand total would probably be brought to between three and four million, which is not far from the corresponding total of the citizens of the United States in 1776.

The negotiations looking toward uniting these numbers into one communion were simple enough in essence. A document called "The Basis of Union" had been prepared, which outlined both the procedures to be followed in securing the union and the principles on which the union would be based. This had been circulated throughout each denomination so that improvements might be suggested. The suggestions coming from the churches had then been considered by the negotiating committee and the text sent out again in its improved form to the two denominations. This process had been repeated time and again in the course of several years until a generally accepted document, which included a set of "Interpretations," was in hand. When the two denominations independently had given their official acceptance to this, the way was prepared for the uniting meeting of 1957.

How many years of eagerness and agony lay behind that meeting! All denominations talk about the reunion of Christendom, but talk is inexpensive; for those who enter into the practical business of effecting a union the need for imagination, initiative, patience, and sacrifice of pride is almost infinite. The minutes of the negotiations referred to are available for those who will read them, but the hours of thought that surrounded the negotiations no one can compute or recapture. Christian groups can be separated with comparative ease, as the melancholy number of them in America attests; they can even fall apart from indifference to each other; but they cannot be brought through the long marches toward union, as all know who have made the attempt, without dedication of a peculiar kind. If it is the mind of Christ that there be unity in his church—and all acknowledge that it is—one mark of contemporary sainthood in a denomination is surely its ability to conceive and accomplish an act of church union.

But there are others besides saints in any branch of the church. The church is partly human, partly divine, and it is the human element that makes church union at once so fascinating and so difficult a problem. The church is divine because it is informed by the real presence of Jesus Christ. He is the soul of it; the closer one gets to its center, the closer one gets to him. Where he has no influence in the hearts of the worshipers, the church is dead. He is the point at which the church comes into touch with God, for God as the church knows him is not the god of the animist, nor of the Buddhist, nor of the Confucianist, but the God and Father of our Lord Jesus Christ. The church, however, is also human and it is human not only in the noblest but in the basest sense. Some of the cruelest and most sanguinary wars of history have been, as we know, church wars. Church dignitaries have been part and parcel of the most fiendish and indefensible political shifts in the world, and though today a milder manner has come over us, the church is still—and while it is of this world will be—filled with what we popularly call "politics." Our hope is for good rather than bad politics—but of politics as such the church in this dispensation will never rid itself. It is this necessity for treating the church, on its earthly side, as the political institution it is that colors every history of church union. When now I mention some of the road blocks encountered and detours necessitated in the establishing of the United Church of Christ, it is for the sake of imparting courage to others whose minds are lighted by a like dream: saints they must be but it does not follow that they must be feeble politicians.

It used often to be said that theological differences keep churches apart. Even the great Archbishop Söderblom, who had so much to do with launching the world-wide ecumenical movement as we know it today, held that practical needs unite while theology separates. The experiences of the Faith and Order Commission of the World Council of Churches disprove this thesis: it has been discovered and redemonstrated again and again in the theological study groups set up by that commission that when theologians make a common enquiry into some Biblical or doctrinal truth—say, the meaning of the Holy Trinity or of the Incarnation—though their several points of departure may be poles apart they tend in a manner really spectacular to achieve community of thought. This is one of the points of brightest hope in the ecumenical movement. There is little of basic difference in the purely theological thought of Congregationalists, Presbyterians, and Episcopalians. It is not to be expected, therefore, that variations in theological emphasis will in the long run prove an obstacle to church union; but, obversely, similarity in the theological doctrines held by two different denominations does not necessarily imply that they will find it easy to get together. We are separated by more than basic belief.

For one thing, denominations contemplating union need to come to know, to understand, and finally to appreciate each other in the apparently untheological human category of cultural customs. In every proposed church union, sociological forces pent in the group mind come out. In the union of the Congregational Christian with the Evangelical and Reformed Churches, the New England boiled dinner and Pennsylvania sauerkraut had to come to terms with each other: the culinary differences had their place with the theological. Perhaps it would be truer to say that in the emotional warmth which attends a union, cultural and theological differences melt together into a mélange, and even incidental manners of living are felt by the thoughtless to reveal deep spiritual tendencies. Some of the Evangelical and Reformed leaders, for instance, were cigar smokers—and smokers of cigars plainly have not the spiritual sensitivity (thought some) of the smokers of cigarettes! Some of the Congregational leaders were from Boston and the State of Maine—and a down-East accent is clear proof of provincialism! In the midst of this kind of nonsense there is no substitute for good hard common sense, of which there is never too much to go around, even in ecclesiastical circles. Situations of this sort call for the treatment that any good politician would give them; narrowness has to be laughed out of court or argued out in the cause of church union as in any other enterprise.

Even human loyalties, which are the best of virtues, bedeviled us—proving once more that there is no evil so obdurate as the corruption of the good. "We" and "they" were pronouns that came to have the status of generals, each marshaling his army behind him, everything good being found under the *we* banner, the bad or suspect or grudgingly conceded to be good usually to be discovered over *there* with *them*. *We*, after all, are the old churches of New England (or Pennsylvania); *they* are not our kind. Approaches to church union provide a field day for the social psychologist. On its divine side the church overrides the societies of men as the sun overrides the nations, but on its human side it partakes severally of the societies from which it draws its people; it is both in and of them. So, we have the Church of England, the Church of Sweden, and other "national" churches which are an amalgam of Christianity and nationality; and in the United States of America we have churches which, instead of the high-sounding Christian names by which they call themselves, might well be called "The Church of the Exclusive Social Set" or "The Church of the Upper Middle Class" or "The Church of the Tradesmen and Artisans" or given some other title drawn from the social make-up of the adherents. The Christian element in the church constantly tries to break down the barriers that divide class from class, but the battle is never wholly won. In a union it is necessary to fight hard, and the achievement of union is a token of victory, on this dim and difficult terrain. In the union of the Evangelical and Reformed with the Congregational Christian communion, it was not a matter of combining a well-defined class with another equally well-defined class but of bringing together two different styles of ecclesiastical-social life; one deriving from centuries of history on the Continent of Europe, the other from a like number of centuries in Britain.

The mythology that one denomination may have built up about the other has to be swept away in the course of preparation for union. The images of other communions that each communion allows to grow up within it are still one of the unhappiest features of our interdenominational life. Thanks to the witch hangings in Salem Village for seven months in 1692, the Congregational Churches descended from the Mathers and the Cottons are sometimes pictured as being stark devotees of intolerance. Because Archbishop Laud, over three centuries ago, believed that he could obliterate opposition to the plans for church and nation which he and the king espoused by the mere exercise of power, all Anglican bishops since have been believed by many to have motives secretly despotic. And when Presbyterians are accused by some of being Calvinistic, the adjective means in the minds of their critics not so much that they are the spiritual offspring of one of the most creative religious geniuses the world has ever known as that they are so closely bound to the letter of a theological system that they too—after four hundred years—would vote for having Servetus burned if his thinking seemed to compromise The Faith. Denominations change—in America rapidly—and it is unsafe to judge any of them by what we knew of them even yesterday; in enterprises of church union there is no substitute for the contemporary fact. Images from the past are likely to be false images that do not take into consideration the factor of inner evolution within the communions, but because they are mere images they are not for that reason easier to dislodge from the minds of the various communions; on the whole it is easier to exterminate flesh and blood than it is to exorcise a ghost. These ghosts are, for church union, as potent as banshees, and unless they are laid by education in understanding they will perfectly prophesy the death of the project. The Congregational Christian and the Evangelical and Reformed Churches had to take a long time to learn the facts about each other wherewith to displace the fancies.

Each church in a proposed union has to learn the ecclesiastical language of the other; they may both speak English, to be sure, but through the preceding generations particular words and phrases become weighted with meanings which differ in the two groups. In the negotiations that led to the establishment of the United Church of Christ, for instance, the word *synod* had particularly frightening implications for the Congregationalists. It is true that it was a word that had been used without necessarily sinister meaning throughout the history of the Christian Church and that it had been the word employed by the Congregational Fathers of New England for their own gatherings, such as the Cambridge Synod of 1646–8 and the Saybrook Synod of 1708; but nonetheless—and partly because the latter synod at Saybrook had passed authoritarian legislation—Congregationalists had come to associate synods with ecclesiastical tyranny. Dimly remembering the Synod of Rome of 1413 (which condemned

Wycliffe) and the Synod of Dort (where Orthodox Calvinism quashed the Arminian case), Congregationalists had to gulp more than once before swallowing the idea of naming the ranking body of the new United Church, the General Synod. On the contrary, the Evangelical and Reformed constituents of the United Church had as precedents for their happy use of the term, the Synod of Rome of 1059 (which had given orderliness to the election of the Pope); the Synod of Homberg (which had stood for the autonomy of the local church); and, most of all, the Evangelical Synod itself, which, after long years of independent growth, had united with the Reformed Church in the United States to become the Evangelical and Reformed Church. And "synod" was only one of scores of words which had to be redefined on each side. Long talks had to take place between the two uniting bodies before they understood the hidden meanings behind the key words each other used; and this understanding had to be established not only among the negotiators at the national level but through all the congregations up and down the land.

The making of the American nation, already referred to, was a colossal task that was not finished in the eighteenth century, as the Civil War, or War Between the States, proved; and the United Church of Christ had its own war of this type, too, but it came not after the union had been effected but before, in the days of negotiation. It was not a war of violence, but feelings ran high, and on the same grounds as in the political combat; Congregational Christian dissidents thought that their state's rights or local freedoms were to be jeopardized by the union.

A spate of pamphlets appeared, some criticizing, some defending the negotiators of the union and their work. At times animosity overcame the mood of reasonableness, but not often, and never in the steadier heads on either side. The spiritual and intellectual battles of the church are unhappy affairs at best, and usually fought, as this one was, on the field of convictions dearly held; but the scars from this one, because they had not been unduly exacerbated by personal recriminations, were in the main curable, except in the extremists.

That the healing process will go on in the future may be argued from a comparison of the vote on the Constitution of the United States of America in 1787–8 with that on the United Church Constitution in 1961. It is impracticable to compare the votes at the town level, but those at the state level are illuminating. Even here an exact comparison is impossible, but it is noteworthy that a majority of the churches voting in all thirty-five of the Congregational Christian Conferences approved the Constitution of the United Church, as did thirty-two of the thirty-three Synods of the Evangelical and Reformed Church. The vote on the Constitution of the United States was roughly comparable, though not quite so overwhelming; that instrument was put into effect after eleven of the thirteen colonies had ratified it, but the twelfth and thirteenth entered the union only eight and fourteen months thereafter. The contrast is greatest in the intrastate vote: the divisions within the largest Congregational Christion Conferences were—Massachusetts, 415 churches for, 39 against; Connecticut, 215 for, 20 against; Illinois, 190 for, 22 against. Those within the largest Evangelical and Reformed Synods were—North Illinois, 212 for, 39 against; Reading, 115 for, 5 against; South Indiana, 156 for, 38 against. In comparison to these the votes in the largest colonies were relatively close: Virginia 89 to 79, Pennsylvania 43 to 23, Massachusetts 187 to 168. If then, in spite of these narrow margins, the United States could rise to unified self-consciousness, there is every prospect that the future of the United Church of Christ has not been imperiled by its less equal divisions during the time of negotiations.

That was a time, however, which tried men's hearts, largely

because the tension on the Congregational Christian side broke into litigation. For several years—from 1950 to 1953 inclusive—the church was forced into the unhappy role of making its plea in the secular courts of New York State. A group of Congregational Christians brought suit against the Moderator of the General Council of the Congregational Christian Churches and asked for an injunction arresting the whole advance of the union. They pictured the denomination as having such a structure that it could not enter into a union with any other group without the consent of every one of its over five thousand congregations. Those who know the individualistic nature of Congregationalism, with its insistence on freedom of thought within the bounds of loyalty to Christ, will recognize that such a restriction would have frozen the denomination into its contemporary forms in perpetuity—and it a denomination that prided itself on its creative and adjustable character!

During the litigation it was necessary not only to bring the negotiations to a close but for the leaders and organizations within the two denominations to take care to avoid contact with each other lest the court might be led to believe that its judgment was not being awaited.

When, therefore, the highest court in the state finally declared against those who had made complaint, the picking up of the broken threads between the two denominations was even more delicate a task than the original process of cultivating mutual acquaintance had been, for now there was less sense of pioneering and all too bitter evidence of the storms that would beset the journey. It was gravely questioned whether the interest in the union had not grown too cold on each side to be revived. The Evangelical and Reformed Church had surely been given ground for believing that litigious personalities in the other group would not cease from their strategy, and that the union even if consummated would be attended by lawsuits and all the unpleasantnesses that accompany them. There were new faces in the committees of both denominations; the camaraderie that had been developed by the negotiators in previous years was gone. No one can depict the apprehension of those days in the minds of those who stood for the union, when it could not be told whether the union would survive or not.

More than once, when the union was being negotiated, the hope for its success hung on a thread of gossamer. There came the time, for instance, when the Congregational Christians were convinced that the Evangelical and Reformed Church was ready to withdraw, and the Evangelical and Reformed leaders believed the same of the Congregational Christians. After several hours of discussion at a joint meeting at which many were heard who took counsel of their fears, a short devotional address was given by the Reverend Ben M. Herbster of Zion Evangelical and Reformed Church in Norwood, Ohio, in which, in a simple and moving way, he stressed one point, one single point—but the cardinal point: What, he asked, is the mind of Christ about this union? Granted that mountains have been heaped upon mountains to obstruct our way, making the sum of difficulties ahead of us seem almost insurmountable, the question for us to ask is not: Is the way rocky? Is the going likely to be rough? Is the process longer than we had anticipated? Is it even painful? Questions of this sort, he pointed out, simply have nothing to do with the case. The only matter we have to consider is whether the proposed union is according to the mind of Christ. This was the turning point: a subcommittee found the courage to report out a recommendation to proceed, for none doubted that union rather than division represented the mind of him who had had his own *via dolorosa*. The whole joint committee, now looking at the matter from a viewpoint higher than that of expediency, accepted the recommendation—and began again its long, slow, unspectacular work. So the expanding will to unite, running like widening ripples on the surface of a pool from this center to the farthest congregations of the two communions, presently assured the consummation of the union. The remembrance of this rescue from a defeat considered almost certain by most of those concerned—a rescue occasioned entirely by a reorientation to Christ—put iron in the arteries of committees facing similar crises subsequently. (It is a pleasure to record that years later Dr. Herbster became the first president of the United Church of Christ.)

But to continue our catalogue of hurdles to be crossed in any process of church union—one of the sighs most often heard in such a period is to the effect that the time is not ripe. It is reminiscent of St. Augustine's "Make me a Christian, Lord, but not just yet." Even when the tide in the affairs of men is at the flood, the fainthearted have difficulty feeling it. They ask for gradualness, which is the respectable name for delay. As an offset to this kind of conservatism, which is the more impenetrable for being honest, there is need for a few unmanageable saints who by their very belief create the tide. No union can be effected if there be a dearth of such souls.

It is this same kind of soul that keeps the vision of union incandescent. One of the most invincible deterrents to a proposed union is the necessary machinery of negotiation. The minutes of innumerable committee meetings are tiresome to keep and grow tiresome to read. And there is work to be done beyond the committee rooms: keeping the public informed within the negotiating churches calls for unsleeping attention—for the union will fail if the people of the churches feel that they have had no hand in its making and that it is, at the last, foisted upon them. Communication to that public is made mountainously difficult if there is a group that believes it is its duty to prevent the union if possible. Such a group, in the case of the forming of the United Church, gave interpretations of committee actions and general situations which from the point of view of the negotiators were tragic *mis*interpretations, but they were spread far and wide. Through all of these hindrances uniting churches have to make their way; and through them all there is only one means of keeping on course and not wrecking the undertaking—the maintaining of the vision of the final end, sustained by the faith that this is what God desires for his people.

This is the prime necessity for the leaders, who have to deal with a thousand details, some of them actually irrelevant and needing attention only because they seem relevant to some: if they do not have the flame of the ideal burning bright in their minds, the enterprise will languish. Many, if not most, unions have failed because of the lukewarmness of the leaders; the bishops and the superintendents, the archdeacons and the executives of ecclesiastical boards who enjoy the security of permanent status, can hardly welcome the uncertainty that union reorganizations lay upon their shoulders—unless the vision of the great end dominates. But it is not the leaders only, it is the whole people who must believe that the union is essentially right, for leaders and people divided can accomplish nothing in this adventure. It is the common apprehension of Christ's desire that keeps them together.

Given all these obstructions to union, some of them as real as boulders or washouts on a mountain road, some of them real only in the sense that hobgoblins of the woods are real, being a source of real fear to the timid, it is a witness to the spiritual vigor of a church that it is able to march ahead to actual union. Some local churches have united because circumstances virtually forced them to, both having gone down in membership and financial support until the only hope of each was to pool resources and reduce expenses. No such contingency haunted either the Evangelical and Reformed Church or the Congregational Christians: both were growing in numbers and properties. Each, however, felt the pain of division in face of Christ's prayer that his people all should be one; it was to alleviate that pain, or some of it, that they began the conversations which led to union. It took nineteen years, in face of all difficulties, to effect the establishment of the United Church of Christ, but it was finally accomplished, and there is every expectation that the qualities which assured the achievement will accompany the new communion into the future.

The Shadow of the Law

When the two communions started their negotiations looking toward union they used the language of ordinary conversation and were not as conscious as the subsequent litigation compelled them to be of the demand of the law for nicely accurate language. The first Basis of Union, for instance, speaks of "a union of the Congregational Christian Churches and the Evangelical and Reformed Church." This was what the two groups desired—a complete mutual marriage. But the words of the Constitution—"the union of the Evangelical and Reformed Church and The General Council of the Congregational Christian Churches"—are different. On the Congregational Christian side, not the Congregational Christian Churches as such but only their national body, the General Council, was a primary party to the union.

This leads to the reflection that there exists a legal world as well as the world which most of us know and live in, and that though the former closely resembles the latter, it is only one aspect of it. It is far more accurate in its detailed expressions, but it is not so ample; it is a fine photograph that brings out definition but does not take in all the perspectives.

The church belongs to the real world and though parts of it—its properties and fiduciary relationships, for instance—belong to the legal world as well, there are other parts that do not. It came as quite a shock to me to discover in the course

of the litigation that the Church of Jesus Christ as a totality
has no legal existence. It cannot sue or be sued. In the Commonwealth of Pennsylvania, a generation ago, a farmer in a
carefully drawn will left his land to "Jesus Christ." Here is a
name which, like that of the total Church of Jesus Christ, is
often heard from the pulpits of a Sunday morning, and there
it stands for an actuality in human life; but in a court of law
it can hardly be said to have any meaning at all. In the Pennsylvania instance the local authorities acted according to
good legal norms, giving all concerned the benefit of possibility: they advertised for the heir and when he did not
appear and claim his property they sold it for taxes. If the
farmer had wanted his property to go to the cause of Jesus
Christ or some part of it, he would have been better advised
to consult a good lawyer who would have made it clear to
him that in order to avail oneself of legal rights it is necessary
to act within the framework of the law. Mystical relationships, such as some of those within the church; relations of
friendship, such as those which are often made the theme of
poetry—these are not easily handled by the law.

On the other hand—and this is the point where our Constitution is brought into consideration—if and when a matter
does come within the context of the law, it is necessary to
make it conform to the law. In the United States the law of
the land does not impose itself upon the law of the church in
general; it accepts for the churches the law which they impose upon themselves. It judges the Presbyterian Church
according to Presbyterian Church law, a Congregational
Church according to its own church law, and so on; and any
church can bring itself under the law of the land by organizing and legislating for itself. The reason the Church of Jesus
Christ as a whole could not bring itself under the law, even
if it should wish to, is because it is unorganized and at the
moment unorganizable—and it would be hard, certainly, to
make Jesus Christ a part of a legal organization. The reason

the Congregational Christian Churches as such could not be a party to the union was because they had not provided for themselves any law to this end that could be recognized by themselves and the state.

The two bodies—the Evangelical and Reformed Church and the fellowship of the Congregational Christian Churches wanted to get together. They wanted a real union with all the richness and strength of a close-knit and well-organized family. This was to be no Hollywood type of marriage which today is and tomorrow is cast into the divorce court because it is essentially superficial; it was to be a marriage in every dimension, the uniting of a whole to a whole. And they wanted a legal as well as a spiritual union. As the papers preliminary to the consolidation plainly stated, it was to be the two fellowships, "the Congregational Christian Churches and the Evangelical and Reformed Church . . . uniting without break in their respective historic continuities." The latter phrase, as we shall see, is repeated in the Constitution itself— but, alas, the Congregational Christian fellowship had never organized itself as such and so had no legal existence. According to the law it belonged as much to the realm of faërie as the Church of Jesus Christ itself. It is true that the fellowship was real enough according to ordinary standards. Innumerable men and women had lived for it; some had died for it— but you could not sue it, and so it was outside the orbit of the law. In order, therefore, not to have the plan for union suffer the fate of the Pennsylvania farmer's bequest and be dissipated for want of legal support, the best legal aid was sought and the wording of the Constitution cast in the form we have quoted.

Here a first difference between the two uniting bodies is to be noted. The Evangelical and Reformed Church could be a party to a legal union because, like an ordinary Presbyterian Church, it could act as a unit before the law. It had a constitution in which all parts of the church had committed to the General Synod (the national body) the power, if supported by two-thirds of the constituent local synods, to effect a union in the name and on behalf of the whole church. The Congregational Christian Churches, on the other hand, though they might have built up such an organization, never had. The General Council was a legal entity and so was each individual church: they could therefore act in their own names but they were legally powerless to act together. In consequence and with the desire to have the union completely within the law, it was decided that the General Council should take the first step which should bring the union into being and provide a way for the churches to follow. The phraseology of the Constitution is legally accurate: the United Church of Christ was indeed brought into being by the Evangelical and Reformed Church and only the General Council of the other uniting group, but one would misunderstand the union completely if he regarded these as the two parties which finally formed it: the Congregational Christian Churches following their General Council have surrounded the latter with their combined powers, and the United Church of Christ in its finality is a union of communion with communion.

The Recent Centuries of the Uniting Communions

The Constitution reads that the United Church of Christ was formed by the union of the Evangelical and Reformed Church and (to paraphrase) by Congregational Christian Churches acting through their General Council. Just what was the Evangelical and Reformed Church, and what were the Congregational Christian Churches? Before we get through, I shall point out that, together with all other Christian communions, these had their beginnings centuries upon centuries ago, but for the sake of identifying them today it is not necessary to go back so far.

The Evangelical and Reformed Church, as may be guessed from the *and* in the name, was itself a communion that had come into being as a result of a previous union. The two communions that had formed it were the Evangelical Synod of North America and the Reformed Church in the United States, each one of which had had a notable independent history until they united their forces in 1934.

The Reformed Church stemmed directly from the Protestant Reformation of the early sixteenth century, and owed its character not a little to the mighty John Calvin of Geneva and the other thinkers and churchmen who surrounded and immediately succeeded him, carrying the Reformation into southwestern Germany. It may be said that the Reformed Church in the United States was that part of the German-speaking church in Europe which accepted the Calvinistic reformation and in the eighteenth century (200 years later) removed to the country that was to become the United States of America. Their local churches in Europe did not cross the Atlantic as churches, but individuals, who themselves were good Reformed Churchmen, having arrived in this country, got together and established new local churches; and the new churches here and the old churches there recognized each other. Recognition came specifically through the Reformed Church of the Netherlands. The newcomers to this country brought with them Reformed hymnals, Reformed prayer books, and the Heidelberg Catechism. A devout schoolteacher, John Philip Boehm, in 1725 conducted the first communion service of what was to become the Reformed Church in the United States. This was at Falkner Swamp, a farming community forty miles north of Philadelphia, Pennsylvania. Later in that century the scattered churches were bound together into a denominational fellowship and, in 1793, became completely independent of aid from Europe. Early in the twentieth century, English supplanted German as the language of worship.

This is the church that established Mercersburg Academy, Franklin and Marshall College, and Lancaster Theological Seminary—to name only the oldest and best known of its institutions of learning.

The Evangelical Synod of North America (the other part of the Evangelical and Reformed Church) had its beginnings in this country in the nineteenth century; though it, too, goes back to the great Continental Reformation of three centuries before. In fact, it may be said to have derived from the Reformation even more completely than any other American denomination, since it came from both the Reformed branch of the Reformation, which looked back to Calvin as its prophet, and from the Lutheran branch, that hailed as its original leader Martin Luther himself.

The local churches of the Evangelical Synod, like those of the Reformed Church, had not been transported to this country from the old world as churches, but the foreign-missionary societies of Germany and Switzerland and the American Home Missionary Society of this country, gave the German groups that began to settle in the upper Mississippi valley such aid in personnel and money as they could, and churches were established. Both in Germany and in this country at the time there was strong feeling against Protestant denominationalism, and to the honor of these pioneers be it recorded that they formed neither Lutheran nor Reformed Churches but gathered both the Lutheran and Reformed members of the neighborhood into inclusive Evangelical (the Continental word for Protestant) Churches. This may be called one of the earliest of the ecumenical movements in the United States.

It was in 1877 that various groups of churches united to become the Evangelical Synod. The teachings of the Synod were those of the historic confessions of the Reformation, such as the Augsburg Confession, Luther's Catechism, and the Heidelberg Catechism. In the points at which these symbols seemed to disagree, the Synod declared that it would adhere "to the passages of Holy Scripture bearing on the subject" and avail itself "of the liberty of conscience prevailing in the Evangelical Church." What more liberal provision could have been adopted?

It was this body that founded Eden Theological Seminary just outside of St. Louis, and Elmhurst College in Illinois.

The other group which had a part, in 1957, in bringing the United Church into being was the Congregational Christian Churches. Originally, like the Evangelical and Reformed Church, these too had used an *and* in their official title ("Congregational *and* Christian"), for in this case, also, two groups had united to become one fellowship—the Christian Churches represented in their national body called the General Convention, and the Congregational Churches in their National Council. Of this union, which occurred in 1931, the Congregational member was by far the larger.

The Christian Church, the other member, itself was the result of an ecumenical movement which had had its beginnings as far back as the second decade of the nineteenth century. Three small denominations of churches came together under the aegis of what was first called "The United States Convention." Methodists in North Carolina under Thomas O'Kelly in 1793 had parted company with the main stream of Methodism on the ground that the latter at that time was too "autocratical." Baptists in New England had developed a group independent of but not hostile to the other Baptist Churches of the area in a search for greater freedom in theological thinking and church practice, baptism by immersion being regarded as only one method of entrance into the church, and the closing of the communion table to any but the immersed as a limitation on the generosity of Christ. Presbyterians in Kentucky under the influence in part of

Barton W. Stone inaugurated, in 1804, a small denomination which played down the theological emphasis then dominant in Calvinistic circles in the interest of direct conversions associated with revival meetings. In its beginnings this group was closely associated with the Disciples of Christ, who also owed a spiritual debt to Mr. Stone and who, under the able leadership of the Campbells, father and son, were to become one of the nation's largest communions. It was these three groups, Methodist, Baptist, and Presbyterian, unknown to each other at their inception, which joined hands to become the "Christian" Church. This name was chosen in the thought that if only every denomination would call itself simply "Christian," at least one stumbling block to unity among the churches would be removed. The Disciples of Christ, moved by the same considerations, also called their local churches in many areas simply "Christian," but the idea went no farther.

The Congregational Churches were brought to this country by the Pilgrim Fathers and the far larger company of Puritans who settled the Massachusetts Bay, Connecticut, and New Haven colonies. The Plymouth settlers had originally broken with the Church of England but had returned into fellowship with it far enough to be able to say that they had never deserted its Thirty-Nine Articles. The Massachusetts Puritans, with whom the Plymouth Church at once assumed church fellowship (long before the amalgamation of the two colonies in 1691), never regarded themselves as having broken with the Church of England at all. They were a school holding their own views within that church, but being three thousand miles from the seat of that church's authority, were not at all subject to its episcopal government. Until their brother Congregationalists in England were forced out of the Established Church by the laws of Charles II—the Corporation Act, the Act of Uniformity, the Conventicle Act, and the Five-Mile Act of the 1660's—it may be said that the Puritans in New England had not separated from the homeland, either in church or state, and another hundred years would pass before the link with the English state was severed.

The Evangelical Protestant Church united with the Congregationalists in 1925. This was a group of congregations in the Ohio Valley from Pittsburgh to St. Louis that had originally been German-speaking. They had been known for their liberal views in theology and for their passion for bettering the lot of the underprivileged. At the time of the union there were about 10,000 members of the Evangelical Protestant Church.

The part that the Congregational Churches have played in the history of the country does not need to be retold here. Harvard College was founded by Congregationalists who desired, as they said, "to advance learning, and perpetuate it to posterity, dreading to leave an illiterate ministry to the churches, when our present ministers shall lie in the dust." Yale College was started by ten Congregational clergymen each making a gift of books to its library. John Eliot became "The Apostle to the Indians." After the Civil War, the (Congregational) American Missionary Association established almost 500 schools for freedom below the Mason and Dixon Line and so helped the South start its Negro education, the ideal from the beginning being racial desegregation and equality of opportunity for all.

Through the years, numbers of individual churches have united with the Congregational fellowship, most notable being a group of Congregational Methodist Churches in Georgia and Alabama in 1892.

So the record goes. For the denominations that make up the United Church of Christ it has been a record of union—of mending, so far as possible, the parted garment of Christ. With such a past it was almost inevitable that the Congregational Christian and the Evangelical and Reformed peoples should hold out their hands to each other.

They knew from the history of the United States that up
to the mid-nineteenth century the Christian Church there
seemed destined to split into an increasing number of divisions as the years rolled on. Already in the world there were
the Roman Church and the Orthodox Church and the Anglican Church, each calling itself Catholic but none of them
in unrestricted communion with the others; and on the Protestant side of the line the situation was far worse, especially
in this country. The saying ran that here there were two hundred and fifty sects and insects. Of the large-sized and growing sects there were about thirty, with any number of small
communions with store-front churches of barely more than a
thousand members.

It was obvious to all thoughtful Christians that even thirty
ranking denominations were too many. If these groups had
been essentially different from each other in faith or order,
there might have been some argument for their continuance,
on the ground that they might satisfy the wants of various
types of people better than if they were united, but this was
not the case. Each of the greater churches itself contained
many different schools of thought within it, many different
kinds of rituals; each had its high-church and its low-church
groups. By whatever names the churches were called there
were basic and growing similarities among them, and one of
the most striking of these similarities was the fact of their
intradenominational variety. It was with this background
that the greater churches of the country and the world had
entered into the ecumenical movement—the movement leading to interdenominational unity—the movement which has
become, in Archbishop Temple's words, "the great new fact
of our time." Part of this movement is simple co-operation
among the various Christian communions, demonstrated in
the hundreds of city councils of churches, state councils, and
the National Council. Co-operation as such, however, does
not reduce the number of denominations; and because it is

felt that Christ desires his Church to be a family and not a mere alliance, the idea rules in Christian circles that the goal is church union rather than mere church collaboration. This does not mean uniformity in every part—perish the thought! —but it does mean, in the midst of multiformity, a Church of Jesus Christ in which the parts fully recognize each other, in which members do not have to be rebaptized or reconfirmed or ministers reordained or bishops reconsecrated if they move from one part of the church to another. Practically speaking, as a first step in the midst of our American disunity, this means union among those churches which can unite. The United Church of Christ has taken this step.

As it has been in the United States, so it has been in the world at large: the history of the Christian Church, until these modern times, has been a history of division.

The lines of the Congregational Christian fellowship, as we have seen, go back, through the English Church, to the time when that church was divided into conformity and non-conformity. That church itself had been divided from the rest of the Western Church, as the Western Church in its own turn had been divided from the Eastern. The strands in the Evangelical and Reformed Church go directly back to the Western Church through the era of the divisions of the Reformation in the sixteenth century, and thence back through the Eastern-Western crisis to the beginnings of the Church.

The lines of ancestry in the United Church antedate division if they are followed back far enough, for they start from the one Jesus Christ and the Hebrew nation out of which he came. If one were to chart that genealogy, he would for the last generations show many streams flowing together into one, but behind that he would show the one stream beginning in Christ parting into the many. In 1960, the United Church of Christ was one; in 1860, it was six; in 1560, it was three; in A.D. 60, it was one. We begin to return to the unity in which Christ gave the church to the world.

This return has not come without trials and tears, as we have seen, but the course of the United Church of Christ is now set: it has purposed and purposes to do all it can to reverse the fissiparous tendency of the Christian Church, beginning with itself. It conceives this as part of the strategy Christ has assigned to it in the history of Christianity in this era. So it has become a kind of nerve center for unity in the body of the total church, its record of union speaking for itself.

Chapter III

FUNDAMENTAL CHARACTERISTICS OF THE UNITED CHURCH

The Purposes of the United Church

The Preamble of the Constitution goes on to say:

The United Church of Christ . . . in order to express more fully the oneness in Christ of the churches composing it, to make more effective their common witness in Him, and to serve His kingdom in the world, hereby adopts this Constitution.

This is to say that the aims of the United Church do not differ in any way from those of the Church of Jesus Christ in general. At the great meeting of the Assembly of the World Council of Churches held in New Delhi, India, in 1961, the very year in which the Constitution was adopted, the three areas of study were the Church's Witness, the Church's Service, and the Church's Unity—which, by something more than coincidence, are the three ends of the church's life named in that Constitution of the United Church of Christ.

Pages might be written on the importance of what is *not* mentioned as characteristic of the purpose of the United Church of Christ.

The United Church's unity of purpose does *not* derive from

any wish to further one culture or one race. It is *not* one church because of the social congeniality of its members, socially congenial though they may be. It does *not* find its cohesion in a common aloofness from other people in the world, including other Christians. It is *not* one because all parts of it enjoy a common tradition, a common interpretation of the Bible, a common creed, a common historic episcopate, or any other form of official succession—all of which, even if they be considered expressions of church unity, are far from being its cause. It is *not* unified by its central organization, its uniformity of worship, its unwillingness to accept new ideas, its determination to stay huddled about some palladium of the past. It *is* unified by its loyalty to Christ: this informs all its worship and its work; everything else which may seem to mark its unity is secondary to this.

The United Church purposes to make its witness to Christ more effective. One deadly disease of churches is that they may witness to the standards of the world, being prosperous, their members socially elite, snobbish. Or churches may witness to their own selfishness—and denominationalism itself, though often mixed with better ingredients, is in part undisguisedly such a witness. There is the church's equanimity in the midst of a world ridden by social and racial injustices; there is its comfort in the midst of homelessness and hunger; what kind of witness is this? It is only sorry testimony to our own self-satisfaction. The United Church of Christ cannot hope, being composed of sinful people, to escape making this kind of false witness, but the inscription on its banner is clear—it exists to witness *not* to any of these things, but to Christ.

In the realm of service, the purpose of the United Church is equally clear. It is dedicated *not* narrowly to meeting human need only where there is hope of increasing the population of the church, but to meeting human need without asking further questions, simply because it is human need. On the one hand it is interested in helping people out of illness, superstition, and poverty, but it amplifies that interest by a sustained attack on the sources of illness, the ignorance that provides a bed for superstition, and the social injustices which create poverty. Its ministry is directed to the whole human race and is applied socially as well as individually.

The ramifications of all these purposes will be made evident as the Constitution unfolds itself.

The Head of the Church

The United Church of Christ acknowledges as its sole Head, Jesus Christ, the Son of God and the Saviour of men.

So begins the second paragraph of the Preamble to the Constitution, and so the United Church is marked not only as Christian but as Christian in the mainstream of the church's tradition.

When Jesus Christ is called the sole Head of the Church, Christianity's extraordinary paradox is touched upon, because Jesus Christ is the very man who lived in Palestine almost twenty centuries ago, a Jew, a carpenter, a preacher of the love of God who for his preaching died an agonizing death on a Roman cross and is yet alive today in a mystical but real way, speaking no words, making no appearances, invading the physical world not at all, and yet exerting an enormous influence on those who are sensitive to his presence. This is a strange belief because it is at once historical and not historical; it binds two worlds together. It has had more to do with giving Western man such decency as he has achieved than any other single force. When this Jesus Christ is called the Son of God, the intimation is that God through him has entered into human life; and when he is called the Saviour of men, it is indicated that through this contact men

have come to realize that the Creator of the universe has
sufficient concern for them to keep them in his care forever.

The Constitution now proceeds:

The United Church of Christ . . . acknowledges as brethren
in Christ all who share in this confession.

This was not always so. When our fathers of the Reformation read of "Antichrist" in the Epistles of John, the word
reminded them not of Satan or any other members of the
spirit world—though these were regarded as being the close
collaborators of Mr. Against-Christ (as the Greek title might
be translated into American)—the only figure that rose in their
mind was that of the Roman pope. When they read in their
Bibles that Jesus had said, "Many shall come in my name,
saying, 'I am Christ'; and shall deceive many," they thought
they knew the chief contemporary representative of the
group our Lord had in mind and could have given any man
his address in the Italian capital. And now the United Church
of Christ calls the Pope its brother—along with all others who
believe that God was in Christ reconciling the world to himself.

This is an illustration of the fact that it is dangerous to
belong to a living church. The danger lies in the possibility
of growth. When one puts himself into the hands of a creative God, one cannot be certain how one will come out.
One's philosophy may be changed, one's attitude toward life,
one's ethics.

That which imparts growth to the church, the matrix of
its life, is the Christ of whom we have spoken. Slowly but
inevitably as the centuries progress he converts every secondary thing within the church into conformity with his own
gracious intent. All the forms of thought, of worship, and of
structure that are found within the church are subject to his
perfecting influence. He and his people, united in love, alone
constitute the real being of the church (its *esse*, as the the-

ologians are likely to say), and no *forms* of belief and action, though they may belong to its well-being (its *bene esse*), do. Christ in the midst of his people is the same yesterday, today, and forever; all shapes of response to his presence are subject to change as his loving will becomes more perfectly understood.

This is the occasion for the difference between the attitude of the United Church of Christ today and that of its Protestant forebears to the Roman Church. Granted that there are profound divergences between the ways of the Roman Church and those of the United Church, granted that no method of reconciling those ways has as yet been conceived or is at the moment conceivable—nonetheless, because Roman Catholics, too, lift up Christ as the sole head of the church, the United Church of Christ approaches them not as old enemies but as brethren with whom Christ can make all things new.

And so the United Church of Christ looks toward the Eastern Orthodox Church and to all other churches which profess and call themselves Christian.

The Bible and the Holy Spirit

The Constitution says:

The United Church of Christ . . . looks to the Word of God in the Scriptures, and to the presence and power of the Holy Spirit, to prosper its creative and redemptive work in the world.

This is a carefully written sentence which repays a careful reading; it relates the Bible and the Holy Spirit to each other and speaks of them as together a force in the world.

When we speak of the Word of God in the Scriptures we mean God's utterance, his expression of his will. The very word, *word*, stands, after all, for something marvelous. Here

I am, setting down various words for the pages of a book—
and there you are, good reader, separated from me perhaps
by continents and by numbers of months or years which I
cannot guess—and yet, thanks to the words, we are able to
share the same ideas and know part of each other's minds.
When words are used by a genius in language their power
seems almost magical. To read, for instance, the simple words
of Homer describing Hector's leave-taking of his wife and
infant before he goes out to the conflict finally fatal to him is
to relive the poet's pathetic admiration for his hero after
three thousand years; it is, after all, something, to be compelled to brush away a tear by the writing of a man who lived
before the dawn of recorded history. This is the *mana* of the
word; it reaches from mind to mind and, when it comes from
a master, reaches deeply. But the Word of God in the Scriptures is something that comes from before history itself, recorded or unrecorded; it is spoken in historical settings but
tells of God's will, which is from everlasting to everlasting.

The Word of God in the Scriptures, however, is more than
an ordinary word: it is God's expression of his will. By his
word he created the world:

> By the Word of Jehovah were the heavens created,
> And by the breath of his mouth all their host.

By his word, God sustains the whole world and in the long
last assures the consummation of his purposes:

> So shall my Word be which goeth forth from my mouth; it
>   shall not return unto me void,
> For it shall have done that which I desired,
> And shall have accomplished that for which I sent it.

This Word of God can be understood by some men and from
them others can learn its meaning. It came to the prophets
as something to be announced. Jeremiah found that even
when he fought against speaking it, there was that within

him which, like a creative thought in a thinker's mind, demanded utterance.

> The Word of the Lord has become for me
>   a reproach and derision all day long.
> If I say, "I will not mention him,
>   or speak any more in his name,"
> There is in my heart as it were a burning fire
>   shut up in my bones,
> And I am weary with holding it in,
>   and I cannot.

This is the Old Testament idea of the Word; it was God's expression of himself in the world, in the underlying forces of the world, and in the mind of man. The New Testament brought the meaning of the Word to its fullness:

> The Word became flesh and dwelt among us, full of grace and truth.

In Jesus Christ, the Word was a person; this was God's supreme expression of himself. When the Constitution speaks of God's Word in the Scriptures as the force behind the church's creative and redemptive work in the world, it points to all those ways in history, epitomized in the Scriptures, in which God has made his character known. In those ways he has *spoken* (used the vehicle of the Word) to the United Church of Christ, and it is as a direct response to his Word that this church exists and goes about its work. It is as much his creation, as fully a carrier of his purpose, as were the heavens and the earth in the beginning; it is the extension of his Word in Christ—and it is good to belong to a church when it is such.

The Constitution refers to God's Word as being spoken *in* the Scriptures; it does not equate the Scriptures with the Word of God, as if everything in them were his own truth. The United Church of Christ does not regard the writers of the Bible as having been protected supernaturally from reporting events erroneously or setting forth inadequate and untrue philosophies. It is said in the Book of Joshua (10:12–13), for instance, that:

Joshua . . . said in the sight of Israel, "Sun, stand thou still. . . ." and the sun stood still . . . and did not hasten to go down for about a whole day. There has been no day like it before or since.

This is plainly folklore, most interesting to any hearer, but imaginative beyond the limits which a modern historian would impose upon himself.

Happy he who taketh and dasheth thy little ones against a rock!

This line from an imprecatory Psalm (137:8) hardly identifies its author as one who knows the loving Will of God. One cannot say that it and other biblical passages like it set forth the Word of God. And yet the Bible as a whole has been a mine in which diamond after diamond of insight into God's ways has been discovered.

The United Church of Christ through its scholars approaches the Bible as any literary critic approaches any book. Every line is investigated until everything about it that can be known is known. The historians are called in, and the experts in language, the students of the sacred books of other religions (so that comparison may be made), and the archaeologists, who can support or question or supplement the writers of the Bible from their delvings into the sands that cover the remains of ancient biblical civilizations. And, after all is said and done, after the Bible has been laid on the laboratory table and all the instruments of modern scientific investigation have been employed to get at the truths it contains, it still speaks to us the Word of God; the man Christ Jesus, quivering on the cross outside the walls of Jerusalem and telling by his very agony what God is willing to endure if only his people will accept his love and live by it, is, if anything, more clearly limned today than ever. In the pages of the Bible, better understood now than in the past, though not magically, God *speaks* to the United Church of Christ and to us all.

Linked in the Constitution to the mention of the Word of God in the Scriptures is the reference to "the presence and power of the Holy Spirit." This is as it ought to be, for no person would know he was hearing the Word of God unless God himself marked the word for him. A contemporary playwright speaks of "the glow of the soul" which occurs when one encounters any event which he feels to have been caused by the direct hand of God. That glow may be said to be itself the result of God's touch. The religious thinkers of yesterday who wrote in Latin called this the *testimonium Sancti Spiritus internum* or the inner witness of the Holy Spirit, for "Holy Spirit" is the name we give to God when he comes to us in this way. God speaking with one voice at these two points—through the historical record of the Scriptures and in the mind of the reader by his Holy Spirit—causes the moment of illumination in the life of any man or any church. It is to the Scriptures and to the Holy Spirit that the United Church of Christ looks, and asks others to look, as it goes about its creative and redemptive work in Christ.

The Faith of the Fathers

The Preamble continues:

The United Church of Christ . . . claims as its own the faith of the historic Church. . . .

This leads to the question as to what that historic faith is. We have already pointed to what the Bible calls the author and perfector of that faith—Jesus Christ—but we have now to ask how he is related to the church and the church to him. It is a marvelously simple relationship, but an inspiring one—

and infinitely satisfying, too. We have space here to describe it only in its broadest features, but it is in its breadth that its magnificence is seen.

Let us begin with you, good reader. There you are standing between two magnitudes—God on the one hand and the world on the other. Put it this way in your imagination: you stand at the corner of a triangle, the world is at another corner, and God at the third. In that sense you stand between God and the world. But this is a triangle of forces, and God is the source of them. He is the giver of all things. All that you have and are came from him; but some of these gifts come direct—along the side of the triangle that connects you immediately with him, so to speak—and other gifts from him come indirectly—along the other sides of the triangle through the corner called the world.

God relates himself to you directly. We have already spoken of his Holy Spirit moving a man to recognize the things of God in the Bible; but God, of course, touches an individual in many ways. The very fact of individuality is his gift; thanks to your Creator you are able to say, "I," and so differentiate yourself from the entire world about you. He not only comes to you but he works through you; individuals like you bring to the world new ideas; they create what has never before been known. God did not cease creating on the sixth day: he goes on doing it, and in the sector of his world called humanity he is likely to do so through the medium of the individual. Our first proposition is that God may make himself known to the world, that he may let one of his streams of creative life flow into the world, through *you*.

But in the second place, consider how much God gives you not directly but through the world, through your friends and neighbors, through the thinkers and doers of the past. Almost everything you have came to you through others—the language you use, the forms of thought you employ, the art you enjoy, the architecture of your house, of your church, the very society in which you live. God is the creator of all things, but most of them were given to others and came to you through them. You are part of all you have met; you are debtor to millions, known and unknown; you have undoubtedly received from God through the human race a good deal more than you have had directly from God and turned over as your contribution to the race. Our second proposition is that a second creative stream from God comes to you through the world into which you were born and now live, and of which you are a part.

There are of course many people who are not aware that God speaks to them either directly or indirectly; we shall hear more of them later, but I take it, good reader, that you *are* aware that God makes gifts to you in both ways. As we think of the faith of the historic church, we can well take as our basic conception the triangularity of forces which we have pictured. This is an utterly inadequate way to represent the coming of God's forces to you, but if you think geometrically, as most of us do, it may help you to understand the faith of the historic church which the United Church of Christ regards as its own.

Up till now, Christian reader, we have been thinking of the points of the triangle as God, yourself, and the world; but now take another step. In order to get a clearer conception of the church, let us reduce the third point from the whole world to only a part of it, that is, the world of your fellow believers. Here we have the three parties to what is known in church history as the Covenant. God has already committed himself to it: he has said in effect, "I will give to you and your fellow believers, and you both must give to each other." If then you and your fellow believers both consciously accept this, you are all members of the Covenant. When we recall that the old word for Covenant is *Testament*, the name given to the two parts of the Bible itself, we can appreciate how much the idea of the Covenant has meant to the church. The history of the church is indeed the history of God's Covenant with his people, and this goes back to the dawn of recorded time.

To the ancient Hebrews, the church owes a debt it can never repay, for it was they who had the genius to see that there existed only one God and not the many gods that the other tribes of that day took for granted. The gods were conceived by those tribes as living lives roughly similar to that of tribal headmen; they fought each other on the plains of history, using their tribes as their regiments. The more powerful overcame the weaker. When, for instance, Assyria captured Damascus, the event was an announcement to all who heard of it that Asshur was a mightier god than Rimmon. These gods were many, and they were out for power.

The Hebrews, however, knew that their God, Jehovah, ruled over the other tribes, though unacknowledged by them, just as he did over themselves. He had created the world and all that is in it. His interest was not in becoming powerful, for he was already all-powerful. His interest was in developing better relations between himself and his people, and among his people. This idea of one God who stood for righteousness and wanted his people—all and each—to be righteous to each other (sometimes called ethical monotheism) is the priceless gift of the ancient Hebrew people to the Christian Church, not to say to Christendom. Their acceptance of that God and what he demanded made them the people of the Covenant.

A "covenant," in ordinary usage, is an agreement between two or more persons to act or refrain from acting in a particular way or ways. Marriage is a covenant relationship, for instance. After the vows have been exchanged between the man and the woman, the minister prays, according to one of the classical forms of the ceremony, "O eternal God . . . send thy blessing upon these thy servants . . . that they . . . may surely perform and keep the vow and *covenant* betwixt them made." A treaty between nations is a covenant; the three thousand miles of border between the United States and Canada is kept free of armaments by covenant.

The Hebrews understood the relation that God had entered into with them as a covenant, though this was different from any ordinary covenant. It was not a contract entered into between equals; it was like that which, our archeologists now tell us, was sometimes used by powerful but intelligent Hittite rulers in the Middle East before the time of Moses to bind to themselves the people over whom they ruled. The party of the first part—the ruler—was the author of it, and the parties of the second part—the people, each and all—though bound by it, had nothing whatever to say about the creating of it or the form of it. The interesting and unique feature of this kind of covenant was that the ruler bound himself. He said, in effect: "You, my citizens, will perform certain duties (all duly spelled out) and I, on my part, will guarantee you certain rights"—trade rights, military rights, limited rights of self-government, or something of the sort. So the Hebrews felt that their Jehovah had put himself under the terms of his own covenant: he would be to them a just and responsible ruler if they, as obedient devotees of his, would be to each other just and responsible fellow citizens. The responsibility of all for each and each for all under God was set forth in what they called the Law. This was the Old Covenant or, as we say, the Old Testament.

The books of the Old Testament and the New Testament —the Old Covenant and the New—are rightly bound together in one Bible, because the New, properly understood, is really an extension and a deeper interpretation of the Old.

The three parties to each of these Covenants, that is, the one party of the first part, God, and the two parties of the second part, the believer and his fellow believers (to revert to our triadic figure), correspond. God is regarded in both as the author of all power and all good, who takes part in history and is concerned that justice shall be done to each and all. Jews and Christians of today, because they each go back to the original Covenant, have the same feeling toward God. They do not regard him, for instance (as thinkers of Hinduism seem to), as the sea of consciousness outside history into which some day they will themselves merge; they do not understand him as that spirit behind or within nature without qualities of personality (an idea that seems to dominate the Taoist and Shinto religions); to Jews and Christians alike he has a righteous character and if his will were only shared as he desires it to be, the race and all its members would have the character of righteousness. Christians and Jews being theological cousins under their skins, the former should hang their heads in shame at the treatment they have sometimes given their spiritual relatives during past centuries. There would be no New Testament (or Covenant) if it had not been for the Old.

The New differs from the Old Testament in that it tells the story of how God conveyed to the race the knowledge that at the heart of his justice there is love, and that what he most desires is to have his love accepted and carried by every man to all men, and by all men to every man. He took the initiative: it was not enough to send the *idea* of his love to mankind through a prophet; this was to be more than an idea. He had to establish a living relationship, and that could be done only by coming himself; and this he did in Jesus, a carpenter in the town of Nazareth in Palestine. I say that he came in Jesus without attempting a theological explanation of this extraordinary fact, simply noting that the presence of Jesus in history has actually given people a new conception of the inner character of God, and that the life he lived and the death he died have given them a new sense of what God's relation to them really is: he is now known as being in a covenant of love with them.

I have mentioned The Law, the religious and ethical demands Jehovah made upon his people as their part in the covenant; but herein lay difficulty for the spiritually sensitive. It was not merely that they could not carry out all the requirements of The Law but that after Jesus came they felt the true relation between the participants in the divine-human covenant to be not one of law-giver and law-receiver but rather of Father and family, the tie between them being the law of love. Jesus did not *discover* this truth, for the great Hebrew seers before him—men like Hosea—had begun to feel it. Verses like the Psalmist's "As a father pities his children, so the Lord pities those who fear him," were well known in Jesus' day; but Jesus gave this truth supreme and absolute emphasis: he singled out the verb *love* as the one word to describe God's attitude to man, and by giving his own life completely to help mankind, even to the sacrifice on the cross, he showed what God's love is in human terms. It is ultimate, final.

God then is not only the only God but he is a God whose purpose is one of love; and this clear vision of God's character necessarily gives clearer vision of the essence of the Covenant. What God wants from men is not sheer obedience, which in any case cannot be perfectly given, but *love*, from which obedience flows, as a stream from a spring. God is a God of judgment, but also one of forgiveness—an attribute which in itself draws forth love from his people. Jesus, as he said, did not come to abolish the law but to fulfill it, that is, to bring out its essence. So he was able to say, singling out two sentences from The Law well known to all: " 'You shall *love* the Lord your God with all your heart, and with all your soul, and with all your mind.' This is the great and first commandment. And a second is like it, 'You shall love your neighbor as yourself.' On these two commandments hang all the law and the prophets."

With this powerful emphasis on love and no slightest suggestion of race as a coefficient in the covenant between God and man, it is understandable that the Gospel of Christ quickly overspread the boundaries of Judaism. God was the God of the Jews, to be sure, but he was also the God of the Samaritan, of the Roman centurion, and of the Syrophoenician Greek woman. God had made his Covenant with the Jews, but it was open, in reality, to any who would accept it, any in the whole of humankind. "God so loved the *world* that he gave his only son . . . that the *world* might be saved through him."

So the United Church of Christ, together with all the other parts of the Christian Church, is united to God in the same way that the ancient Hebrews were, by Covenant—and by an extension of the same Covenant—for Christians believe that from the first God loved mankind and bound himself to them in a promise of love, which we today, since the coming of Christ, understand better than our spiritual forebears before Christ.

The Covenant is a vehicle of life. To go back to our three-cornered figure, it is a relationship in which life is imparted by God through individuals to their society and through their society to them. Society and individuals pass it to each other from generation to generation. As you sit in a pew of the United Church of Christ or any other part of the Christian Church, you are a direct inheritor of the Covenant God established with the Hebrews in the first days of history. There never would have been a United Church if there never had been such a Covenant. Oliver Cromwell once gave the message to his daughter's husband: "Bid her be cheerful and rejoice in the Lord once and again; if she knows the Covenant, she cannot but be so." This sense of enjoying and being animated by the life relationship which God has established with all men and each man—and explicitly with all believers—is the substance of the faith of the historic church, which the United Church of Christ makes its own.

The Creeds

The Preamble goes on:

The United Church of Christ . . . claims as its own the faith of the historic Church expressed in the ancient creeds and reclaimed in the basic insights of the Protestant Reformers.

The "ancient creeds" here referred to are the Apostles' Creed, the Nicene Creed, and the Athanasian Creed, sometimes called from its first word in Latin, the *Quicunque*. The Apostles' Creed was apparently used in the very early church in association with the rite of baptism. What could have been more natural, when an adult was baptized, than that he should briefly give voice to his beliefs by way, as it were, of showing his credentials for membership in the church—and that this expression of belief, repeated by many in almost the same form, should finally become a regular formula? The appropriateness of this creed for occasions other than baptismal services became apparent with use. It is recited by many of the congregations of the United Church of Christ to express at once their own common belief and their community of faith with the church of all the ages past. In many other congregations it is not used, chiefly because their members have come to believe that a phrase or two in it is not true. The Nicene Creed is longer, and not nearly so frequently used, and the Athanasian Creed, much longer, is hardly used at all, and then sung rather than recited.

Although these creeds may not seem to all today, as I have said, to express the truth in every line, they contain, in relatively simple form, a statement of Christian essentials that are the same yesterday, today, and forever. Granted that they also may contain single sentences or phrases that some critical minds of today, disciplined to seek the truth in Christ's name, cannot accept, these are like the incidental folklore and unchristian vagaries of the authors of the Bible: they do not prevent the broader and essential truth about God from shining through the whole.

This essential truth, as the Preamble says, is claimed in the basic insights of the Reformers. Here the reference is to the Christian leaders involved in the tremendous upheaval which took place within the church of the West—that is, of Western Europe and Great Britain—in the sixteenth century. History remembers the Augustinian monk named Martin Luther who, risking his very life in those murderous times, nailed to the wall of the local cathedral at Wittenberg, Germany, a set of theses—ninety-five of them—in which he tried to make clear the essential truth of the Gospel at a time when the church as a whole seemed to have forgotten it. Ulrich Zwingli of German-speaking Switzerland, a contemporary of Luther's, and also a reclaimer of the basic Christian faith, actually lost his life in battle in the religious wars of the time. John Calvin, born in France, lived in Geneva in French-speaking Switzerland, and there put the world in his debt not only by the writing of books to re-establish the faith but by establishing in and about that city a little civilization built on the insights of what now came to be known as "Protestantism."

The Constitution speaks only of the "insights" of the Reformers, though it might in the context have spoken of their creeds, which were an attempt to put their insights into words. The Evangelical and Reformed Constitution, like that of the Evangelical Synod before it, had mentioned in a corresponding section the Heidelberg Catechism, Luther's Catechism, and the Augsburg Confession, all of which are creeds in the sense that they set forth the faith in brief compass. Luther himself was the author of the "Small Catechism" of 1529, which bears his name; though at first it was only one of many to be used in the instruction of the young, it quickly won its way to pre-eminence. Luther's friend and co-worker, Melanchthon, was responsible for the final form of the Augsburg Confession, in 1530, which was written in the hope that from it the Roman Catholic leaders might understand and appreciate the Protestant position. The Heidelberg Catechism was published in 1563 by two theologians, Zacharias Ursinus and Caspar Olevianus, and is an admirable presentation of the position of the "Reformed" (Calvinistic or non-Lutheran) Churches of Germany. It is more theological and less adapted to the teaching of young children than the Lutheran Catechism, but on the other hand surpasses it as a systematic description of Christian truth. Taken together, these three may well be understood as expressing "the basic insights of the Protestant Reformers."

The Congregational Reformation in England came so much later than the great Reformation of the Continent that the "insights" referred to in the Constitution can include those of the Puritan founders of New England only if the period of the Reformation is extended to cover several generations. Corresponding to the three great Continental symbols just named might then be mentioned the one Westminster Confession, which was produced by the Puritan Westminster Assembly in 1647, and accepted by the New England fathers "for substance of doctrine" except for the sections on church government. The substance of doctrine alluded to was virtually the same as that of the Heidelberg Confession of the previous century. The Westminster Confession, like its Continental predecessors, was designed not for liturgical use but for teaching purposes.

The "Christian" parts of the Congregational Christian Churches studiously avoided the attempt to reduce the faith to brief conceptual form. One of the five principles which they taught (and teach) reads: "The Holy Bible . . . is our only Creed or Confession of Faith." They interpreted (and interpret) the Bible, however, in the general way of the Calvinistic Reformers.

This sentence in the Constitution about creeds calls up

questions that in the past have agitated some groups now part of the United Church of Christ and undoubtedly still remain a concern to them.

There are those who think that creeds of any kind, whether they be for use in worship or in teaching, are dangerous to the freedom wherewith Christ has made us free. In the later centuries of the church there have been groups in many denominations who have fought against creeds as against shackles. They have felt that when faith, which is properly a sense of relationship between person and person, is put into words and then, in that shape, lifted up as a definition of what one must assent to in order to qualify for church membership, it becomes a casing that prevents the expansion of the free mind; and I suppose that in some intervals of the church's life the creeds, partly because of the antiquity they achieve and the high reverence in which they then come to be held, and partly because of the possibility of their being used for procrustean purposes by reactionary leaders, have actually arrested the full play of uninhibited Christian thought in the church. In any case there are persons, and persons of the highest type, who simply do not like the idea of assenting solemnly, as if for eternity, to a set of propositions; it seems to separate them from Christ, rather than unite them to him. With persons of this kind of sensitivity, the United Church of Christ has every sympathy.

All parts of the United Church—Congregational, Christian, Evangelical, and Reformed—possess a seasoned and positive belief that the basic relationships of faith whereby the human soul and the church of souls are hid with Christ in God can never be fully represented in a theological statement, long or short. A creed can no more be equated with the reality which it describes than a snapshot with its subject. A form of this sort was called by our fathers "human," by which they meant that it was not absolute, but must be changed with the changing times in order to be kept focused on the changeless absolute to which it points—God, who loves us. A creed has the same use as the simple diagram of forces I have ventured to employ—intended to illustrate how God's grace in Christ comes to each person both in a direct and in a roundabout way—but to regard this as anything but a mnemonic or pedagogic device would be to miss its point entirely. In a similar way a creed is a human device to picture a divine fact or relationship.

On the other hand, the United Church does not hold the naïve view that creeds can be dispensed with. If a man should rise up and say, "I do not believe in the use of creeds," that statement in itself would of course be his creed, albeit in negative form. There is no substitute for short statements of belief when there is need to communicate the faith in teaching or in worship. It is part of the miracle of human life together, as Plato pointed out long ago, that a spark can fly from the flame in one soul to another, and set up a flame there; the spark itself is not the flame, but it has powers of igniting one. So a word, a sentence, a statement of belief by one man, leaping like a living spark into the questioning mind of another, may cause there the same fire of belief as warmed the mind from which it came. It is as a means of communicating faith and not as a fixed interpretation of that faith that the United Church of Christ views theological statements, short and long.

The United Church of Christ uses not one but many creeds —a fact which in itself proves that no one of them is regarded as absolute. In some of its congregations are recited the classical creeds of Christian antiquity; in its theological classrooms are studied not only these but the longer Reformation symbols; in its catechetical classes, where young people are prepared for church membership, like studies are made; and in the old Congregational parishes, each church has a creed of its own, written by its own minister and members, either in a former century or this. Creeds, in a word, are here taken seriously, but not absolutely. They are of many forms, but their plurality does not betoken variety of subject matter; all of these creeds point, though in differing phraseology, to the fact of God's love made available to all men and each man in Jesus Christ. They are many flowers open toward the one sun.

Where one of the catechisms of the Reformation is used, or a more modern one, in the training of youth for church membership, it is the practice of many ministers of the United Church of Christ, in helping their young charges give shape to the beliefs forming in them, to ask them not only to study the answers of the catechisms to the fundamental questions of life:—"What is the chief end of man?" "What rule hath God given to direct us how we may glorify and enjoy him?" and the others—but also to write out their own answers in their own words. This is to assign the statement of faith to its proper station, as an aid and not a straitjacket to the religious life. Even in the formal service of confirmation, the young people are not ordinarily asked, even indirectly, to profess their belief in articles of faith contained in the Apostles' or any other creed of the church, but are more likely to be invited simply to tell about their own relation to God in Jesus Christ. Acknowledgment of him is more basic than assent to a creed, however good the creed may be.

When ministers in the Congregational tradition are ordained they are not required to give assent to propositions drawn up by the church, but are asked, instead, to set forth their own faith in a carefully prepared paper, on the basis of which the representatives of the church judge whether or not they are fitted to become its ministers. In the United Church of Christ, originality within the framework of consecration and good will always enjoys priority, and in the case of the personal creed of an ordinand, the church, believing that all good creeds are symbols pointing beyond themselves, stands ready to review any original presentation of his faith by an intended minister in the expectation that from it may be determined whether or not the reality to which it points is the same as that apprehended in the faith of the church itself.

The statements of faith written by young people at the time of confirmation or by young men to be ordained to the ministry of Christ's Church help them to use creeds as instruments and not as ends, but they lack one important attribute of an ordinary creed: being merely statements of individuals, they have of themselves no social sanction. They are not the product of the church itself, as a creed normally is. And such a creed—a creed of, by, and for the whole church—is indispensable. Not seldom a person asks, "I should like to be able to tell people what the essential beliefs of my church actually are." In such a case a brief statement meets the demand. We have already spoken of the advantageous use to which such a statement can be put in the instruction of the young. But the greatest benefit of all lies in its liturgical possibilities. What is more thrilling than to hear a great congregation stand, as at attention, and out of full conviction recite its common belief? A church creed, to have its full effect as a vehicle of worship, must be believed by the individual worshiper and by his fellow worshipers to be true. When God (to go back to the thought of our diagram) imparts faith direct to a worshiper who hears the congregation about him saying words which can mean only that God has imparted the same faith to it, this meeting of the two streams of faith from the one God is an experience sometimes too wonderful to describe. It gives a sense of being at home at once with the congregation and with God.

As we have said, many in the United Church of Christ attain to this at-home-ness when they stand with the church and recite the Apostles' Creed or the Nicene, but there are those who have desired a statement of common faith that carries not only the truths of the ancient confessions but also the insights that God has given to his church since the early centuries. Though the old creeds imply the fact of God's love, they do not give it the centrality the church has come to feel it deserves. They have nothing to say about the Kingdom of Heaven, though this was our Lord's central theme. And so in our day there has been a felt need for a brief confession in which the complete church can meet the complete contemporary man and invite him to join it in a declaration of common faith. An Apostles' Creed for our own day has been called for, and the United Church of Christ has in humility responded to what it has believed to be the urging of the Holy Spirit by composing a Statement of Faith.

It was a first great act of the United Church in its corporate existence to cause this statement to be written in order that all within and all outside the church might know the beliefs commonly held in the communion. The original Basis of Union had promised a committee to be appointed at the first meeting of the General Synod, the national body of the church, consisting of members of the uniting denominations in equal numbers, which should draw up a brief statement outlining the general beliefs of the uniting groups. The committee took two years for its work, being careful to submit its drafts, as they emerged, to the leaders and people of the churches for suggested improvements. When it was finally presented to the General Synod at its second meeting there were a few last-minute revisions asked for, but it was passed substantially as the committee had prepared it, and passed unanimously. The swiftness of its acceptance and usage throughout the church subsequently was a source of surprise even to those who knew the church best. It is now used liturgically as an affirmation of faith in churches large and small, rural and urban, and in all quarters of the country. Its cadences, its independence of the now somewhat archaic language employed in the creeds of the ancient church and of the Reformation, its setting forth of truth largely in simple

Anglo-Saxon monosyllables, lend it strength and beauty for contemporary believers:

Statement of Faith

We believe in God, the Eternal Spirit, Father of our Lord Jesus Christ and our Father, and to his deeds we testify:

He calls the worlds into being,
    creates man in his own image
    and sets before him the ways of life and death.

He seeks in holy love to save all people from
    aimlessness and sin.

He judges men and nations by his righteous will
    declared through prophets and apostles.

In Jesus Christ, the man of Nazareth, our crucified
    and risen Lord,
    he has come to us
    and shared our common lot,
    conquering sin and death
    and reconciling the world to himself.

He bestows upon us his Holy Spirit,
    creating and renewing the Church of Jesus Christ,
    binding in covenant faithful people of all ages,
        tongues, and races.

He calls us into his Church
    to accept the cost and joy of discipleship,
    to be his servants in the service of men,
    to proclaim the gospel to all the world
    and resist the powers of evil,
    to share in Christ's baptism and eat at his table,
    to join him in his passion and victory.

He promises to all who trust him
    forgiveness of sins and fullness of grace,
    courage in the struggle for justice and peace,
    his presence in trial and rejoicing,
    and eternal life in his kingdom which has no end.

Blessing and honor, glory and power be unto him. Amen

Most statements of faith have come out of times of great tribulation in the church, when it was necessary in order to keep the faith pure to cast up a bulwark of written beliefs to enlighten the ignorant, strengthen the faithful, and fend off the heretical. The Nicene Creed itself, for instance, was a kind of summary of the beliefs of one of the two great parties within the church in the fourth century, each trying to gain the ascendancy. When one of them finally defeated the other, both by votes in the church synods and politically in the Empire, the victory was consolidated in the creation and propagation of the famous Nicene statement. In the case of the Statement of Faith of the United Church, however, different circumstances held. The United Church was confronted by no major heresy; a conciliatory mood had descended upon the entire church and the united part of it was in no frame of mind to condemn those who did not see eye to eye with it in all things. So instead of being an instrument of war, as many a creed had been, this statement came out as a declaration of gratitude to God—and the more one thinks of it, the more one is likely to agree that this is the best form for any creed to take.

It was specifically pointed out in the Basis of Union, in which the Statement of Faith was authorized, that this declaration was never to be brought to bear as a test on prospective members or any others. It is not designed to prove anything, as a test is. It is rather a testimony: it witnesses to the faith held by the church, and offers opportunity for men of free mind to unite with the church, if they will, in praising God for his mighty works.

Worship

To return to the Preamble to the Constitution: it now speaks of the necessity for keeping the church relevant to its age, that is, to each age as it appears:

The United Church of Christ . . . affirms the responsibility of the Church in each generation to make this faith [the faith of the historic Church] its own in reality of worship. . . .

The United Church of Christ tries to keep its worship meaningful to the people among whom it ministers. It regards forms which have only antiquity to commend them as an abomination unto the Lord. The worship of the God and Father of our lord Jesus Christ must be a living thing, since it is the very heart of the church's life. Worship breaks down the barrier between the concrete human situation in which men find themselves and the world of eternity over which God presides; it therefore has a human as well as divine side: it is a changeless God who is worshiped but human beings who worship; in their prayers they must use human language—which is always in process of evolution; they must think in human ways—and emphases in thought alter; they must in all things see that their changing forms are kept pointed to him who changes not.

The liturgy of the United Church tries to keep these facts in mind. *Liturgy* is a word often saved (though from the viewpoint of its etymology incorrectly) for the modes followed in highly formal services we associate with the Catholic branches of the church. Its original meaning, however, refers only to popular or public worship in general, and it is in this sense that we use it here. The liturgy used in a service need not be an elaborate one; it may have even the simplicity of a Friends' meeting, where the silences are many and unpremeditated and eloquent. *Liturgy* becomes the useful word to describe a form of public worship, and in the United Church of Christ such forms are many.

The liturgical life of the United Church of Christ is a response to God, bearing gratitude and confidence for all that he has done and is doing for the worshiper both directly and, through the world, indirectly. We still have in mind the dual flow of life from God, and in public worship, which is a kind of happy counterflow toward God, the same duality is evident: the worshiper sends his praise and the other offerings of his worship directly to God but at the same time sends them indirectly to him through the worshipers of the surrounding congregation. When the direct prayer is lacking, a fundamental law is broken: the worship becomes a third-person matter, God in Christ being "he," "him," whom one worships only as part of the congregation. On the other hand, when one cannot feel that the company about him is worshiping God, and therefore carrying one's own adoration indirectly back to him, one has a sense of spiritual isolation that is not good for the soul. Public worship at its best always has both an individual and a social dimension.

Now the society of the church in which one worships is far larger than the congregation gathered about. The congregation, to be sure, is all important, for in it there is immediate play of feeling between yourself and the others whom you can see and hear and who can see and hear you; you are a worshiping group of the highest degree. But the company around you represents the entire church, and not only the contemporary but the historic church. It is for that reason that liturgical forms that not only have meaning for today but also come out of the church's history have incomparable value for worship. When, for instance, my fellow-worshipers and I assume the posture of prayer and together say the "Our Father . . . ," it is not a little something to realize that this form, at least according to tradition, was taught by our Lord himself over nineteen hundreds of years ago, that it has certainly been on the lips of millions in ever widening circles ever since, and that it ascends as incense today in many languages from almost every nation under heaven, announcing the oneness of the human race. The Lord's Prayer is over-toned by a sense of the unity of the church as no private prayer of my own could possibly be. The United Church of Christ is therefore not averse to using prayers and other forms of worship which by broad usage speak the voice of the entire convenanted people.

In this practice the United Church bears heavily upon the need for each person in the congregation to participate. Read prayers and read responses, to say nothing of read hymns, in which each person in the congregation may share, are coming more and more to supplement (though not to displace) the prayers and other readings taken by the minister alone. This is not to say that solos and choir work, and sermons and prayers by the minister, and others in which the congregation does not immediately participate will ever be done away. They themselves are a manifestation of devotion to God on the part of individuals or individual groups that redresses the balance often lost where worship is so traditional as to have forfeited the charm and reality of the spontaneous and creative. The moment these individual parts in the worship become vehicles for exhibitionism—the solos the showing off of a prima donna, the choir anthems concert numbers, the sermons poorly veiled egoisms—they are damned. But if they really lead in worship, if they are the putting of some peculiar talent to the service of the Lord, if they are really devotional or interpretive of worship, they are happy aids to the greatest experience a human being can attain.

The United Church of Christ banks on the quiet power hidden in the public worship of God. God being the creator of all things, the habit of opening one's soul to him periodically and submitting to his guidance has possibilities which even the worshiper cannot foresee. It is as if clay could act and speak, and putting itself into the hands of a sculptor infinitely skilled would say, "Make me into what you will!" For most of us, to be sure, this kind of being-created experience does not come to us in the public worship of the church because we carelessly take the purpose of the occasion to be like any other. Church is just another thing to go to, another engagement on the calendar; but it might, even for us, be what it is intended to be—the most important encounter of the week. God works upon his worshipers slowly and always by mysterious means; but who will fail to see the difference after, say, thirty years between two men, likeminded at the start, one of whom worships (in the true way) weekly and the other not at all? God, of course, does not appear in person, and anyone who thinks he does, or believes God communicates with him by direct talk or action, had better see a psychiatrist; but upon the worshiping mind God does work through that mind's contemplation of and comparison of its ideals, its balancing of values—exercises that are given first priority in the time of worship.

There are communions in which the congregations, as such, have little individuality, since the forms of worship are prescribed by the denomination as a whole. There are others in which there is, as it were, little but individuality, since the norms of worship that the historic church stands ready to supply are completely neglected in favor of innovations, eccentricities, and unfitting informalities that separate rather than unite the single congregation to the rest of Christendom. In the United Church of Christ complete freedom is left to each congregation to worship as it will the Father of our Lord Jesus Christ and our Father, but the sense of fellowship with the rest of Christ's Church (especially the United part of it) is so strong that identical forms symbolizing unity are constantly employed, with a resulting happy balance of creativity and solidarity. The United Church of Christ finds itself, as do many other churches, part of the stream of the contemporary liturgical movement, in which the mighty instruments of worship which the past has known are being rediscovered and new ones being developed to parallel the new theological understandings of the day; but in the United Church this movement is probably felt even more keenly than elsewhere because the confluence of the two rivers of tradition adds force to it. As for the relation of worship to art in general, the whole Reformed tradition from which the United Church is descended has emphasized the need to make art the servant of worship and not to allow worship to become the servant of art. In the United Church today there is a revulsion against artistic barrenness in worship, but this does not mean that the church has deserted its ancestors' love of simplicity. The traveler who remembers the infinite collection of religious gewgaws—supplicatory plaques, vigil lamps, inscriptions in disorganized profusion, in the midst of debased and busy architectural appointments—which surround the so-called holy places of Christianity in Palestine will have an illustration of the kind of overstressing and over-massing of forms that the Reformed Church, and especially the Puritan part of it, dislikes. What refreshment to go from one of these spots where the arts of Christian worship are seen at their intensive worst into a Moslem mosque across the street where there is quiet to the eye as well as to the ear (for the mutter of the disciple by the pillar reciting the Koran only enhances the silence), and where no image of anything in heaven above or in the earth beneath or in the water under the earth serves to fasten the mind to things terrestrial! Of course Moslem arts of worship are quite different from those which make their special appeal to the United Church of Christ: the only resemblance is in the freedom from multiplicity and plethora of symbol. Closer to the United Church ideal—if one is to seek for parallels in faraway places—is the art inspired by Buddhism and usually called simply "Japanese." In both there is the same love of the austere. There is some consanguinity between the picture of Sakyamuni sitting under a weather-beaten pine—direct, of few lines, colors subdued—and the service of a United Church in a New England village, say, or in a frontier village in Wisconsin settled by Germans. There is in both a strain of economy and ruggedness. There is no shying away from the arts (as there was in Puritanism before it came to its essential and positive self) but there is also no such abandonment to the medium as would obscure the single purpose of worship.

To help toward an understanding of worship in an average congregation of the United Church of Christ, let me take you, reader and friend, to the church where my wife and I worship of a Sunday morning. It is in a town of a little less than three thousand. The members of the church number about two hundred and fifty. Here is our usual order of service:

Organ Prelude
Call to Worship
Processional Hymn
Prayer of Approach to God
    Response
Responsive or Unison Reading
    Gloria Patri
Prayer of Confession
    Response
Scripture Reading
Anthem
Prayer of Petition, Intercession, and Thanksgiving
    The Lord's Prayer
Offertory
    Doxology and Offertory Prayer
Hymn of Devotion
Sermon
Prayer of Consecration
    Response
Recessional Hymn
Benediction
Organ Postlude

Many of the shades of meaning of the word *celebrate* are present in the prelude and postlude of a church service such as this. As I grow older, music becomes an ever holier language for me: it penetrates to an inner area which ideas do not seem to reach. Silence has its own spiritual luxury, it is true, but what is more natural than to make the joyful noise unto the Lord? By it both primitive and sophisticated men seem to declare their common gratitude. What substitute is there for a voluntary such as comes from the exaltation and glowing genius of a César Franck? When such music is played in a church today it is sheer celebration; it celebrates not only the composer's quest for the beauty of God in melody, consonance, and rhythm, but also, the organist's own identification of himself with the composer. Through them and with them, therefore, the congregation celebrates the grand fact of contact which has been made between man and God in the gracious realm of sound. The United Church of Christ is a church which believes in music as a medium of worship.

All that has just been said may be applied also to the singing of hymns, but here a new element is added—the words. It has long been noted that the hymnbook and the Bible are the two symbols of the unity and interdependence of Christians which persist in spite of the denominationalism that has divided the Church. If any of the several hymnbooks used in the United Church of Christ are opened (including what might be called the two official ones), they will be found to contain the expressions of the spiritual moods of poets in every corner of Christendom. I pick one of them up at random and find that the first in the book was written by Isaac Watts, an English Congregationalist; the second by Nicolaus Decius, a German Lutheran; the third by Gerhardt Terstee-gen, a German Reformed Churchman and mystic; the fourth by William Kethe, a Scottish Presbyterian; the fifth by Robert Grant, an English Anglican—and so on. It is an ecumenical volume, and the United Church of Christ takes pride in drawing into its worship hymns from as many parts of the great church as possible. Since there is probably no part of the

Christian life which is left uncelebrated in these hymns, the minister in selecting three or four for any particular service may cause them to emphasize any phase of the Gospel which he believes ought specially to be brought before his people at the time. Nor are the hymns mere words: they are the distilled hopes and fears of generations of men, the lonely but triumphant agonies of many, the finally inexpressible delights of others in the presence of that God who made them for himself—and all of these are available to the congregation as gates to the more abundant life, gates that swing open at the moment of true celebration.

The prayers in the United Church of Christ are in part classical, in part prepared in advance for the particular service, in part extempore. In general it may be said that prayers which come out of the past—such prayers as the communion collect, which appeared in English in the First Prayer Book of Edward VI, in 1549, and in Latin before that—carry with them an inevitable aura of the church as the church, and by the use of them one binds himself to all the saints by whose lips they have been uttered, their joy of communion with God becoming his.

In the seventeenth century there were leaders in Puritanism who felt that all forms of what they called *set* prayer, that is, prayers quoted from the past, were likely to do harm to a minister and the church that used them. They feared that the employment of forms already written would cause minister and people to lose the gift of praying extemporaneously and from their own heart. John Owen said, "We daily see men napkining their talents until they are taken from them." He saw that the universal use of classical prayers might cause some to believe that these were the only kind that could be prayed. John Norton notes in his quaint manner: "One's own free words that go with his own momentary sighings reach the emotions in a more exciting, warming, and moving way than can any set form whatever," and others questioned whether any book of prayers, however voluminous, could fully meet the myriad moods of the spirit. Furthermore, repetition is the enemy of freshness and therefore breeds the hypocrisy of saying something without feeling it.

These criticisms of the use of classical prayers, however, in the long run have had the effect of setting up guards against dangers which may be encountered in the excessive use of such prayers rather than of driving them out of public worship altogether. It is generally believed in the United Church of Christ that a minister who is prepared only to read prayers or to recite those he has learned by rote is unqualified for his high office. The usual prayer that one hears in a United Church congregation is one which the minister has himself prepared, in language hallowed by the liturgical uses of the past and therefore not so full of novelties as to draw attention to itself, but which, being prepared for a specific congregation for a definite occasion, is pointed, relevant, and in empathy with the needs of the people.

The responsive or unison reading in the United Church of Christ is from the Holy Scriptures, chiefly from the Psalms, the ancient liturgical treasury of the Hebrews, which recites the struggles and triumphs of the human soul before God with the same appositeness to the twentieth century that it had to the centuries before Christ. There are churches in some denominations in which literature from the pen of humanity's thinkers like Confucius and even Ralph Waldo Emerson is read alongside the Bible, but it is seldom so in the United Church. These writers may be quoted in the sermon, but only the canonical authors are called into service for the basic liturgy. The entire church, and not one segment of it alone, has accepted the Scriptures as the United Church knows them, and every time the minister opens the pulpit book and reads from it, he and his people celebrate their membership in an old and ever new tradition. The teaching potentialities of the reading of the Scriptures, either by the congregation in unison or antiphonal mode or by the minister from the lectern, are of course beyond compute, and here the individual as well as the social demand in true worship comes into evidence: the minister of the United Church asks his people to bring their brains with them to church, for worship there is more than a periodic emotional social stimulation. The reading from the Scriptures needs to be understood as well as accepted as a congregational form.

The sermon takes all the wisdom on a particular spiritual matter that the minister can garner from the world of spiritual knowledge, his own being added. Since the time for the sermon in the United Church of Christ is usually from twenty to thirty minutes, it is evident that the minister must be highly selective in his material. At no point does the minister more clearly evidence the degree of his own spiritual depth. The Saturday-night grasper who depends upon headlines he has read, is soon revealed. Though the sermon is a channel for teaching and learning, it is also an ideal component for worship, for it not only permits an explanation of the meaning of the worship but also carries the congregation from the mood of prayer, basically important as that is, into that of commitment—commitment both to God and to the works of God in the world inside and outside the church—but of this more later.

These comments have indicated, between the lines, that the minister of the congregation has not a little to do with the preparation for and conduct of the service. Worship is not an art, but like every other expression of the human spirit, it involves art. The minister, in choosing from the store of patterns of worship which his tradition lays to his hand, or in deciding at what points he should make a new departure in general structure or detail, must choose the forms which he believes best illustrate his intent and will therefore best woo his congregation into the adoring celebration of God's presence in their midst; and this choice involves art. If he chooses ill, he is a poor workman; if well, a good one—and any workman who needeth not to be ashamed is, in his way, an artist. Concerning the minister and his further duties, we shall have more to say later.

Historically, one branch of the United Church of Christ, the Reformed Church of the United States, has had a great deal to do with making the American churches aware of the meaning of liturgics. In 1840, John Williamson Nevin was elected professor of theology at the Seminary in Mercersburg, where Frederick Augustus Rauch was already teaching. The latter dying suddenly, Philip Schaff of the University of Berlin, Germany (1819–93), was elected to take his place in 1843. This election was one of the greatest gifts ever made by any part of the American church to the church as a whole, for Schaff brought to this country the magnificent achievements of German religious thought. He not only introduced to American theological classrooms what is known as the historical method, now accepted in every leading institution of learning, but with Nevin he also helped the whole church to see the importance of time-honored and meaningful ordinances of worship. Stress was laid upon the place of the early church fathers in the shaping of proper forms and upon the real spiritual presence of Christ in the Lord's Supper (of which the whole United Church is today fully aware). To the Mercersburg Theology, as the thought of the two men came to be called, the United Church of Christ owes its own special debt. We shall have more to say about this happy turn in the tradition of the United Church when we treat of the sacrament of communion.

Honesty of Thought

The ordinary congregation of the United Church of Christ in an ordinary American town orders its worship, or tries to, with the intent of keeping it relevant to the needs of the times. And relevance involves honesty. Says the Constitution:

The United Church of Christ . . . affirms the responsibility of the Church in each generation to make this faith [the faith of the historic Church] its own . . . in honesty of thought and expression. . . .

The United Church of Christ feels this responsibility most intensely. It is ready to admit that the church, of which it is a part, has too often allowed the essential truth of the Gospel —God's love for the world expressed in Christ—to remain cluttered with ideas which, though they may have seemed true in one day, have been in a later day definitely proved untrue. The bronze serpent which Moses sets on a pole does very well as a psychological cure for people superstitious enough to believe in its efficacy, but Hezekiah, years afterwards, has to break it down in order to deliver the people from superstition. So the United Church of Christ, resolved to get at the truth in life, ceases to acknowledge beliefs of yesterday, however beautiful and even useful they may have seemed, if the shadow of falsity creeps over them. As we have said, the United Church approaches the Bible with all the instruments of research that modern science can supply, taking nothing for granted except that God favors enquiry and accompanies the enquirer; and if it is found out that some beliefs of the fathers—such, for instance, as their idea that the world was created in six days—is found not to square with the facts, it is dismissed without tears. A discovery of fact is regarded as a new revelation from God.

Truth!—the honest search for it and the honest living by it when found—this is a constant concern of the United Church of Christ at its best; it does not follow, however, that when an ancient belief is found to be untrue, it is forgotten. It is dismissed from the realm of essential faith, to be sure, but if it has in it qualities of truth, such as a fictional story or a piece of poetry or even a myth may have, it is not dropped out of the life of the church. Take the Christmas story in Luke, for example. I am sure that there are few adult members of the United Church of Christ who believe that angels, such as the medieval artists were fond of depicting, actually appeared from heaven and talked in Aramaic with a group of shepherds about the birth in the stable. What then is to be done with the story? Some denominations take the attitude that the fathers knew better than we, and that the story should be accepted as part of the belief of the church although we cannot believe it as individual Christians. This seems like an invitation to schizophrenia. Other denominations on the extreme left of rationalism have thrown the whole tale overboard and substituted for the Christmas legend the kind of abstract and unadorned recital which might be acceptable in a classroom where objective study rather than imaginative celebration of the great event is in order. The United Church of Christ holds affectionately to the Lucan account, tells the story over and over again every Christmas, identifies itself with the shepherds, making their wonder and delight its own—but in any moment of reflection carefully distinguishes between the true kernel of the story and the elaborations of devoted fancy. The truth of Christ's coming, however enveloped in happy folklore, is truth, and is not injured by its association with fantasies beloved by the race from its racial childhood.

The United Church of Christ is an heir of the Reformation, but it is also a child of the earlier Renaissance; and many of those who were its spiritual ancestors were steeped at the time of the Renaissance in the recaptured wisdom of the classical age. When, much later, modern science was beginning to make its entrance into the mind of man, the conservatives in the Church were fundamentally indifferent to the new learning except as it could be used for homiletical purposes; and the extremists among the sectarians on the other side, though they professed interest in it, used it chiefly as a club against the conservatives. In distinction to both these schools, the ancestors of the United Church of Christ were interested in it as an instrument for the betterment of man. They were the ones who called for a reformation of university learning so that it might become relevant to the social and personal needs of the day. It is this same spirit that prevails in the United Church today.

In the thought of the United Church there is no more conflict between religion and science than there is between religion and art. Religion treats of God, science of the world that God has created and is still creating—as art treats of the forms of that world. The kind of religion that is preached in the pulpits of the United Church is an assistance to science (as to art) because it points to a God who made man in his own image, and desires him to rise to the greatest heights of discovery and creativity. If one asks if it is not to be feared that science will discover something that will prove that God is not a God of love such as Christ showed him to be, the answer to be given is that there is not a thing in the world, discovered or to be discovered, which can prove the moral character of its maker. Even an apparently evil thing can be put into the world by a benign creator for a good end; and just as we cannot conclude from the fact of evil things in the world that God is evil, neither can we legitimately hold that good things in the world prove that God is good. Our recognition of God is not dependent upon the physical circumstances which are the stock in trade of science: it comes to us in the midst of good or evil surroundings, through the relationship with him called faith. This is a sense of life in the soul—something really impossible to describe in an ordinary way, because the only words we have for such description are those borrowed from the world of things, and God is not a thing. God is the eternal subject, who never can be made the object of brain activity, as all the things of science are. God is God and the world is the world—and science has to do only with the latter.

The United Church of Christ sees the world presided over by a God of love as Christ makes him known—a world composed of things that can be seen, heard, studied into by scientific methods, and so progressively better known in physical dimensions. God wants man to know the truth, all of the truth achievable. Wherever truth is found it is God's truth; it is all one; and a person who believes in God, as Christ revealed him, is encouraged by that very belief to cut ever more deeply into the truth of things. The faith of the thinker in the United Church is a faith that enquires.

To the religious life of North America the United Church of Christ and its fathers have contributed an unusual number of thinkers. By way of illustration, let one individual and one school of theology suffice for all.

The individual who has often been called the greatest religious philosopher this continent has produced was Jonathan Edwards (1703–1758). During the greater part of his life he was the minister of Congregational churches in western Massachusetts, one of which, interestingly enough, was the first, over two hundred years later, to ratify the Constitution of the United Church of Christ. A busy and practical man, as well as a metaphysician, he faced the problems of the small town on the wilderness frontier and all the while lived as a thinker facing the problems of man as man. He is not to be explained fully by his times, for he looked at his age through the eyes of the timeless, and therefore made his contribution to all times. His fierce determination to put his brains to work in the cause of interpreting God to man is an inheritance he bequeathed to his successors; the idle talk about keeping theology (that is, thought about God) out of religion is not heard in the United Church.

A school of thought that deserves mention, since it colored the attitudes of the churches in this country for a century and more, is that of the so-called "New England Theology." It would be inappropriate to detail the emphases of its thinkers here, for those emphases have long since faded into forgotteness; but during the latter part of the eighteenth century and the best part of the nineteenth, these were people who kept vigorous thought alive in the churches of the land. Some of the names associated with the movement are still widely remembered: Joseph Bellamy (1719–1790) and Samuel Hopkins (1720–1803) of the first generation after Edwards; Nathaniel Emmons (1745–1840) and Timothy Dwight (1752–1817) of the middle generation; and of the last generation (if they may be held to be of the same school), Lyman Beecher (1775–1863) and Horace Bushnell (1802–1876). The New England brand of Calvinism was provincial enough, in all conscience, but its relevance to the needs of the people of that time and that place gave it strength. Auguste Comte wisely remarked that if a thing is not local it is not alive: the New England theology was both local and alive.

The thinkers in the United Church today are not merely heirs of the New England theology (heaven forbid!) but of all the thought of Christendom, especially that which has been wrought out in the area of the Western and the Reformed Church. I venture to name here a few who already have had a record of guiding opinion in the church (and younger men not named stand ready to take their places when the time comes):

> Roland Herbert Bainton
> John Coleman Bennett
> Robert Lowry Calhoun
> Nels Fredrik Solomon Ferré
> Walter Marshall Horton
> Wilhelm Pauck
> Liston Pope
> Paul Sevier Minear
> Helmut Richard Niebuhr

Reinhold Niebuhr
Paul Tillich
Amos Niven Wilder

And some there be who have no memorial. As a matter of simple fact, the vast task of teaching the people of the churches to look for truth and to recognize it when they see it does not belong to those who will leave a name behind them but rather to the ministers and teachers in parishes who, year after year, week after week, break to their church members the bread of the reality by which they themselves live. They try to keep the thought of the church honest and relevant.

The sentence in the Constitution that we are considering speaks of honesty not only of thought but of the expression of that thought. This is an area to which the United Church of Christ almost at its very inception gave profound attention, and one of the earliest plans it made was for an "Office of Communication," as it was called. Part of the purpose of this office (to be described on a later page of this book) was to let the world know what the United Church was doing in the manner of what has come to be known as the promoting of good public relations—but the philosophy of it goes much deeper than this: the office is to be an instrument and a reminder to the whole church that the Gospel, being a bridge between God's world and the world of man, is not itself if it is not communicated to the people in language they can understand.

The fact is that a good deal of the language heard in the church service needs translation. A man without any background of the church would feel a touch of bewilderment as he sat through the service on a Sunday morning in almost any of the great churches of our metropolises. In some of them he would hear Latin spoken—which often even the devout do not understand. All praise to the Roman Church in the United States for its mighty determination to see to it that the worshipers do understand what is being said and done in the Mass! In some churches the stranger would encounter words and phrases in the sermons, prayers, and other offices that have very little meaning for Americans today. There is a school of thought that would eliminate these words altogether, but the fact is that they—or many of them—have become so richly laden with connotations supremely important that there is no substitute for them. "Salvation," for instance, is today wholly a church word: it does not have its original simple and general meaning of *saving*— we never speak of the "salvation" of a drowning man—and so it is argued that this word, lacking the universality it once enjoyed, is unfit for use by the church that wants to make contact with the world's larger realities. Words like this are in constant employment in the United Church of Christ, however, but with interpretation. It may take an entire sermon, a series of sermons, a life of sermons, to explain the full meaning of *salvation,* but once the understanding of it is arrived at, the word itself becomes a marvelous concentrate of meaning—a whole sermon or set of sermons in itself, as it were. The United Church of Christ is not frightened by the employment of words whose significance can be found today only within the church, but it does try to make their meaning clear to modernity. On the other hand, there may be some words used in the church for which better words are available. In such case the old word can die, and the sooner it does, the better. The important point in the mind of the United Church is that the words of ritual, sermon, and church teaching in general must be made emotionally affective for the modern man.

Purity of Heart

The Constitution in its Preamble now preaches the United Church of Christ a sermon:

The United Church of Christ . . . affirms the responsibility of the Church in each generation to make this faith [the faith of the historic church] its own . . . in purity of heart before God.

This is obviously true but as obviously reflects a counsel of perfection. If only all the members of the United Church might show a crowning relevance to the needs of this age by revealing a simple saintliness in their dedication to God! A church, in the long run, must be judged by only one set of statistics: how many and how profound are the saints it produces? It is through saints, singly and in companies, that God binds the world to himself and lets flow into it his wisdom and his grace; and it is by his purity of heart that a saint may be known. More than one writer has compared this purity to that of the forest pool uncontaminated by surface dust, which reveals the spring bubbling at the bottom with crystal clearness—and I know no better comparison, for the saint, likewise, is a source of refreshment from God unpolluted by the selfishnesses and social prejudices of life lived superficially. What is the *use* of saints? Nothing: but they delight God and delight other human souls, being a kind of open doorway through which he and these others can reach and touch each other.

This my own story of the United Church of Christ is necessarily an idealized version—for who can help but idealize what he loves? I have seen in it incredible examples of sainthood—missionaries who sacrificed all they had for the people to whom they were sent but who in their joy never seemed to know that they were sacrificing anything; ministers who wore themselves out through the years in making life bearable for others; but most of all, men and women of the pews who seemed to have a special calling from God for moral splendor in their business and family life—yet I know the church too well to think it escapes, at times, politics of a baser sort, the play of perverted ambitions, and all the other ethical ills the flesh is heir to. It stands always in need of reformation at some point or other; with the entire Reformed branch of the Church of which it is a part, it has as a motto, *Reformata Semper Reformanda,* and may well take the meaning of it to heart; it is reformed *to be* reformed wherever there is need. And reformation starts ever with the pure in spirit. God grant that human forces will never so completely muddy the heart of its members and the common mind of its congregations as to make them unavailable as relevant channels of his grace.

Chapter IV

THE SACRAMENTS

In accordance with the teaching of our Lord and the practice prevailing among evangelical Christians, it [the United Church of Christ] recognizes two sacraments: Baptism and the Lord's Supper or Holy Communion.

As the constitution here announces, the United Church of Christ joins all the great communions except the Orthodox and the Roman Churches (where seven are counted) to limit the number of the sacraments of the Gospel to two.

It is usually said that the two sacraments of Protestantism are so called because they are the only ones ordered by our Lord himself: of the breaking of the bread, he said, "This do in remembrance of me"; and his last instructions, according to the Matthaean account were: "Go ye therefore, and teach all nations, baptizing them. . . ." It is understandable why some churches take with equal weight Christ's word, also recorded in the Bible: "If I then, your Lord and Master, have washed your feet, ye also ought to wash one another's feet." There are actually some obscure congregations that have a tenuous connection with the United Church to be found in the hill country along the Ohio where the rite of foot washing is practiced—and those who have participated say that there is simply nothing comparable as an act of humility. As a

whole the United Church, however, with the rest of sophisticated Christendom, Catholic and Protestant, knows little of
this practice. It is better said, not that Baptism and Communion are the only sacraments ordained by our Lord himself but that they are the only two of the seven authorized
by the Western Church so ordained. Of the five others we
shall speak later.

Baptism

In the United Church of Christ, baptism is the rite of
initiation into Christ's church. The United Church accepts as
its own the baptisms performed and accepted by any other
part of the church. Here it identifies itself with the Catholic,
and distinguishes itself from the Baptist, strain in Christianity. Normally its own baptism is by sprinkling, but in areas in
which people are generally committed to baptism by immersion, it may suggest to its ministers there that they too
utilize this same method, in order to obviate theological controversy with their neighbors at too trivial a level. It would
have no quarrel with the practice of pouring—affusion—at
baptism, but that is a practice not often encountered in this
part of the world in this day. When a person with Quaker
background, or some other, who has conscientious scruples
against the use of water or any other particular material at
baptism, desires the adoption into the church which baptism
signifies, some special arrangement is usually made whereby,
in some mode or other, the baptism of the spirit (which is
the essential matter) can be betokened.

What does the United Church of Christ mean by baptism? For one thing, baptism provides the occasion for focus-
ing the mind of the one to be baptized (if adult) or those
who are to sponsor him (if an infant) on the basic meanings
of church membership. The water used is the symbol of

washing, and washing means renewal, so that the total rite comes to mean that the person baptized is thereby adopted into the new life which is hid with Christ, and Christ's people, in God. That baptism also has moral implications is apparent. The adult when baptized takes an oath to strive to know the will of God as taught in the Scriptures, to walk in his ways, and to be a disciple of Christ not in name only but in deed and in truth. An infant obviously can make no pledge, but his parents or other sponsors do, and this is a direct pledge, binding them themselves to do what lies in their power to cause the child to grow up in the knowledge of the love of God. If promises are made in behalf of the child, these are confirmed in the normal course by the child himself on reaching the age of discretion. No difficulty is felt at involving the infant—that is, the in-fant or not-speaking one —in the rite, because the symbolism is that of Mother Church reaching out to the helpless one and taking him into her care. The parents or sponsors pledge themselves as mediaries between the church and the child, and in due course the child, when able to speak for himself, consciously accepts the hands which were stretched out to him in love before he could appreciate the act.

Here it may be of use to bring forward again the idea of the Covenant and the complex of forces involved in every act within the church. God is always the prime mover, and his action comes to a person partly directly, partly through the mediation of the church; it is when the individual and the church acknowledge the work of God in each other that the Covenant, always a triangular one, is sealed. This could hardly be more perfectly illustrated than in the rite of baptism. In the case of the christening of an infant, the only willed line of blessing goes from God through the church to the child. Since the latter can self-consciously will nothing at that age and cannot understand anything of what is done, the church awaits his coming to the age when God can speak to him and he can complete the circuit of the Covenant by acknowledging his responsibility to the church. Though his parents or his godparents or sponsors may at the time of baptism speak for him, this is hardly enough for a fully sealed Covenant. Infant baptism is then the action of the church and does indeed make the child a member, though not a self-committed and self-communicating member. It is thought by the United Church of Christ better to make him such a member—better so to illustrate its own concern for its little ones—than to ask that the child wait till adolescence, when he himself can make his promise to the church, for the church to make its reciprocal promise to him.

The Lord's Supper

As for the Eucharist, it is regarded in the United Church of Christ, as generally throughout Christendom, as the central act of Christian worship. Everything about it lends it excellence as a Christian symbol. It is biblical, being modeled on the last supper our Lord had with his disciples while on earth. It is associated with his crucifixion, which was the climax of his life. Its form is that of the high moment of any family in any age in any place—the gathering together for a common meal. One of the best descriptions of it is the earliest of the Reformation statements concerning it. In 1518, Luther wrote:

Its name is communion: its essence is the uniting of hearts. . . . And this is set forth in the very elements of the sacrament, in which many grains of wheat, their individual differences lost, are brought together in the one bread, and many grapes, their differences also lost, into the one wine.

In the United Church of Christ are undoubtedly to be found as many interpretations of the Eucharist as there are in Protestant Christendom, since all the major strains of

Protestantism are in the United Church, but these are dominated by the one certainty that the Lord's Table is a means of grace to those who partake, and that, because the real presence of Christ is available there. Doubtless this presence is made known to human hearts elsewhere, too, but at communion time the veil that time and space spread between Christ's living spirit and our living souls is at its thinnest. If Luther's idea that Christ's body is everywhere but that it is brought, as it were, into special focus at the Eucharist, could be translated from its medieval connotations to mean that the essential Christ, his spirit, himself, is indeed everywhere available but in a special way in the sacrament, then it might be said that Luther's thesis is held by the United Church. Certainly the emphasis of Zwingli is maintained in the United Church: the Eucharist is not a repetition of the sacrifice of Christ, as had been believed and still is where Mass is celebrated, but rather a commemoration of the death of Christ made once and for all for all people—the giving of the only life he had, and therefore consummately precious. Most of all it is to Calvin that the United Church of Christ owes its views of the sacrament: the bread and wine are signs of the body and blood of Christ and symbols of his presence, which make the rite a real means of grace, strengthening the union with him.

It is sad to think that historically the communion table, which should bring all the grains and all the grapes into the one bread and wine, has been a point of disunion. Here Protestantism separates itself from those who believe that the priest at the altar is actually the instrument through which God changes the substance of the elements into the body and blood of Christ. Here Luther and Zwingli (at least Luther) found that they had a different spirit—Luther being a monk wanting nothing so much as assurance of grace and Zwingli a parish priest wanting to make the rite above all a welding point of community. Now, in the twentieth century, there

are suggestions that the old chasm between the Lutheran and
the Reformed Churches may be closed, and there are even
signs on the horizon, no bigger than a man's hand, that even
Roman Catholics and Protestants may together enter into
conversations to resolve their eucharistic differences. In
the United Church of Christ there is a yeasting hope that
all Christians may one day meet around the one table of
their Lord.

There are two main schools of thought as to the churchly
meaning of the Lord's Table in Christendom. Those churches
commonly called Catholic (though there is also a Catholic
base in Protestantism) tend to regard the Table as the symbol
of the ecclesiastical unity of those who communicate there.
At an Anglican altar, for instance, when communicants
gather, the Holy Communion is, among other things, a
declaration that they belong to the one church family. But
Anglicans do not draw the line of definition closely, for they
open their communion to members of certain other churches,
like the Church of Sweden, on the ground of a determination,
long since made, that that church accepts what the Anglican
family of Christians regard as marks of true churchmanship
—the Holy Scriptures, the Apostles' and Nicene Creeds, the
two biblical sacraments, and the historic episcopate. The
circle of what is known as intercommunion is wider than that
of any one communion, and within it admission to the Holy
Table stands not merely for the unity of the one church
family but for the mutual recognition of two church families
as members of Christ's one church. The other school of
ecclesiastical thought, loosely called Protestant (though there
are Protestant churches which do not agree), takes one
further step. It extends intercommunion not merely to the
members of other churches which can exhibit a number of
marks of being true churches but to all which possess the
one and only necessary mark (as they conceive it)—acknowledged belief in the Lord Jesus Christ as the revelation of

God. They think that the acceptance or refusal of bishops in apostolic line, for instance, is not of the same nature or consequence as the acceptance or refusal of Jesus Christ as Lord of the Church, and they do not with equanimity see persons shut out from the Lord's Table on the ground of their opinion about church government. It is to this group of churches that the United Church of Christ belongs, and it prays for the day when intercommunion will be the order among all parts of the church of Christ or, better yet, when all parts of the great church shall be members of a single, though not of a uniform, communion.

Holy Communion is the event *par excellence* in which the tripartite quality of the Covenant and the directions of the force of grace may be traced.

When a man communes with God (in Christ) and his fellows at the holy table, he stands at the conflux of the two vital streams which flow from Christ's spirit. On the one hand he receives what Christ gives him through the church, and on the other hand he imparts to the church what he receives directly from Christ. Christ is the source; and one course of his grace flows through all to each, another through each to all.

When either one of these moments of grace is interrupted or in any way reduced, the communion is misunderstood and impaired. Take two historical examples:

The warm reciprocity of receiving grace both through the brethren and directly, which we believe to have been the experience of the early Christians, slowly gave way in the course of the centuries to a one-sided conception. By the early sixteenth century, when the Reformers began to lift their voices, the grace that came through the church had become so greatly magnified as to obscure that which came directly from Christ to the faithful communicant. Who could forgive sins? The priest alone, according to the then theory, because he could act for the *church*. Justification was through penance, appointed by the *church,* and not through faith, which is an attribute of the single human soul in touch with Christ. Who could set up new congregations in growing towns or villages? Only a bull of the pope, or fiat of the local bishop, representing the *church.* The whole spirit of the Mass was one in which the individual had simply nothing to give except implicit, that is, folded-in, obedience, and everything to receive.

The Reformation, with its concern for the priesthood of all believers, redressed the balance.

What John Williamson Nevin and Philip Schaff (to return to these important ancestors) found in this country about a hundred years ago illustrates the swing of the pendulum in the direction of individualism. People on the frontier did not easily remember that they never would have been Christians if it had not been for the church of the past, for there was little there to remind them of the past. Communion was celebrated from time to time as a kind of extra bonus not part of the regular rhythm of the church, and the real sacrament, the only one that truly counted, was conversion. People in general thought that churches were created by the converted getting together and creating them. The church, therefore, seemed more directly the result of their own efforts than a response to the work of Christ. Nevin and Schaff and their aides cannot be said in the Mercersburg Movement to have achieved perfect success in their attempt to bring the doctrine of the church back into American Protestantism. They may even have gone to extremes we should not condone. But the United Church of Christ regards this shining episode in its tradition as an endeavor to keep the stream of grace, which flows from Christ through the many to each, as strong and fecund as that which flows through each to the many. The leaders of that movement desired an Evangelical Catholic— that is, a Protestant Catholic—Church, and that is precisely what the United Church deems itself to be.

The two streams of Christ's grace take color from the channels through which they pass.

The grace which enters your soul at the time of communion, giving outreach and concern for every other soul, takes on your own character and possibilities. Whatever your characteristics—whether you be a man of few words or many; of scientific or artistic frame of mind; quick thinking, deep thinking, or both—the grace of Christ in you will not go out from you in a sheer or wooden way; it will take the shape of your own interests and abilities. Christ never reduces a man to a given mold, he brings him up to his own best capacities and expressions. At the time of communion it is appropriate for each person to consider how he can best channel the grace of the Lord Jesus to his neighbor: this self-examination is part of the cost of grace.

And the grace which comes to you through the others who gather with you at communion, brings with it the characteristic flavor of those others—and the cost of the grace that comes through them is always high, for behind them stands the entire church which they represent, and only as you appreciate them and the church can you partake of their blessing. The more you know of Christ's life, the better you can commune with him. The more you know of the church's heroes, the better you can understand the blessing which the church brings you in its communion. Communicants at the Lord's Table in the United Church of Christ drink the words of Augustine and the other thinkers of the ancient and the Western Church in proportion as they know them. They eat the thought of Luther, Calvin, Zwingli, if they are acquainted with them. They take the bread of the Pilgrims at Plymouth (hard to break, being frozen on the paten); they sip the wine from a common cup with those at Falkner Swamp whom John Philip Boehm has gathered about him; they stand behind the spiritual defenses made for them by Louis Nollau and his colleagues in the early days of the Midwestern synods

—all in ratio to their knowledge of them. The stream of strength which flows to us from the prophets and apostles of the past is limitless in its potentialities, but the price of it is study and acquaintance with them. The United Church of Christ urges its people to know so well the saints and martyrs who have made the church what it is, that when they eat the bread and take the cup they will feel toward them a personal gratitude for having transmitted to them the communion of Christ and given it new meaning.

CHAPTER V

UNITY AND DIVERSITY

Now we come to an extraordinarily important milestone in our journey through the Constitution:

The provisions herein [in the Constitution] define and regulate the General Synod and those instrumentalities of the United Church of Christ which are recognized, established by or responsible to the General Synod, and describe the free and voluntary relationships which the local churches, Associations, Conferences and ministers sustain with the General Synod and with each other. The pattern of relationships and procedures so described is recommended to local churches, Associations, Conferences and ministers, to enable them more effectively to accomplish their tasks and the work of the United Church of Christ.

Here the Christian-political genius of the instrument is shown—but first, some definitions of the terms which are used:

The General Synod is the representative body of the United Church of Christ at the national level.

Its instrumentalities are the mission boards and other agencies appointed by the General Synod to do the work of Christ and the church in areas in which special expertness is required.

The Associations are the representative bodies of the United Church at the level of counties or groups of counties.

The Conferences are the representative bodies of the United Church at the state level.

Even the government of the United Church of Christ is an expression of its faith. It believes, as we have many times pointed out, that God works with mankind both socially and individually and that his church should for that very reason provide him an instrument which, on the one hand, may be used by him as a whole and as a whole respond to his will, and yet, on the other hand, be made up of individuals and individual parts which may each be used by him and each respond to his will without awaiting action by the great whole.

So far so good: God's pure will making itself effective through an individual will not conflict with his pure will expressing itself through the church to which the individual belongs—but God's will is seldom if ever found in its purity in our humanity. It is likely to be stained by the individuality of the individual and by the ecclesiasticism of the church it uses as a channel. A member or a minority within the church may interpret his will in one way, and the church as a whole, that is, the majority, in another. Each may be wholly honest, wholly convinced that its point of view best reflects the mind of Christ, but still the two do not agree. What does a Christian church do in this situation? Three general solutions are available: (1) to lodge final authority with the church as a whole, represented in the governing body, in such a way that nonconforming parts of the church are regarded as disorderly; (2) to lodge authority with the various parts, so that any authority on the part of the whole is virtually nonexistent; or (3) to hold strongly to the idea that all authority is with God in Christ, that no human person or organization can quite represent him, that it should be taken for granted that he may be heard both through the church as a whole and through any part of it, that therefore both the authority of the whole and that of the individuals and individual parts that compose it should be maintained at a maximum, and that when they differ, each should be given the chance of following its own insights, holding to the belief that Christ will eventually show them a way to synthesize them. The United Church of Christ takes the third alternative.

In denominations where the first course is pursued, the national body, corresponding to the General Synod, makes rules for the entire church, including all its parts—rules which, if followed, mark the good churchmanship of those who follow them. It is a solemn moment at the national gathering of such a denomination when the judicial commission makes its report: the entire assembly is likely to rise as it enters to announce decisions which, if approved by the assembly itself, may affect churches, ministers, or laymen on the extremest periphery of the communion. There is nothing undemocratic about procedure of this sort, which gives to a central body legislative and judicial authority over the entire communion, since the constituent groups which are affected by the legislation and judgment delegate this power to that body and make their own choice of delegates to represent them there; but such groups do not, however, have the power of taking the initiative and trying out new measures that do not conform or are even opposed to the authorizations of the national body. No local part of the greater church can in good order adopt a form of life which differs from that prescribed by the higher body. If it wishes to make a change in its habits at this point, it must work through its delegates to the higher body to have an amendment made in the constitution or bylaws of that body permitting it.

The opposite of this system—the second alternative mentioned above—is found in those areas of the church which are sometimes called, from the best known illustrations of it in church history, Anabaptist. As has been brought out in recent

17805

studies of sixteenth-century Protestantism, the opprobrium attached to this name is unjustified by the facts. That rascals sometimes attached themselves to the credulous groups that made up the Anabaptist movement and led them into deplorable excesses is beyond doubt, but rascality no more reflects the heart of the movement than the character of the pirate who in 1410 claimed to be Pope John reflected the character of the church with which he was associated. The heart of the movement was the sense that God can speak directly to any person he selects as a prophet—a forth-teller—of his will. The doctrine of the necessary separation of church and state, which is basic to our American political philosophy, had its historical rise among the people who, knowing that God might sometimes select an individual to be his mouthpiece, felt to the point of defiance and, when necessary, of willing self-sacrifice that no state could interpose its own mandate between the Deity and his chosen instrument; and in consequence the United States owes to them, through Roger Williams, a very great debt. But the same determination not to allow any state to interfere with the prophetic voice and the prophetic act may be directed against church authority and, indeed, when unqualified, denies any kind of social authority at all. Theologically, extreme Anabaptism takes it for granted that God speaks only through prophets, that is, individuals, and never speaks through a society to individuals.

As we have said so many times, the theology of the United Church of Christ holds that God speaks through each of these channels. The church at its best is a company of believers among whom the living Christ is at work, speaking to each through all and to all through each. The Constitution of the United Church of Christ, taking this truth as its foundation, finds its peculiar genius in avoiding either the authoritarian or the Anabaptist extreme. It is designed to draw the best out of the totality and out of each individual and individual group within it. Lincoln Christian College

Taking for granted the individual-social polarity of God's Covenant with his church, the United Church of Christ sets up a point of entry for the whole church—a pole, as it were, on which his lightning may most easily strike and whence his grace may flow through the church as a unit to its parts. This point of entry must be at the very nerve center of the church, whither the needs of the whole can be most easily carried and whence they can be seen most clearly and in best balance. It must be such that from this point the place of the whole church in the economy of Christendom can be gauged and the service of the whole church to the world may be programed. Its lines of communication must connect all parts with itself, and all parts through it must be able as a unit to respond to God's call, so that it becomes a symbol and demonstration of the whole, by the whole, and for the whole. This is the General Synod, which, serving as a symbol of the one church, has one set of laws governing it, and these are those given in the Constitution.

The other pole is a multiple one: it is every individual, every individual grouping within the church, through whom God may speak and who may respond to him in worship and service. Through these many points of entry, creativity, patient study, mystical illumination, and all the other virtues of the mature individual and the small group, are utilized by Christ as the carriers of his grace into the church and so to the world at large. It is because the United Church of Christ believes so deeply in the individual and individual groups like congregations as indispensable crucibles for God's spirit that it protects their individuality in every way it can. They must be allowed to make their own contact with Christ: the church will provide the best environment it can, but the will to believe and to serve must come from within them. They must be allowed to worship in the form that they themselves know best suits them; the larger church will be ready with suggestions, but the decision must be theirs. They must be allowed to witness and minister as they will; the church will supply instruments if necessary but the initiative must lie with them.

So the United Church of Christ, conceiving itself a member of God's Covenant in Christ, its individual communicants another member, and God himself the chief member, who initiates the impulse in the others to unite in witness, worship, and ministry, consciously sets up a government which will permit action by the total communion without waiting on the parts, and by each part without waiting for the total. The one does not make rules for the other: the total church appoints the General Synod its agent but no communicant, congregation, Association, or Conference within the church takes his (or its) rules from that Synod. Similarly the Synod looks not to its parts but itself for its own rules. The United Church is neither authoritarian nor Anabaptist. It is a church free to act for Christ as a church but with its parts free to act for Christ for themselves, too. The parts are free at any moment to depart if they will from the whole, and the whole to let go the parts; but he who said, "I, if I be lifted up, will draw all men to me," draws them to him and so to each other. This combines the maximum of establishment with the maximum chance for creativity.

But there is more: the General Synod, representing the whole church, is made as receptive as possible to the creative touch of the parts. It is not a monolith, standing invariable from age to age. Since it represents the whole church it does indeed make haste slowly to change its procedures; but at the suggestion of delegates coming from the various parts of the church it is ready to consider proposed improvements—and when the proposals are made through stated authority, due advance notice of them given, a two-thirds vote of those present and voting supports them, and two-thirds of the Conferences ratify them, the changes are actually made. The General Synod pole (to revert to our electromagnetic figure) is ready to pick up messages from the other poles, and even to receive charges which alter its own form, always provided these do not jeopardize the essential Constitution which keeps it representative of the whole church.

In the other direction, the parts of the church—the Conferences, Associations, congregations, and even individual members—make themselves as receptive as possible to the advice and counsel of the whole, represented in the General Synod. Without giving up their freedom to listen themselves for the voice of God and respond themselves to new commandments which the living Christ may give them, they treasure their fellowship with the entire church as free men treasure friendship. This fellowship gives them enlargement and security in Christ. They know well enough that there was never any religious innovator of consequence who was not nourished within a church organization—the Reformers within the Western Church, the Puritans, and, later, John Wesley, within Anglicanism, for instance—and so they devote themselves to the limit of their ability to the whole church and its forms, given shape by the General Synod.

To this end the General Synod is requested to provide what it believes to be the best standards of conduct for all the parts of the church—for "local churches, Associations, Conferences, and ministers," says the Constitution. These standards are set forth in those parts of the Constitution which do not have to do with the General Synod and its immediate instrumentalities. These standards provide for action throughout the entire church, but they are of the nature not of the laws of the Medes and the Persians but of highly recommended norms, from which if exception be taken by any local church, Association, or Conference, no stigma of bad churchmanship attaches to the act. The United Church of Christ is a church which trusts its minorities; it even expects them at times to step out of the routine in order to make a new and signal contribution to the church in Christ's name. The result, it is plain, will sometimes be a plurality of procedures within the total church, but it is a healthy kind leading to no untoward consequences.

The whole church, on the one hand, acknowledges the power of any part of it to move ahead in areas where it (the part) thinks it can better serve the Lord of the church; but on the other hand, no part is left uncertain as to what the total church considers best. The two ideas come to tension, and tension is always the point of growth. Two procedures may exist within the one church—and if so, the Lord of history has his chance to teach the sensitive by the process known on the human side as the survival of the fittest. It may be that some experiment deemed advisable by the local church will prove abortive; the theological idea behind it may show itself to have been ill thought out and not consonant with the general corpus of belief—it may reveal practical infelicities which annul it—and in any case of the sort the practice can be discontinued. Or it may be that the new experiment will open up unexpected avenues of Christian statesmanship and action, and in that case, the trial-and-error stage having been undergone in one congregation, it will be imitated in another until there is common sentiment sufficient to have the norm in the Constitution of the greater church itself amended. Or the new departure may prove to be a blessing to the church that has tried it in its own community, but not at all successful elsewhere. In that case a permanent plurality will seem to have established itself, and the effect on the Constitution eventually will be not amendment as such but amplification.

A new local church just establishing itself is not without advice and counsel as to how to organize its people and what to aim for in worship and service, for the General Synod stands ready to offer basic blueprints; but, on the other hand, it need not feel bound by these standards in a way not suitable for free Christian minds. The United Church at once supplies the authority of long experience and provides for experimentation.

Viewed from the abstract side, the Constitution might be expected to occasion no end of deviations from the norm. These would be as possible theoretically as they are rare actually. The recommended standards are the result of generations of experience which the churches gratefully recognize. Though the congregations realize that they are free in the United Church of Christ to utilize such forms as seem to them best to accord with the mind of Christ, it does not follow that they seek novelty for its own sake. Most of them lean confidently on the standard ways and means suggested in the Constitution. This combination of freedom and reliance on experience would seem to be one of the marks of maturity.

If it be asked what measures of discipline can be used against a part of the greater church, let us say a local congregation, which enters upon a line of conduct that the church at large considers antagonistic to the mind of Christ, the answer is one which follows the injunction of Matthew 18: to tell the erring congregation that its action seems unbecoming to a part of the church of Christ, to use all persuasive powers available to convince it of its error, and then, if it still refuses to listen, simply to break fellowship with it. There is no attempt to confiscate its property or to use any but spiritual pressures. The whole desire of the communion as a whole would be to maintain fellowship with the straying sister, for else the lines of redemption would be severed. If, however, there were no way of maintaining agreement with the local church, the break would have to come, but it would be only a break. Punishment, especially that kind which is a cloak for vindictiveness, would be out of the question. Cases of this sort, it may be added, are so rare as to have been nonexistent in the later years of the uniting communions, and it is expected that this precedent will carry over into the United Church.

If, contrariwise, a part of the church should feel that the church as a whole had strayed from the ways of Christ, it would also be free to break away from it, though it too would be restrained from so drastic a step by its sense of being a possible redemptive agent. Its tie to the greater church is not a legal one; the tie is only the Covenant in Christ—but that, after all, is everything.

To the very important matter of unity in diversity and diversity in unity we shall return again in other connections.

Chapter VI

NAMING A CHURCH

Now we come to the constitution proper:

Article I.   Name
The name of this Church shall be UNITED CHURCH OF CHRIST.

The first point to note here is a fully intended omission: the name is not *The* United Church of Christ. This United Church of Christ recognizes that every true church is a church of Christ, and every church of Christ is a United Church. This United Church of Christ does not regard itself as unique in this regard. Indeed, if it could have found a name equally good but not so subject to being misunderstood as presumptuous, it would have chosen it.

The fact emerging from a review of many possible names is that every good name seems somewhat arrogant, for every communion has the same general ideal image of itself and, in choosing for itself an appropriate designation, necessarily selects one that others would find applicable and might fairly covet. Contrariwise, names which no other denomination would want are not wanted by any given denomination. In the case of the United Church of Christ a name announcing the church's polity might have been singled out—but what church today believes its government to be its most important feature? Episcopal, Presbyterian, Congregational—it is a tribute to churches so named that by their consecration to Christ and their good works through the generations, they have caused us to forget that originally their names suggested nothing more than government by Overseers, Old Men, and Assemblies. A name like "Methodist" might have been selected—but procedure is not exactly the chief attribute to be advertised in a church. The Methodists, too, are better than their name, which was given them by those who did not love them. A name suggesting a rite, like "Baptist," might have been chosen, or a name commemorating an individual, like "Lutheran" or "Waldensian." The churches bearing these names were christened by history; they did not name themselves—and it is safe to say that if they had enjoyed an opportunity like that given to the United Church of Christ to fix upon their own titles, they would have chosen names closer to the heart of the Gospel. The United Church at least felt that its name should point to Jesus Christ. On the other hand, names that seem to come close to the heart of Christianity—Catholic, Disciples of Christ, Society of Friends—belong to the whole of Christ's church and therefore (it might be argued) ought not to be pre-empted by any one part of that church for particularized use. The answer to this argument is that though a name may be pre-empted for a title, it cannot be monopolized as a description. The fact that there are Catholic Churches, so named, does not rob others of the possibility of being truly catholic, too. Any such title soon becomes a mere means of identification, and the presumption in choosing it, if any has actually existed at all, soon fades into the realization that a name is only a name, and its ultimate meaning depends wholly upon the content put into it by the one that bears it. So at least the United Church of Christ hopes that its name will be taken as one name among others—one having good connotations today, to which, it is hoped, the work of the United Church will add in the future.

The "of Christ" in the title picks up the emphasis we have been making throughout. His is the banner nailed to the mast of the good ship *Ecclesia Unita Christi*. The stream of life that runs historically through the whole church to each individual member has its source in him, and that which animates the heart of each member directly, causing him to respond as a free soul to the Christ of history, is due to the mystical presence of his Holy Spirit. There are many forms of belief and action which belong to the well-being of the church and which we should relinquish only with regret—forms of worship, forms of government, forms of thinking—but Christ alone and the relationships he establishes belong to the veritable *being* of the church. Acceptance of God as he reveals himself in Christ—not in the Buddha, not in Mohammed, but in Jesus Christ of Nazareth—is that which makes the church the church, and nothing else does. This is not to say that God does not make a revelation in Gotama, in the great prophet of Mecca, and in innumerable others: our affirmation that God *does* make himself known in Jesus Christ in a saving way, in judgment and in love, is without negative reference to others. The United Church is *of Christ* because it is through Christ that God created it, redeemed it, and continues to shape it.

The word "Church" in the title of the denomination has more meaning than might meet the eye of the casual reader. The Congregationalists, who are one of the companies who make up the United Church, never used the singular form of the word to describe their fellowship officially; they were always the Congregational Church*es*, never the Congregational Church. They saved the singular word for the uses to which the Bible devoted it: the local congregation was called a church—"the church that was at Antioch"—and so was the entire church throughout the world—"Upon this rock I will build my church." The Bible knew nothing of modern denominations, and it was in the mind of this communion that it might be well if it did not recognize any of them either by so exalted a title as "Church." But it is the whole people that make a language and not any particular group in it, and in American usage the word church has come to mean, among other things, a denomination—and in this sense the United Church of Christ has come to call itself such.

If any word in the official title of the denomination has special significance, it is the word "United." Consideration was given at the beginning of negotiations looking toward union to the idea of calling it not United, but Uniting Church of Christ, because it intends to go on uniting with other bodies in the belief that the one God should have one people. The Basis of Union had declared the hope "that in time soon to come, by further union between this church and other bodies, there shall arise a more inclusive United Church," and there was a companion fear lest the sense of achievement in drawing together the two denominations in the United Church of Christ—a name that suggests a *fait accompli*— would stop the clock of endeavor and leave the new combined group to the unprofitable business of self-congratulation. The warning as to the danger was taken, but not the suggestion as to the name. It was felt that the title "uniting" would, if accepted, have had its own disadvantage, expressing a sense of unrelieved inconclusiveness. Granted that United Churchmen are pilgrims on the road, they are not completely unhoused: as the Psalmist speaks of "the house of my pilgrimage," they can speak of their unitedness in the midst of their continuing endeavor to unite. It was thought that the word "United" in the name would not necessarily imply that the church had foregone its ecumenical élan—and so that name was taken.

CHAPTER VII

GENERAL ORGANIZATION

Article II. Structure
The United Church of Christ is composed of local churches, Associations, Conferences, and the General Synod.

WE HAVE ALREADY BRIEFLY DEFINED ASSOCIATIONS, CONFERences, and General Synod; and the local churches, having the same function in all denominations as in the United Church of Christ, need no definition here for ordinary Americans or Europeans.

In passing, it may be remarked that every denomination in the United States has this type of structure, being pyramidal, the local congregations serving as the base, with county and state bodies (or something corresponding thereto) composed of representatives of the congregations in the intermediate position, all reaching an apex in the national body of delegates. Whatever theory of government may have been held by the several communions at the start, they have all grown to look very much alike. The relations between the parts of the pyramid differ from denomination to denomination, to be sure; the lines of authority passing from lower to higher in some, from higher to lower in others, and in many in both directions, but the skeletal outlines of all resemble each other and undoubtedly owe their shape partly to the political configurations of our United States.

CHAPTER VIII

THE OFFICE BEARERS

Article III. Officers
Officers of the United Church of Christ shall be a President—

LET US STOP HERE FOR A MOMENT, FOR THE MENTION OF THE President in the Constitution brings up the whole question of personal leadership in the church, a question which has caused the shelves of our libraries, age after age, to groan under the weight of the books written about it.

If the United Church of Christ were the heir of a different tradition, the President might fairly be called a bishop or even the archbishop—though probably not the pope, since that name has a flavor all its own and connotes a unique authority to which the President of the United Church makes not the slightest pretension. He is, however, *the* minister of the United Church of Christ, and as such is "charged with the care and nurture of the spiritual life of the Church." He is the official representative of the church in ecumenical and interdenominational relations. He is, in a word, one who watches over, an overseer, a guardian, an ecclesiastical superintendent, commonly called, from Ignatius downward, a bishop.

The Presidency of the Church is an office that gives content to the assertion that the United Church is, on its administrative side, episcopal. But that is not the whole story: each Conference has its own *episcopus* or bishop. This office derives from that of the Area President, so called, of the Evangelical and Reformed Church and that of the Conference Minister (or Superintendent) of the Congregational Christian Churches. The task of this officer, among others, is to supervise all pastoral relationships within his area. He is the *pastor pastorum*, as is every bishop. He meets with congregations to give advice and counsel in helping to solve any problems which may arise. He is not a monarchical bishop, to be sure, but his are episcopal functions. His actual constitutional authority over the churches and ministers of his Conference is less than that of the corresponding office bearers in many a connectional church, but his office, combined with the wisdom given him by his ecclesiastical experience, makes him a leading figure—even a liturgical figure—among his churches.

I call the President of the Church and the chief office bearers of the Conferences episcopal, however, only to deny it to a certain degree immediately after, for episcopacy on the "Catholic" side of the church means always episcopacy in acknowledged line, and for this the United Church of Christ has no zest whatever.

In its extreme form the theory of episcopal succession is that the line of connection between the present church and the past is through the bishops, the bishops of today having been consecrated by bishops of yesterday, those of yesterday by those of the day before, and so back to St. Peter and the Apostles gathered by our Lord himself; only those ordained by bishops are truly ministers, and only those confirmed by bishops are full members, of Christ's church. This philosophy of the church gives the bishops the importance of being the primary carriers of the authority of Christ from age to age. In the more democratic Episcopal Churches today the people actually select their own bishops, but in many cases even among them the formal setting apart of the bishops to their task is performed by other bishops, and none who are not bishops—a reminiscence of the day when episcopacy was self-sufficient and self-constituting. The theory of episcopal succession—as theory—still dominates the life of many churches as purely as it did in the days before democracy was heard of, or regarded as anything but anarchy. It is not, however, held by the United Church of Christ: its "bishops" are not in this succession—though, as we shall see, under certain circumstances bishops in historical line would not be excluded from it. At present there is an allergy to the very title *bishop,* which the churches forming the United Church of Christ inherit from the time of the suffering under unwise if not unworthy holders of the office in the sixteenth and seventeenth centuries.

In the United Church of Christ the absolutely basic matter is that apostolic succession lies in the whole church. The church comes before its officers, whether they be bishops or others. If, as a result of some terrible catastrophe, all the bishops of the church should be cut off, or even all the ministers, the church would not thereby cease to exist. As long as there were two or three to gather together in Christ's name, recognizing the promises of God in Christ and accepting each other as beneficiaries of his Covenant, the church would continue to exist. Most Christians hold to this belief, but the United Church of Christ lifts it to a position of great emphasis. This is not to deny the need for ministers or even bishops: indeed order, which expresses itself in the principle of good leadership, is regarded as a presupposition of good churchmanship; but office bearers do not make the church the church in its essence. They enhance the church; the church cannot be at its best without them; they are like eyes to the organism, but like the eyes, they do not create the organism nor sustain it, as does the heart, for instance. Office bearers and nonoffice bearers alike belong in the Covenant. There they are one. This relationship is brought out by the fact that there is no house of bishops or house of ministers over against a house of laymen as a governing body in the United Church. The United Church minister has his standing as a minister in the Association, which is a combination of local churches consisting of both lay and ministerial members. Laymen are as much in the apostolic succession, according to the doctrine of the United Church of Christ, as are bishops or any other office bearers.

The whole of the paragraph in the midst of which we interrupted ourselves reads:

Officers of the United Church of Christ shall be a President, a Secretary, a Treasurer and such other officers as the General Synod may from time to time determine. They shall be responsible to the General Synod.

There is nothing here requiring prolonged comment, since the officers named have duties that are customarily associated with their offices. The Secretary keeps the records of the General Synod and of the ministers and the general statistics of the local churches; and he is a member of the ranking committees of the church. The Treasurer receives, holds, and disburses moneys contributed to the General Synod for the support of the church and its instrumentalities; and he also is a member of the church's highest committees.

CHAPTER IX

THE IMPORTANCE OF
THE CONGREGATION

THE NEXT ARTICLE IN THE CONSTITUTION IS A LONG AND IMportant one, which begins:

Article IV. Local Churches
The basic unit of the life and organization of the United Church of Christ is the local church.

The local church is basic even in a historical sense, for the great church throughout the world began as such. The United Church of Christ, looking back to those beginnings, does not find them, as the Church of Rome seems to, in our Lord saying to his fisherman follower, "Thou art Peter, the Rock—and on this rock I will build my Church." That scene may have been the beginning of a ministry within the church, but it can hardly have been the first moment of the church itself. The church involves Christ and people, not Christ and a single man; its true beginning was the gathering of the disciples about their master and friend, through whom they found their salvation. The church came into being when "he sat down with the twelve"; it began as a congregation. The pattern for a congregation today is displayed even more accurately in the

117

scene where the disciples are gathered together after the crucifixion, and Christ is with them not merely as the carpenter of Galilee but as a Presence—the presence of one who has passed through the experience of death and in God's loving grace has been brought out on the other side, victorious, so that life now has a new meaning for all. This is precisely the same Presence that we encounter in the twentieth century when two or three are gathered together in his name. To keep the church essentially like this—devoted groups of disciples recognizing the gift of God in Christ, submitting to his judgment, depending upon his forgiveness, strengthened by his Spirit, and gathered about him for worship and for the service of mankind—this is the deeply felt determination of the United Church of Christ; and this means vital congregations.

The congregation is basic to the church in the even more important sense of being the essential church at any given point. If in theory one divides and subdivides the whole church into lesser wholes, he will finally have it in congregations. To dissect it into anything less than congregations—that is, into mere individuals—is to get to something which has lost the character of the church, for the church is a society whose indivisible part is two or three gathered together in Christ's name. Without a society the Covenant is no longer a triad of forces. The local church is the atom, full of power, out of which the great church is made. We have already said that the United Church of Christ bears heavily upon the conception that the vehicle of apostolic succession—through which the abundant life brought to the world by Christ is carried on from age to age—is the entire church; and this means its congregations, for they are the great church in microcosm. All that makes the great church its essential self is in the local church—this is, Christ and his people. In the congregation can be encountered those same living forces to which we have alluded, that are the blood of the Covenant in Christ. There the dual flow of inspiration from God can be felt, the individual enjoying his gifts made available to him by the church, and the church the obvious beneficiary of the faith of its members.

Because the essence of the great church can be best seen in the congregation, the Congregationalists of the seventeenth century argued that the mighty Covenant of grace, by which God binds the whole church to him and imparts to it its strength, should be reflected and acknowledged in the local church; and so in every congregation they entered into a *church* covenant. In view of God's promise to them—which was part of both the great Covenant and their church covenant—they would stand and repeat together a pledge indicating their acceptance of it, not forgetting that this also involved the mutual promise of all of them to each of them and each of them to all of them to maintain Christian communion. In the many churches these covenants took various forms, but all of them sounded the note which is found in that of the church of Salem, the first church established on New England soil:

We Covenant with the Lord and one with an other; and doe bynd our selves in the presence of God, to walke together in all his waies, according as he is pleased to reveale himself unto us in his Blessed word of truth.

This symbolizing, within the walls of the local church, of the universal Covenant of grace has a good deal to be said for it. Many of the old Congregational Churches still use the seventeenth-century forms they have inherited; some have amended them or adopted new ones; it is to be hoped that the practice will be examined by all the congregations of the United Church of Christ and more widely adopted, for if the text is properly written, it brings out in a striking way the commitment made by God and accepted by all and each in the local church which makes that church a foundation stone of the great church.

The Congregation Organized

The Constitution now defines the composition and purpose of a local church:

A local church is composed of persons who, believing in God as heavenly Father, and accepting Jesus Christ as Lord and Saviour, and depending on the guidance of the Holy Spirit, are organized for Christian worship, for the furtherance of Christian fellowship, and for the ongoing work of Christian witness.

Now we come to the word *organized*—but though the word itself is used, very little is said about the organization of the local church in the Constitution. This is because it is expected that all local churches as they enter the United Church will go on using the procedures they have been accustomed to, whether "Christian," Congregational, Evangelical, or Reformed. New churches, as we have said, will have made available to them model constitutions of various types which they may adapt to their several needs.

In general, however, each church has its pastor, about whom a good deal is said in the Constitution and about whom we shall have our own comments to make when the time comes.

The pastor is surrounded by a governing committee, called by different names in different places. In the early days of Congregationalism in New England each church had both its Ruling Elders and its Deacons, but very early the two offices coalesced into one, the Diaconate, and for the last three centuries the lay officers of the ordinary Congregational Church, with general supervision (with the minister) over all of its spiritual affairs, have been the deacons. Most of the congregations in the United Church of Christ which come of Congregational parentage continue the office, title, and over-all duties of the deacons. The Evangelical and Reformed congregations, curiously enough, have been accustomed to elect officers more along the lines of ancient Congregationalism than have the later Congregationalists themselves, for they have had both elders and deacons. The difference was not a matter of great moment, for the same work was done by the Congregational deacons as by the Evangelical and Reformed elders *and* deacons. The division of work between the two in the latter case is carried over into most of the United Church congregations which are descended from an Evangelical and Reformed past: the elders are advisers and assistants to the pastor in all the spiritual affairs of the church, but the deacons have the specific work of securing the funds necessary for the support of the church, educating the people to the principles of good stewardship under God, and taking charge of the church's charities.

The actual organization of the life of an ordinary congregation in the United Church of Christ is under a council which, in Congregational Christian areas, is usually composed of the minister, deacons, and heads of the various organizations within the parish, such as the superintendent of the church school, and, in Evangelical and Reformed parts, is made up of the pastor, the elders, and the deacons. In the latter churches the elders and deacons themselves are as a rule— and wisely—made the trustees of the congregation. As such they are the liaison officers between the local church and the state. In the former churches, owing to their different history, the trustees are a group specially elected.

In the busy churches of today there is a good deal of division of labor, and beside the standing committees not a few committees *ad hoc* are set up from time to time to meet particular and nonrecurring needs. And our forte becomes our foible: too often the susceptibility of American churches to proliferation into committees robs them of the experience truly thrilling (when entered into under good leadership and with understanding) of acting upon the issues confronting them as *whole local churches*. What is called in England the church meeting, where business and worship are combined, has been utilized in this country to a certain degree but, in view of the spiritual dividends it is able to pay, rather feebly. Deriving from old New England days, however, it is part of the heritage of the United Church of Christ.

The church meeting is a meeting in which God's will is consciously sought for the solution of a specific problem by the whole congregation and in which, in the light of that will, decisions are arrived at. The meeting of the church previous to the church's settling on its budget for the year, or the meeting at which it calls its minister, or at which it decides where its special benevolent contributions should be made, or at which it considers the findings of some denominational or ecumenical gathering, such as those that are arrived at in the gatherings of the World Council of Churches—all such meetings are of the kind at which both prayer and mutual consultation among members are called for. Such church meetings permit God to speak to the whole group through the persons that compose it and to the persons individually through the group.

Sometimes church meetings are held monthly, sometimes on Sunday morning after formal public worship, often on week nights, not seldom after church suppers, sometimes even in series during one week. No end of preparation goes into them if they are to yield the best results. Painstaking study of the issues involved in the problem must be made by the people in general, and sometimes technical studies by a committee. The meeting needs a leader, who is normally the minister of the church; and in advance he must have taken the issues in personal prayer to the Head of the Church and be ready in public to open the Scriptures to appropriate chapters and to seek light from above. When the discussion begins, each person speaks as in the presence of Christ and of Christ's people. Not always is the answer found, not always are the tensions between groups relaxed, but time and again I have witnessed the coming to pass of such results as by a miracle.

Usually a common mind is discovered, and always the opinion of the minority is carried over to be met and accommodated to in the future if not then. Formal votes may well be taken, even if there be a dissenting minority which cannot in good conscience vote with the majority. If, however, the opinion of the minority is not listened to with the attention that the shepherd of the ninety and nine gave to the one, it is not worthy of the name of a church meeting.

A local church organized to use such meetings well in the study and determination of forms of worship, fellowship, and witness (to quote the purposes of the congregation named in the Constitution) ordinarily acquires a glowing sense of strength. By this means it brings itself to spiritual maturity, discovers lay leaders, melts the personal self-centeredness of its members into the life of the fellowship, and gives them the consciousness of taking the initiative against the evil forces of the world and siding with the eternal God against current fancies and hysterias. It welds them into a kind of corporate conscience.

This kind of meeting, which combines organization and consecration, and provides openings for God's grace to fill the mind of the local church and its members, is in the blood of the United Church of Christ, and it is hoped that the years of the future will see it increased in power.

Membership in the Congregation

In accordance with the custom and usage of a local church, persons become members by (a) baptism and either confirmation or profession of faith in Jesus Christ as Lord and Saviour; (b) reaffirmation or reprofession of faith; or (c) letter of transfer or certification from other Christian churches.

The first phrase in this paragraph of the Constitution once more indicates the diversity that is to be expected in a denomination like the United Church of Christ, in which the local churches have come out of more than one ecclesiastical background. Experience has proved that this is not a weakening feature, however, and that this kind of diversity is even to be encouraged in the members of a healthy body.

We have already spoken of baptism and its complementary rite, confirmation; the one of which is the church taking the child to itself, the other, the grown child accepting the church for himself as his parents or godparents had done provisionally for him when he was an infant. When a person has not been christened as an infant, he may be baptized as an adult in a ceremony wherein he makes profession of his faith in Christ.

In most of the larger denominations of the United States, when a member of a local church desires to transfer his membership to another local church, either because of removal from the neighborhood or for some other reason, provision is generously made to grant him a letter certifying that he is a member in good and regular standing and commending him to the good offices of the other church. If, however, the church to which he goes happens to be one of a different denomination from that from which he comes, some denominations will not give him such a certification—but the United Church of Christ is not of this type. It would feel it its Christian duty to show every courtesy to that other church, whether it were of its own communion or not, and would therefore grant a letter of transfer, if requested, without ado. On the other hand, if the congregation to which he came were of the United Church of Christ and that from which he went refused a letter, the United Church would not dream of confirming him again. It would accept the confirmation of any other Christian church on the statement of the person transferring his membership and would ask him to reaffirm or reprofess his faith in a rite having quite a different meaning from that of confirmation.

Says the Constitution:

All persons who are or shall become members of a local church of the United Church of Christ are thereby members of the United Church of Christ.

This is further evidence of the fact that the United Church of Christ regards its local churches as basic. It is to them, and not, for instance, to a bishop, that power is given to receive members not only to themselves but to the entire communion.

The Constitution continues:

Congregational Christian Churches and the Evangelical and Reformed Church unite in the United Church of Christ without break in their respective historic continuities and traditions.

We have already referred to this all-important matter. It indicates, among other things, that the United Church of Christ has a healthy though conditioned respect for a living tradition. There are churches that seem to have no sense of continuity with the past at all; others that have a most fragmentary sense of it. Many an American Protestant church, if one may judge from its literature, regards the great upheaval of the sixteenth century not as a reformation but as a restitution of authentic Christianity, as if the Holy Spirit had been on holiday from the church from the time the last words of Scripture were penned until the denomination concerned was organized. Other churches seem to go to the opposite extreme: they appear to have plenty of history but little theology. As Cyprian long ago observed, our Lord did not say, "I am the tradition"; he said, "I am the way"—and this way leads not merely back into the past but out into contemporaneity and on into the future. By this time the reader will know that the United Church of Christ, with its companion emphasis upon *both* the grace of God that comes freshly to an individual and so is made serviceable to the church *and* the same grace as it comes through the church to the individual, is avidly interested in the tradition of the church as one of the channels through which God mediates his life to it. We have spoken of the local church as the channel through which that life comes from God to the church member; we have spoken of the larger communion performing the same function, but actually the *whole* church with which God has made his Covenant and through which he makes his saving gift to the members is nothing less than the entire company of the redeemed in heaven and on earth—and the visible church (with which we are concerned in this book) is that same company as they appear or have appeared in history. The United Church of Christ regards itself as a branch of that visible tree and has no ambition to be cut off from the trunk of it. It cherishes all that has come to it from its continuities with the past, and studies them, learning ever new secrets from them. Its reverence for that past is conditioned only by its reverence for the present and future, for it knows that God still speaks directly to his prophets in pulpit or pew or even outside the church entirely.

The United Church of Christ does not take the attitude that its tradition alone is the truly Christian one. When I was a good deal younger than I am now, I used to stop in at times at a church in a Massachusetts city in order to look with incredulous eyes at a chart hung in the narthex designed to indicate to the worshipers there how blest they were in their tradition and how impoverished most other churches were in theirs. At the top of it was depicted the suffering Saviour upon the cross, and from his riven side flowed blood—the grace of our Lord Jesus Christ—which was caught in a container just below; and from the base of the container ran a great pipe (full of grace) labeled *The Church (Anglo-Catholic, Roman Catholic,* and *Orthodox Catholic*), which at its very bottom was divided into seven branches—the seven sacraments—with faucets attached to each, so that if the proper fingers opened them, the grace of the Lord Jesus Christ poured out. In parallel to this system were others which, instead of having Jesus Christ at the top, had the several founders of denominations. There was Martin Luther at the top of the Lutheran system, John Calvin at the top of the Presbyterian, John Wesley heading the Methodist—and there were others. These, too, had containers below them, with pipes leading down from the containers, having single faucets at the end—all open—but never a drop of grace came from any of them since none of them were in any way connected with Christ. I stopped in at that church not so long ago and discovered that the chart had been put out of sight. Let us hope that it has also been put out of mind. Even Catholics today are likely to hold that though some churches are more catholic—that is, more truly in the apostolic line—than others, even to such an extent that their own is called *the* Catholic Church, none of the churches are wholly separated from Christ. The thought of the United Church of Christ on this subject is not complicated: this church believes that it had its beginnings many centuries ago, that it owes an immeasurable debt to the church which has carried the message of Christ to it from that time to this—but it does not for a moment imagine itself to be the only church with such hallowed beginnings, and the only one with a debt to the past.

God's Covenant with his people is a chain which links Abraham in the gray dawn of history to the last member confirmed in the church this week. Paralleling the "begat" tables in the Bible, which are lists of ancestors in the Messianic line —"Abraham begat Isaac; and Isaac begat Jacob; and Jacob begat Judas (or Judah, in the Hebrew spelling) and his brethren. . . ."—one could construct a table of what might be called covenant recognition. It would begin like the table in Matthew, but the ligature which bound the generations together would not be biological begetting but the more important one of mutual recognition: Abraham recognized Isaac as a member of the covenant, as Isaac, coming of age, recognized his father; and so Isaac and Jacob recognized each other; and Jacob and Judah the like. Instead of the actual fifteenth verse of the first chapter—"And Jacob (a later Jacob) begat Joseph, the husband of Mary, of whom was born Jesus, who is called Christ"—we should have a verse cast in covenant language: "And the chosen people recognized as fellow heirs of God's promise, Joseph the husband of Mary, of whom was born Jesus, who is called the Christ." The continuity of mutual recognition within the Hebrew nation runs on through St. Paul, who was himself, as he said, "an Hebrew of the Hebrews." But here occurs the first fork in the line, for some members of the old Abrahamic covenant conceived it, properly understood, to be restricted to the Hebrew people and to point to a messianic future, while others, equally good members of the old covenant, were convinced that it was a bond of love in Christ, the present Messiah, that embraced the whole of mankind, and so allied themselves with St. Paul to preach the good news to the gentiles.

There therefore came a division between the Jews and the Christians, but there was no break between either and the line from Abraham. They became separate streams but neither was severed from the common source of both. There are many places on the continental divide of North America where one can watch a mountain stream divide into two rivulets, one eventually to find its way to the Atlantic, the other to the Pacific. They themselves are two different streams, but each carries the water of the one original. A break between brothers (to change the figure) does not necessarily imply a break between either brother and the parent. So it was with the early Christians: they regarded themselves, as we regard ourselves, as children of the same God who spoke with Abraham; St. Paul, as a recognized participant in the covenant, had as much right as any other member of the Hebrew community or any other number of members, to trust the insights God gave him and in his turn to recognize others whom he conceived to be members of the covenant. The thread of mutual recognitions which unites the covenant people was not cut.

To continue with our catalogue we should record it that St. Paul and the other members of the early church recognized and were recognized by their immediate successors, and they by theirs, until the church had grown virtually to the dimensions of the Roman Empire itself. In 1054, occurred another terrible cleavage, for then the Eastern and the Western Churches fell finally apart; but then also the cleavage was between those two and not between either and the undivided church which gave them birth. The two before the break were undifferentiated parts of the great whole, the complete heirs of the past, and in the break there was nothing to jeopardize that inheritance for either. Each part had been fully recognized by the whole.

These considerations should be borne in mind by those who say that the Roman Catholic Church of today *is* the old Western Church. It is certainly part of the old Western Church but no more so than were—and are—the Lutheran and Reformed Churches, whose bonds with the church of the Middle Ages make them as catholic as Rome itself—and in this catholicity the United Church participates. Before the Reformation the whole church accepted into its Covenant those parts which presently elected to become Roman and Reformed, and with that acceptance the two parts each became conveyors of the Covenant to others who would accept it from them. So also separation came between the Church of Rome and the Church of England, but not in such wise as to sever either one from the church which contained them both. They might excommunicate each other, but that excommunication could avail only at the contemporary moment and could not affect the relationships preceding.

So it was also that the legislation under Charles II of England, though it surely separated the Church of England from all the nonconformity of the day, including Congregationalism, could not separate either the Church of England or Congregationalism from the old church *in* England. Congregationalism (and so the United Church of Christ) is as much a child of English Christianity as is the Episcopacy of the present Church of England. The Covenant today has many strands, but they all lead back to God's revelation to the early Hebrew seers and, in the Christian connection, to the supreme gift of God in Jesus Christ. The United Church of Christ regards itself as a sister to all other Christians, and a cousin, as it were, to the Jews.

Looking back at the long past of the church, the United Church of Christ does not view it as a history apart from its own. The United Church has been part of the great church from the beginning, and can truly exclaim, as it views the advancing sequence of Christian events, "I was there!" It was there in the church's sins and failures as well as in its strength. It can indeed cry, "I was there when they crucified my Lord," but it must also mournfully admit, "I was there with Peter who betrayed him—and so I even helped crucify him. I stood with the early church in the arena: I remember the roar of the lions and the prayers of my brothers there—but I cannot forget my other brothers who thought it expedient to hide from the emperor's will. I was there in the great days of the church but accept my share of remorse for my part in its meaner moments. I take pride in what was good in the Crusades, for instance, but take shame for the evil they wrought—as a son takes the shame of a father." On the whole, the record need not be regretted. "I was there," the United Church of Christ can say, "when the breath of the Gospel carried new health to the circle of lands about the Mediterranean, and then out to Europe, and so to America and the farthest parts of the world. It was my own ancestral church that lifted to heaven the sublime beauty of the cathedrals of

Europe and England. I have been in the dream and purpose of my fathers through generation after generation; and if only I could join myself to them more understandingly I should be wise with the wisdom of ages and almost as patient of the human race and as eager for its happiness as the loving God in covenant with whom I have stood watch over it."

It is understandable that a United Church of Christ with such a memory, and with such a sense of obligation growing out of it cherishes its "historic continuities and traditions."

Many in One

Now the Constitution deals technically with the composition of the United Church of Christ:

The following local churches compose the United Church of Christ:

a. The local churches of the Evangelical and Reformed Church;

Since these by constitutional provision had entered the United Church *en bloc*, there was no need for action on their part.

b. The local churches of the Congregational Christian fellowship which vote to become a part of the United Church of Christ, or which approve this Constitution;

At the time the Constitution was declared in force, 3,547 of these churches had voted to approve it, 342 not to; and 3,665 had voted to become part of the United Church of Christ, 367 not to.

c. Any Congregational Christian local church which, although it has not voted to become a part of the United Church of Christ, or to approve this Constitution, votes to join the United Church of Christ after this Constitution is declared in force;

It is too soon, as I write these lines, to know how many of these there will be. It is to be hoped that every church in the two fellowships will eventually join the United Church.

    d. Any local church which, after this Constitution is declared in force, may be accepted into an Association, or Conference, of the United Church of Christ. . . .

Just as a local church acts for the United Church of Christ in receiving members into the denomination, the Association, in consultation with its Conference, does the same in receiving local churches into the United Church.

    e. The local churches of any denomination which after this Constitution is declared in force unite with the United Church of Christ; and . . .

Since the United Church is a uniting church, a provision of this sort is a natural anticipation of the future.

    f. Any local church in a category not otherwise defined in this article, received upon its request, subject to such provisions as in consultation with the Conference may be specified by the Association within whose bounds it is located, and which are not inconsistent with this Constitution and the By-Laws of the United Church of Christ.

This is another illustration of the combination of firmness and flexibility that characterizes this Constitution. Dangers involved in having no constitution at all and dealing with what in the banking world might be called wildcat situations are equaled only by those encountered in having a constitution so rigid that exceptions cannot be allowed for. This paragraph provides for exceptions but makes it clear that they must be acted upon in an orderly way, authorized by an Association in consultation with its Conference (the Association being in general the body which deals with local churches) and consonant with the spirit of the Constitution. Often local churches which are federated with other denominations need to have special regulations worked out for them: this paragraph indicates how these may be arrived at.

Local churches of the United Church of Christ are represented in the General Synod by the delegates from the Conferences to which they belong.

Here the Constitution indicates the representative character of the United Church. We have already stated that the United Church of Christ is administratively episcopal; here it is seen to be legislatively presbyterial. Actually both the uniting denominations had used the representative system for generations, but the local churches in the Congregational Christian group had been represented in the General Council (as their national body was called) both through their Associations and through their Conferences, and churches having a membership of a thousand or more had been allowed to nominate to their Association their own representatives. So numerous a representation, coupled with the growth of the denomination, had been on the verge of producing a General Council too large to house except on college campuses and unwieldy for skilled and studied legislative work. The advantage of the large national body, however, had been that by permitting a major number of local churches to keep close to denominational decision-making through their representatives, it had been an organ of responsible churchmanship for a large section of the denomination. It is expected that this advantage will be retrieved in the United Church of Christ without expanding the actual membership of the General Synod to mammoth size, by encouraging members of as many local churches as possible to attend meetings of the Synod as associate members or visitors without vote.

An Association or a Conference of the United Church of Christ may, under such provisions as it deems wise, admit, or continue in fellowship with, any Congregational Christian local church which is not part of the United Church of Christ. The names and statistics of such churches shall be kept separately; their members shall not be counted in determining the number of delegates which the Conference is entitled to send to the General Synod; nor shall any member of such a church be a delegate to the General Synod or hold elective office in that body. No direct or indirect participation by any such local church in, or support of, the work of the United Church of Christ, or of any of its instrumentalities, or of any Conference or Association, shall be construed as making it a church of the United Church of Christ.

This paragraph of the Constitution is designed especially for the Congregational Christian Churches which have not yet entered the United Church. The United Church of Christ is committed to allowing not the slightest shadow of a gesture to occur which might be interpreted as shutting out of the fellowship any local churches that belonged to the constituent denominations. The decision of the Congregational Christian Churches which have not yet joined the United Church is their own, for they are free in Christ; but they are still members of the Congregational Christian fellowship, and the United Church on its part will do nothing to break the ties that still unite them to the Congregational Christian majority which is now part of the larger communion. There are a thousand ties of affection which bind members of the majority and the minority together, and the United Church of Christ in its eagerness for union will spare no pains to keep its doors open to those just outside. In order to protect the separate status of the latter, which they themselves desire, a separate roll of them will be kept by the United Church of Christ. Though no responsibility for the United Church of Christ will be attached to them, all the innumerable services of the United Church will be proffered them, just as if they were part of it. Even their participation in some of the work of the United Church, such as that of the Board for World or Homeland Ministries, will not be construed as making them a part of the United Church if they themselves do not so elect.

The local churches of the United Church of Christ have, in fellowship, a God-given responsibility for that Church, its labors and its extension, even as the United Church of Christ has, in fellowship, a God-given responsibility for the well-being and needs and aspirations of its local churches. In mutual Christian concern and in dedication to Jesus Christ, the Head of the Church, the one and the many share in common Christian experience and responsibility.

Now the Constitution returns again to the local churches which are regular members of the United Church. It again emphasizes the dual course of God's grace in the Covenant, from each one to the many and the many to each one, joint and individual responsibility meeting and mingling in every part of the church.

The autonomy of the local church is inherent and modifiable only by its own action. Nothing in this Constitution and the By-Laws of the United Church of Christ shall destroy or limit the right of each local church to continue to operate in the way customary to it; nor shall be construed as giving to the General Synod, or to any Conference or Association, now or at any future time, the power to abridge or impair the autonomy of any local church in the management of its own affairs, which affairs include, but are not limited to, the right to retain or adopt its own methods of organization, worship and education; to retain or secure its own charter or name; to adopt its own constitution and by-laws; to formulate its own covenants and confessions of faith; to admit members in its own way and to provide for their discipline or dismissal; to call or dismiss its pastor or pastors by such procedure as it shall determine; to acquire, own, manage and dispose of property and funds; to control its own benevolences; and to withdraw by its own decision from the United Church of Christ at any time without forfeiture of ownership or control of any real or personal property owned by it.

This paragraph of the Constitution spells out in greater detail the basicity—to borrow a word from the chemical laboratory—of the local church, already touched upon more than once. The companion paragraph which follows is shorter because it does not contain, like the former, a point of previous controversy:

Actions by, or decisions or advice emanating from, the General Synod, a Conference or an Association, should be held in the highest regard by every local church.

These two paragraphs point to the two ports of entry—to borrow now from the sociologists—by which the sense of God's covenanted grace comes into the church. Always it enters both through the whole and through the parts. In these paragraphs the part is not an individual but an individual group, that is, the local church; and the whole is not the entire church but the General Synod which represents it at the national level, the Conference that represents it at the state, and the Association that represents it at the county level. The same principle holds in any Christian society, whatever be considered a whole and its parts. Always the whole must be protected against the parts and the parts against the whole; always the parts must succor the whole, always the whole succor the parts. To interchange the wording of the two paragraphs: in the United Church of Christ the autonomy of the whole is inherent and modifiable only by its own action, and no single part can dominate it; and actions by or decisions or advice emanating from the local church should be held in the highest regard by the Association, Conference, and General Synod. Neither part nor whole is subject to invasion by the other, and each, being in Christ, is strengthened by the other.

The paragraph about the privileges of the local church recites these in great detail because some of the Congregational Christian churches feared that in the United Church of Christ there would be less liberty in Christ than they had enjoyed in the past. It is the actual future, however, rather than any paragraph in a constitution, even one written with the finality of this one, that will be required to convince a few of these churches that their fears on this score are groundless.

Chapter X

THE MINISTERS OF
THE UNITED CHURCH

THE CONSTITUTION NOW REACHES AN IMPORTANT SET OF DE-
scriptions:

Article V. The Ministry

The privilege and responsibility of witnessing to the Gospel belong to every member of the Church. The United Church of
Christ diligently seeks, therefore, to provide opportunities for its
members to exercise such gifts of teaching, evangelizing, healing,
preaching and administration as God has bestowed upon them.

The Congregational strain in the United Church inheritance, with its reiterated insistence on the importance of the
congregational meeting and of lay witness outside the church,
is not the only one in which the laity is lifted into importance.
To Martin Luther we owe not only the phrase, *the priesthood
of all believers,* but also thorough-going theological support
of the idea that every member of the church, clerical and lay,
has his own peculiar part to play in witnessing to and demonstrating the meaning of the Gospel. Calvin, also, as might
have been expected from a man of his own lay status, was
not without reasons for proving that the hierarchy was only
one half of the church. The entire river of tradition which
fills the thought and impulses of the United Church of Christ

138

carries a conception of the church in which the laity have an apostolate as real as the ministry. Of this we shall be treating later.

The United Church of Christ recognizes that God calls certain of its members to full-time service for various forms of ministry in the Church. This call is recognized by ordination, commissioning or other appropriate services of dedication.

As the Constitution presently brings out, *commissioning* is the term usually employed for the consecration of a special "commissioned worker" to his task; the "other appropriate services of dedication" referred to in the text include, among others, the formal setting apart of "lay" ministers; but at the moment we confine ourselves to a consideration of ministers normally so called, whose solemn authorization to perform their work in the church is called ordination.

The ordination of ministers in the United Church of Christ is the end of a long process since, as will be pointed out, the United Church of Christ believes in a learned ministry. A student desiring to prepare for the ministry applies in the normal course of events to the Association in which he is best known, to be received into the status called *Care of Association.*

A *Student in Care of Association* is a member of the United Church of Christ who has been called of God and who, under the care of his Association, is preparing himself for the Christian ministry.

Application is made to the Association through the student's pastor and the local church of which he is a member. The Committees on the Ministry of his Conference and Association co-operate in examining the student as to his fitness and Christian commitment. If found to be qualified he is received into the care of the Association. The Association extends fellowship, counsel, and assistance in every possible form to the student during the time of his academic preparation for the ministry, and the student in turn keeps responsibly in touch with the Association. The student is expected to pursue a course of study in a college or university of standing which will lead to a bachelor's degree; and after graduation he goes on into a divinity school where he can get his specific training for the Christian ministry.

A *Licentiate* is a student in care of an Association who is given a temporary license by an Association to perform such ministerial duties as it may determine.

This constitutional item points to the second step in the process leading to ordination. Application for licensure is made by a student through a local church to its Association. The Committees on the Ministry of that Association and its Conference work together in examining the student as to his growth in the Christian faith, his character, and his ability to do the work expected of him as a licentiate. If he is found to be qualified, he is granted licensure by the Association for the period of a year or less—not more—and licensure is normally granted only after one year of divinity studies and only for services in designated local churches. In very special cases and at the request of the churches they serve, licentiates are sometimes granted the right to administer the sacraments and other special rites of the church, even (if the laws of the state permit) that of marriage.

The reader will have borne in mind that because these procedures are not part of the life of the central unifying General Synod, they are normal but not mandatory—but though every part of the church has the privilege of modifying them where it deems it wise to do so, there is remarkably little deviation from the standard here set forth.

The Constitution now reaches the matter of ordination proper:

Ordination is the rite whereby the United Church of Christ through an Association, in cooperation with the local church, sets apart by prayer and the laying on of hands those of its members God has called to the Christian ministry. By this rite ministerial standing is conferred and authorization is given to perform all the duties and to exercise all the prerogatives of the ministry.

Not more than six months before the completion of his theological training, a student for the ministry applies through his local church to his Association for approval as a candidate for ordination. The Committee on the Ministry of the Association and the Conference again join forces to examine the student as to his abilities, his reason for seeking the office of the Christian ministry, his educational and theological attainments, his knowledge of the history, polity, and practices of the United Church of Christ, and his growth in faith and the wisdom that comes with experience. If he is found qualified, the Association authorizes his ordination: he becomes an ordinand. To his final examination are usually invited the members of the entire Association, that is, the ministers and duly elected laymen from each church. Here is often seen enacted a custom which illustrates the United Church's great concern that originality be not stamped out among its members—the custom already mentioned when we were treating of creeds. In many if not most other churches an ordinand is expected only to answer the questions his examiner may put to him—often constitutional questions that do not differ from candidate to candidate and which are designed to determine whether the candidate accepts the beliefs contained in a theological statement, long or short, already adopted by the church. In this situation, too often the implied demand for conformity leads the weaker young men to twist their own thought into accommodating forms, and the stronger ones to acquire a distaste for ordination to the ministry in favor of some profession in which value is attached to their own individual ways of thinking and doing. In contrast, many ordaining Associations in the United Church will invite the person seeking ordination to write a paper in advance outlining his own religious experience and his thoughts about God and the things of God; and on the basis of this paper and the questions the examiners ask about it and other germane matters, they will decide whether to authorize the ordination. Here there is no burden laid upon the candidate by unadorned affirmative answers to fit his views to the church's massive or epitomized body of theology. Here the church seeks to learn the candidate's own insights into the Gospel. Here there is a two-way motion of the spirit, the church seeking to understand the man, the man seeking to understand the church, all within their mutual commitment to God as he reveals himself in Christ.

Is the ministry an order different from that of the laity? There are two different answers to this question within the one United Church of Christ, though the matter of semantics plays a part here. The Presbyterian influence within the church gives us the doctrine of the two orders, that of the ministry and that of the laity. According to this, candidates for the ministry are ordained only by ministers, and ministers normally give up their membership in individual congregations on being received into membership in the Presbytery or Association. Even the Congregational theory works out in practice in such wise that laymen often have no part in the formal service of ordination, the essence of which is the ordination prayer with the laying on of hands on the head of the ordinand, though the fundamental Congregational idea that the laity and ministry belong to one order would seem to indicate that at least one layman might have a place in this liturgical act. Laymen always have a part in examining a candidate preparatory to ordination, and if the latter does not pass that examination, he is not ordained; and no theory is more sedulously carried out in Congregational areas than the doctrine that a minister belongs as a member to the local church he serves.

Throughout the United Church it is recognized that the

life of the ministry is functionally different from that of the laity. The minister must devote his entire life to the church as such—and whether, therefore, he is regarded as belonging to a different order from the laity or to the same order but with a special assignment, the actual human relationships of minister and people in all congregations of the United Church of Christ are essentially the same.

In the United Church of Christ the laying on of hands is by ministers and, in some cases, a layman specially designated, but not necessarily by a bishop, or superintendent, or anyone in episcopal status. Episcopal ordination, that is, ordination which *must* be by the hands of a bishop, creates a symbolism that the United Church of Christ believes erroneous, for this seems to imply that the power to ordain has been relinquished by the church to the episcopal order. The United Church believes so strongly that full apostolic succession is in the whole church and not in a single set of office-bearers that it seeks the symbolism in the ordination of its leaders that bears out this conviction. It therefore selects for the ceremonial laying on of hands, ministers (or appointed laymen) of congregations, who are the integral and indivisible parts of the church. It was an old Alexandrian custom, at the moment of ordination, for the officiating clergyman to take the hand of the worshiper nearest him, he the hand of the one nearest him, and so on until the whole assembly had been symbolically linked into a unity; only then would the hands of consecration be laid on the head of the candidate. This would also seem a fitting form for the rite in the United Church of Christ, for it also emphasizes the fact that it is an act, not of a self-consecrating line of authorities over the church, but of the church itself.

On the other hand, there is nothing in the United Church system that would prevent bishops (if ever this title, as such, came to be used for its ranking office-bearers) from ordaining its ministers. That is to say, if some Association or Conference of the United Church desired to have it so, the freedom in Christ that characterizes the whole church would permit it—but, as we have said, the same freedom would have to be permitted all other parts of the church *not* to practice episcopal ordination. It is the absolutizing, the exclusiveness, of episcopal ordination as ordinarily practiced that would offend the spirit of the United Church. And, if practiced at any point, it would have to compete in the realm of symbolism with ordination by Association; it would hardly survive as a normal procedure if it could not be proved to be better representative of the church as church than the act of the Association.

In the United Church of Christ the laying on of hands is authorized not by the local church alone but by the Association of Churches. Ordination by the local congregation sole—a practice which is well known in some denominations—might, like episcopal ordination, be permitted where the Association or Conference desired and approved it, but it could not be made exclusive of other procedures; and it also, like ordination by the hand of the bishop, would in the long run have to prove itself to be a better symbol of action by the church as a whole than ordination by Association. As a matter of fact in the evolution of the Congregational Churches this type of ordination, which was supported by some leaders in the beginning of New England, early went by the board; ordination by representatives of the churches in fellowship seemed superior from every point of view to ordination by representatives of one congregation alone—and this has been the custom since the mid-seventeenth century.

At one point the United Church of Christ in its immediate ancestry has been a leader in the general progress of the larger church: it has long since given up the idea that men alone, and not women, are fitted for the ministry. It is true that the average church, having been used to the ministries of men from the beginning of its history, prefers their ministries to those of women, but there are many churches that are not average. Many congregations which have had the imagination to make the try have discovered that a woman of parts can minister to their people quite as effectively as, and sometimes more understandingly, than the men they had grown accustomed to. At the first assembly of the World Council of Churches, one of the world's most eminent theologians was surrounded by a group of reporters who wanted to know his opinions about the ordination of women. "There is nothing I can find in the Bible," said he, "which would seem to forbid it. On the contrary, except for St. Paul's antifeminism, the entire trend of biblical theology seems to give to men and women complete equality in the rights and responsibilities of the church. But," he went on, "when one considers practical matters, it is evident that women are not by nature fitted for the pastorate. For instance, a woman's voice is too light for preaching."

The leader of the group turned to a woman present and asked, "When you last spoke in the Chapel of the University of Chicago [which is larger than many a European cathedral], did you have trouble making yourself heard?" "Oh no," was the reply, "since in all modern buildings acoustical devices make it unnecessary for a speaker to lift his voice above normal." "But," said the theologian, recognizing that his first argument belonged to yesterday, "there is another practical reason against feminine ordination. The minister is the head of the local church family, and therefore ought to stand at the head of the family table at communion; a woman would look out of place there." Then up spoke Dr. Sarah Chakko, one of India's leading Christian women: "Doctor, I never realized until this moment why the communion table with a man presiding at it always has about it a hint of unreality in my India—for there it is the part of the woman of the household to preside at the family table."

The doctor had only shown himself provincially Western;

and in any case practical reasons or illustrations drawn from secular life outside the church are insufficient to disturb the solid theological foundation fact that God calls every individual to serve in his church at the point where he (or she) may perform the service for which he (or she) is best designed—and in any age only God (not the tradition of a past age) can show what that designation is. A denomination that vetoes the ordination of women to the ministry would seem to be still clinging to a social order that, without its realizing it, is gone forever. By their fruits ye shall know them: the United Church of Christ has reason to be proud of the record of its women ministers, few though they are.

The Character of the Ministry

Now the Constitution outlines with telegraphic brevity the specifications for the Christian ministry:

An *Ordained Minister* of the United Church of Christ is one of its members who has been called of God and ordained to preach and teach the Gospel. . . .

There is more, but let us stop to consider what this preaching and teaching mean.

(In parentheses it may be pointed out that being "called of God" as a prerequisite to the ministry is as unascertainable as it is indispensable. Only those are ordained who are thought to be called of God: all the tests there are, are invoked; personal examination is made, as we have said, but the will of God remains to man the will of God, and in the end man's best judgment of God's having called a person to the ministry must be substituted for exact knowledge of it. No person can do the work of the ministry who has not really so been called; but whether he has, actually, only time, which is one of the languages God uses, will tell.)

The minister's task is to preach and teach the word of God.

The verbs go together, for preaching to men is teaching, and teaching about God is preaching.

But who can preach or teach about God? One can preach or teach about created things, for these can be described by words and apprehended by the mind, but God is not like that. He cannot be lured from heaven by any trick of preaching. The man in the pulpit is not a professor at a desk, to bring God out like the neat conclusion of a syllogism; not a chemist at a laboratory table, to conjure him from a bubbling test tube. When God's awful sovereignty is understood, no one dreams that he can be netted by the soft light of stained-glass windows or the languor of an organ prelude or by a series of emotion-whetting hymns—or by preaching and teaching. He remains God. As instruments for commanding him, preaching and teaching are a failure. This one fact alone should serve to keep humble the preacher and teacher in the church.

The preaching and teaching that the United Church of Christ desires in its pastors is of the nature of witness. The preacher and teacher does not need to persuade God to enter the human scene; by faith he knows that he is already here. God has penetrated human history and stands, like the Christ in the Holman-Hunt painting, outside the door of every human heart, knocking to come in. This is the fact to which the minister can testify, and must. The presupposition of every word he utters can be an unspoken acknowledgment that God has come to him in Jesus Christ and changed him; and he can draw out from the contemporary life and opulent tradition of the church the histories of a thousand thousand other men who have made the same acknowledgment. He can make his own witness and witness to the witnessing of others. He can make mention of the grace of God that has come to him directly and that which has come to him through others. For this last he has the enormous resources of the church to bring to his people.

The United Church of Christ believes in what is historically known as the learned ministry. In none of its branches has it ever been seriously troubled by the anti-intellectualism that has bedeviled some parts of the Christian Church. There have been rural areas in this country and abroad in which the minister was expected to go from the plow to the pulpit, and hope that the Holy Spirit would fill his mouth with the appropriate word of the Gospel; the congregations had not noticed that even the Holy Spirit does better when he speaks through the mind of a man who has studied his Bible and the thoughts of the world's thinkers before he preaches to his people than when an undisciplined and empty-minded man presents himself as a mouthpiece. It is surprising that so many groups in the history of the church have felt that "book learning" would unfit a person for the ministry and that matriculation at a university was the beginning of the descent to Avernus. From this attitude of mind the United Church of Christ is free.

The learned ministry is not one, however, that cultivates learning for learning's sake. There is no joy in the life of a student comparable to that which is given in an opportunity for study, and this may indeed constitute a temptation to self-centeredness for some. At the coming of the renaissance of learning many a medieval scholar's delight with the new knowledge was dulled by the hazy apprehension that the pursuit of it might somehow be contrary to commitment to the austerity of the Gospel. In the case of the learned ministry, however, the acquisition of knowledge is not an avenue of sheer selfishness. All the joy of learning is there, but this is actually multiplied by the thought that it is to be employed for the service of Christ and humanity. When the minister meets his people—at any time, but especially when he stands before them to preach—he serves as a bank teller of the church's intellectual capital. Through the ages the church has acquired vast treasures of knowledge, most of which is accounted for in the books of Christendom; and this the minister tells out to the people. Of course he can only know the smallest fraction of it, for the church has a longer memory than any man, or than any ten men. It is the only institution still extant which saw the world under the regime of paganism. It is older than our civilization because it is a parent of it. For ages it has had its prophets and apostles, whose wisdom it has held in trust for coming generations—and this the learned minister makes available to his people.

The learned minister must on the one hand be aware of the riches the church treasures but on the other must also know how to deliver them to the people of his congregation. In the language of the business world, he must be acquainted with his stock but also know how to sell it; or, to draw a figure from the realm of language, he must know how to translate the truths which he finds stated in the classical tongue of the past into the everyday words of modernity. This takes a bit of doing. It is all very well for a minister to quote directly from the King James Version of the Bible—but what does the quotation *mean* to a man who has slipped into a pew from the street outside? Sometimes very little. Often the Bible cannot be used with relevance without interpretation; and to interpret it adequately a minister must know about the Hebrew people who wrote it, about their history and their hopes; he must have learned what the Bible has meant to people in the long history of the church; above all, he must have made its truths his own by systematic thinking; and after he has done all this, he must still be sufficiently well acquainted with the history and hopes of the people in his congregation to be able to tell the truths of the Bible not in its terms but theirs. Like any ambassador he must be able to speak two languages, that of the country from which he comes (in this case, the far-horizoned country of the great church) but also that of the country to which he is sent (the country where the pew sitters really live).

The temptation of most young ministers of the United Church of Christ, and perhaps of other communions too, is to preach and teach in the imperative rather than the indicative mood; they feel the inequities of life so keenly and are so eager to rectify them that they press hard on what their people *ought* to do and, in their public utterance, make too little of what God *has done* and *is doing* both as Judge and Saviour for them and all mankind. As a result of this emphasis some people believe that religion is a matter of morals. "Thou shalt not kill; Thou shalt not commit adultery; Thou shalt not steal"—these and the others of the Ten Commandments have been so much the stock in trade of the preacher that not a few young people, even college students, believe religion to be no more than a code of sanctions.

That ethics is not enough is known to the mature minister of the United Church as he preaches and teaches. His parishioners are not likely, therefore, to feel themselves hammered into accepting a particular code of morality made up of this-thou-shalt-do's and this-thou-shalt-not-do's, but they do, nonetheless, find themselves controlled by the forces of a moral, as of a kind of magnetic, field. The minister stands not for law but for love, and in effect takes the Augustinian attitude: Love and do what you will. "Do you mean to say," said one of Dr. Talmage's hearers on one occasion, "that if I love God I can sin all I like?" "Yes," said the divine, "and how much sinning would a man like who really loved God?" Persons who live within the influence of the Gospel unfortunately, or fortunately, do not find in it a code of conduct to which they can refer as to a blueprint in building their life, but they do find there motive power for doing their best.

And they find more. A man's level best, since he is a man, is not perfection; he does not reach an absolute standard in the realm of loving God any more than he does in that of good conduct. What then? Does he confess failure, acknowledge that he has been untrue to his love, and thenceforth cease to look in God's direction? The great discovery of the Protestant Reformation was of something that is always of the essence of the Catholic faith, though in the sixteenth century it was obscured: that faith in God is the main matter and that even the inability of a person to live up to his own obligation to God—as who can?—does not break the bond between them; God is ready to forgive—and so a life in which a man really tries to do his best even though he fails, as fail he must, is tolerable. One's very failures, in fact, bind him to a God who is ready to forgive, as any person is bound to another who is ready to let him make a fresh start. This matter of being accepted in spite of failures is, as every psychiatrist knows, of simply supreme moment in the life of every one; here the Gospel helps to keep society and its members morally sane. In the midst of our failures the declaration of the love of God for mankind—for you and me—gives us a consciousness that lends to life a meaning in spite of our inability to achieve perfection. His love for us and his willingness to forgive where there is true repentance washes through our own attitudes to our fellowmen and provides the atmosphere of forgiveness in human councils which lead to good workable (though not absolutely perfect) relationships.

Imperatives and indicatives—both are needed in preaching. The former without the latter are desiccated and tasteless; the latter without the former, fruitless and irrelevant to living. With preaching that combines both, the United Church of Christ hopes to make its contribution to the world's sanity and the world's moral progress.

The Rites

But to return to the description of the minister's work as the Constitution outlines it:

An *Ordained Minister* of the United Church of Christ is one of its members who has been called of God and ordained . . . to administer the sacraments and rites of the Church. . . .

We have already treated of the two sacraments, but what are the rites? These are those other regular and solemn acts of the church in which God's special presence is invoked. In the churches before the Reformation most of these rites were also, like baptism and communion, known as sacraments. In the Eastern Church, besides the two named, there were five more: the chrism, the priesthood, penitence, marriage, and unction. In the Western Church, roughly corresponding, there were: confirmation, order, penance, marriage, and extreme unction. The Evangelical and Reformed Church had had five rites: confirmation, ordination, consecration, marriage, and burial. The first two and the last two of these have some correspondence with the classical sacraments, but there is no sign of the rite of penance here, for that was let go at the time of the Reformation when the rediscovery of justification by faith (rather than works) was made; and here has been added the rite of consecration, which is for the eldership and diaconate within a congregation what ordination is for the ministry—the formal setting apart of a person to a stated and standing duty in the church. The Congregational Christian Churches had listed no special rites. The reference in the Constitution is specifically to those which the Evangelical and Reformed tradition brought into the United Church, though there is no prohibition against including other sacramental acts when and if there appears to be need to do so.

Truth to tell, it is difficult to distinguish theologically between a rite and a sacrament. Though the United Church of Christ does not, for instance, officially call *Confirmation* a sacrament, it believes, nonetheless, as in the case of a sacrament accepted as such, that if God is not understood as taking part in the act, its deeper meaning is lost. Something similar may be said of all the rites.

The Order of the Western Church, the Priesthood of the Eastern, and the *ordination* and *consecration* of the United Church of Christ are obviously related, having all to do with the setting apart of leadership. The word *priesthood* must be taken in the large, as covering the consecration of bishops as well as the ordination of priests proper; it is equivalent to the *ordo* of the West. The act of ordination, applying only to ministers, is classed by itself in the United Church of Christ and, as we have just said, distinguished from the act of consecration, by which other office bearers are set apart in the church. All offices in the United Church are filled by election or appointment by others already elected. There are no hereditary posts; none which may be purchased. The more important offices are all filled by direct election by the people, and after the election, which is regarded theologically as a kind of nomination on the part of the people, the act of consecration or ordination is thought of as the point at which God, as it were, accepts the nomination. This analogy should not be pressed too hard; the acts are all symbolic. This procedure is used in the case of the President of the Church and the officers of the General Synod, not to mention the officers of the Conferences and Associations, as well as those of the local church.

Marriage in the United Church is a rite shot through with sacramental meaning. In the early days of New England a serious attempt was made to relieve the ministers of the burden of executing civil affairs, which had been something of an evil in England. As part of this attempt, weddings were put completely into the hands of the state. Apparently the idea of dividing the responsibility as we do today—giving the state the right of issuing licences and the church the right of performing the ceremony—did not occur to the fathers. In any case, the custom was not as irreligious as it might at first seem to those familiar only with today's conditions, for there was abundance of magistrates in those days who were devout

Christians well able to conduct religious services, and they not only presided at the acceptance of the marriage covenant by bride and groom but also asked God's blessing on the union in appropriate prayers.

In the close association between church and state in those early days, it was possible as it would not be today for an officer of the state to take on functions we ordinarily associate with the church—but the custom did not last. Before the seventeenth century was over, young people were going to the parson to be married and, for well over two hundred and fifty years before the United Church of Christ took shape, the Congregationalists of Massachusetts and Connecticut sought the church rather than the state for the solemnization of marriages. The Evangelical and Reformed Church, having never gone through a Puritan revolt, had never experienced this type of interlude.

In the United Church, marriage becomes a covenant within the Covenant: the man-and-wife-to-be respond to God's gracious concern for them with a pledge of loyalty to him and to each other.

Since the United Church with the rest of Christendom takes the family as the fundamental social unit of society, and since, in these days of dissolving sanctions, the brittleness of family life is one of the scandals of this country, the minister of the United Church of Christ looks upon his function, in behalf of the church (and the state too) with anything but nonchalance. His concern takes the form of deep religious solicitude. He will do all he can to make the marriage Christian; and this is the reason he normally will not marry persons he does not first interview at length—sometimes at great length and more times than once. Couples to whom marriage is not a responsibility had best not stop at the door of the United Church parsonage for a quick wedding.

All of the courses in counseling the minister has had in his seminary work, all of his churchmanship, all of his experience with the human race will rise as a conscience within him to prevent the haste at a wedding which must be repented of at leisure. He can be counted upon to help the prospective husband and wife to acquire the vision of the Christian home in which the love that unites it is not merely the chemical attraction of the sexes but that kind called Christian which is willing to give all and ask nothing in return, in which all the arts of the home are used to celebrate this love, and the time for business by the man and for housekeeping by the woman are proportioned to the needs of the home—the whole lighted by the faith that God is also interested in their union.

Of the failures in marriage, when the minister is called in to help prevent the shipwreck which one or the other or both of the two defeated homemakers see coming on, nothing can be said here—since each case carries its own causes and the shadows of its own tragedy—except that the minister, working perhaps with the local psychiatrist, will lend such healing as he can. In this relationship he will not enter as the moral judge to whom all human action is either black or white, right or wrong. That day is past, if ever it existed; he will recognize the under-dimensions of the human soul and the curious way in which its highest motives pick up strange impurities. He will recognize that God alone can look into the inner depths of a person and make adequate judgment; and at all times he will try to envelop the stricken couple in an atmosphere in which genuine contrition and forgiveness can grow.

When the question of possible divorce comes up, he will not take the view of some parts of the Christian Church that marriage is once and for all, and that no kind of divorce is possible on the church's books. Today, even the most Catholic of churches finds ways and means to dissolve a marriage that is leading obviously to evil rather than to good. It was years ago, when ethical pioneering was needed, that the forerunners of the United Church of Christ began to see clearly that when spiritual divorce had already divided man and woman it was not for the church to intervene against the legal divorce of the two, and that the time for the church to do its work was not when the end had come and there was no issue save separation, but at the start, before the start, and following after the start, to remove the causes of separation.

The last of the Protestant rites is that of burial, and death is indeed an occasion when the church—with its hold partly on earth, partly in eternity—seems to have a specially appropriate function. At that time the minister can give his own testimony—often so hard to be believed by the bereaved— that life has a meaning which is not bounded by time and space, and that the grave is not the end. He is often the one who, more than any other person except the members of the immediate family, has called upon and talked with the one who has died; he thereby becomes something of a link between the living and the dead, and it seems altogether natural to call upon him for the funeral service.

The United Church of Christ is informally joined with all other forward-looking denominations in trying to separate American funeral rites from the pagan and commercial elements that in some areas have grown up around and cling to them. Death is not an event which can be treated with dripping sentimentality, nor does it provide occasion for panic, when as a last tribute to the departed—too frequently by those who have neglected the amenities of affection during the person's lifetime—expenses are contracted out of all proportion to the ability to pay them. Here the minister may be a useful adviser in matters severely practical, as he will surely be useful in preparing the order of service and preparing the family for it. As he grows older he sees more and more of death and acquires a wisdom concerning it which makes him a staff of support to those who are unfamiliar with and fear it.

The sacrament having most closely to do with death in the Western Church was extreme unction—the anointing with oil of a person who seems to have only a little longer to live. Roman priests, among whom the rite is of course still used, tell of innumerable instances in which the patient, relieved of apprehension by the solemn ceremony, has mustered the will to live of which his fears had bereft him, and so has recovered from his illness. In the Eastern Church, unction is given to any sick person with the definite intent that it will lead to recovery. In the United Church of Christ there is no formal act of the church corresponding to this; its place is taken by the conversation which the minister has with the patient at the bedside. This has an advantage of flexibility; the minister, learning from doctor and nurse, and from the sick man himself, in what mental state the latter is, may choose his words so as to bring home the particular phase of the Gospel's truth which seems most needed.

The other sacrament of the Eastern and Western Churches not continued in the United Church of Christ even in the form of a rite is that of penitence or penance. This in the older churches consists of penitent oral confession of sin to a proper priest, who assesses the penance or discipline that is to be undergone because of the sin, and finally pronounces absolution, or complete forgiveness for and release from it. Again the place of the formal rite is taken by a more flexible procedure; it is at this point that counseling comes into its own. No minister can know too much of human psychology and though he must never assume the role of the well-trained and experienced psychiatrist, he ought to know the symptoms of the main diseases that affect the human psyche well enough to recognize, when he sees them, the deeper troubles which only the psychiatrist can remedy. It is of course often a grateful relief to a person who is in sin to have someone to talk to about it; this, with contrition, becomes the first step back into social acceptability and consequent mental health.

This has ever been one of the best effects of the rite of confession. As for the penitential discipline that follows confession, ministers of the United Church of Christ, who take their theory from contemporary codes of psychotherapy rather than from Tridentine authorities who lived before Sigmund Freud, and do all their work against the Reformation insight that justification after sin is only by faith in God's forgiveness —these ministers have no set of penances to match sins of various sorts, since in their mind each particular case requires a discipline suited to itself. They know that the discipline required should be of a redemptive nature that will restore the person who has gone astray to a normal and healthy path of life. To be sure, there is no reason—if the minister thinks it advisable and the person being counseled desires it, or at least acquiesces—why the counseling should not be concluded with a formal act. To this end, sometimes the minister will give communion in private to a needy soul as a sign of complete return to the church. More often he will privately talk over with the person the meaning of communion as a sign of God's life-giving Covenant with his people, and then arrange to have him take the sacrament with the rest of the congregation in the near future in normal fashion. He takes the point of view in all of these matters that sin is a sickness of the soul that only God can finally cure.

The Christian Pastor

Now to complete our paragraph from the Constitution:

An *Ordained Minister* of the United Church of Christ is one of its members who has been called of God and ordained . . . to exercise pastoral care and leadership.

What is the chief end of pastoral care and leadership? Is it not to bring the people of the parish into so close a walk with God as he reveals himself in Christ that prayer to him and confidence in him will become to them as natural as breathing? Faith which speaks its gratitude in prayer is at the heart of the United Church of Christ, as it is at the heart of every Christian church. Just here it is made evident why the minister's fundamental task is so difficult. He has to get his people to turn regularly to God in prayer, for that is the way of spiritual health; but how can he do so unless his people believe that there is a God to turn to? The minister when faced by an unbeliever finds himself in the position of a man trying to explain to a blind person what light and color are, or to a deaf person what sound is like. There is nothing in the experience of his hearer on which he can base his description. God is a person, but a person infinite in wisdom, righteousness, and power—unlike any we have ever known apart from him. The best way for a minister to teach a wholly secularized person to pray, is undoubtedly to have him begin on a conditional note—"O God, if there be a God"—and then depend upon his finding the exercise so natural, so germane to his inmost self, so much a part of his whole humanity, that he comes eventually to recognize it as ancillary to a full life, like blood in the arteries. The minister is the catalyst of communion between God and his people.

Of public worship, which is also one of the means through which a minister of the United Church of Christ and of the church in general exercises his pastoral care and leadership, we have already spoken. The minister of the United Church of Christ cannot be at his best unless he is familiar with the liturgies of his own vast tradition. That tradition, unlike any other in this country, is more than merely Anglican or European: it is both—and the use today of services reminiscent of the Ancient Church, the Western Church, the old Lutheran Church, the Church of England, the Reformed Church of the Continent, and the Congregational Churches of Britain, bind our congregations of today to their own past. But because

Christ is alive and his spirit has to be mediated to modern people in language and action that have modern meaning, every minister has to be on the alert to cut out of the service that from the past which has become dead wood—that is, elements now meaningless or untranslatable into current thought—and to add to the service parts that speak to the modern mind. It is clearly easier to do this sort of thing in a church in which the congregations are not committed to a form prescribed by the denomination than in one in which no congregation can move faster than all are willing to move together. In the United Church of Christ, the form of public worship is left to the consecrated judgment of each local congregation working with its minister. This gives opportunity for experimentation combining commemoration and venture without involving the entire communion.

A chief arm of the minister's pastoral care and leadership is personal counseling, the time-consuming but dividend-yielding rediscovery of our era. The ministers of old did a good deal of counseling, to be sure, but they did not make the science of it that psychiatry and the seminaries have made of it today. Its roots, like that of psychiatry itself, go back to the days of Sigmund Freud, and have been generously cultivated by Adler and Jung. One of the main benefits of studying counseling, as we have already hinted, is negative; it keeps ministers from becoming amateur psychiatrists who know a little of the language and fancy themselves in their undisciplined experience to be as well qualified to impart advice as men trained in the profession. The minister and the psychiatrist must work closely together; the minister must have enough knowledge of the symptoms of mental disease to know when a case is beyond him; but the minister must realize also that, though he has the resources of the Christian religion at his disposal, his education does not equip him to do more than a superficial job where illness has set in. The positive benefit derives from the fact that no man can draw the line

between the ways of sanity and those of insanity. Moments
of sanity can be identified as well as the opposite extreme,
but at the median point between them they shade off into
each other.

It is for this reason that many United Church candidates
for the ministry find the knowledge of mental difficulties that
is offered them by the seminaries of the denomination serviceable in ordinary parishes; while they are students they may
act as nonprofessional internes in mental hospitals during a
summer or for a longer period under the direction of physicians and chaplains. The experience gives them acquaintance with the various types of psychopathic aberrations,
familiarizes them with their symptoms, prepares them to deal
in co-operation with psychiatrists with borderline cases, and
above all teaches them about the human race: its instinctive
tendencies, its willingness to make the socially acceptable
cover over and obscure the true but selfish reason for acts
and attitudes, and in general its unlimited exemplification of
the original sin spoken of by the older theologians.

The psychiatrist in any community can usually count upon
the minister of the local United Church of Christ as a useful
aide. And the minister has one instrument to work with which
even the psychiatrist lacks—the congregation. Most ministers
can give evidence of mental cures that have been effected in
the bosom of the church circle. There, a person ridden with
fears of being disliked or hated or even persecuted by others
can build up an awareness of being genuinely respected and
loved by the other members of the worshiping company. The
warm communion in Christ felt by a congregation of real believers has a therapeutic value second to no other single circumstance outside the more intimate relations of the family,
and the consciousness of being accepted by God himself,
through his grace, offers a cure to some that is not available
even in some families.

Most of the counsel offered by ministers of the United

Church of Christ, as by other clergymen, is given to people who are far removed from the mental ills to which the human flesh is heir. There is advice to be given about married life—and United Church ministers, as we have already indicated, do not ordinarily marry any without knowing something about them and helping them to see the points of magnificence in the Christian home, as well as the pitfalls that are likely to lie in the path of those to whom marriage has no spiritual side. There is advice to be given about children. There is even advice to be given to children about parents. Most of this counsel is given not at all directly but in the hundred and one contacts that a minister has with his people through committees, through joint work of various sorts, through chance meetings. If the minister has constantly in his mind the beloved community he is helping to build, all his meetings with his people will be such as subtly prepare them for membership in it. The local church becomes a microcosm of the great world, and within it, the kind of relationships are built up that, if they could become dominant in the vast community of the nations, would give us the peace and happiness of which we dream. This thought plays its leading part in the mind of the United Church minister.

Sometimes the minister himself must be protected by the communion as a whole in his right to be Christ's minister. I am not thinking of those magisterial men who get in trouble because they want to lord it over their congregations; I have in mind only those whose desire to serve Christ humbly but genuinely sometimes causes them to clash with the mores of their local community. Take a situation where the problem of race relations is acute, for instance, and there are social pressures that would squeeze the juices of idealism out of any ordinary minister. The Rev. John Doe is the minister in a pulpit in a part of the country where, let us say, the segregation of races has become as much a part of popular white social philosophy as it was in the South Africa of the Boers. He is necessarily pulled in two directions. On the one hand he knows from his contacts with the great church that God is no respecter of persons and that segregation as it is practiced —enforced separation of the races by one of them—is a sin against the laws of God. To maintain those contacts—the highest and best that he has—he must do what he can to live up to the standards they call for. On the other hand, there are his own people, sons of their fathers who in turn were sons of their fathers, all of whom believe that segregation is the basic structure of the good society and that to suggest a change is virtually to indict their fathers and their fathers' morals. The congregation, if Christian enough, would allow the preacher to follow the leading of his own conscience, but in a cold-war situation it is seldom disposed to do so.

It is easy (for others like us) to *say* what the minister should do between such upper and nether millstones: he should maintain his touch both with his own Christian conscience on the one hand and with the people of his charge on the other; but saying and doing are often two tragically different things. Thousands of ministers are thus trapped. To give the slightest hint that there is any side to the question save that of segregation is to cause the people to feel that they have been betrayed—and yet, not to do so is to sell one's soul. In this particular area, the United Church of Christ is at work to aid such a minister. It provides literature to help him educate his people not only to the idea of desegregation but also to the even more basic matter of letting a person follow the lead of his own Christian convictions. It supplies the fellowship of other ministers and of church assemblies where the ideals are not likely to be so faded as those in the minister's own parish. And if the minister is compelled to leave his people as a result of their own intransigeance, the denomination through its boards sees to it that he does not go abegging and helps him to a new pastorate.

We have already indicated that it is normally the Association which, on behalf of the entire communion, ordains a man to the ministry. From this fact it might have been guessed, as the Constitution now goes on to say:

Ministerial Standing in the United Church of Christ is held in an Association.

It is natural that the body which can give a man standing as a minister should hold it for him and protect him in it. It follows that in the case of moral delinquency the Association has the power also to remove the standing.

The By-Laws of the United Church have a good something to say about this whole matter of standing: A minister, moving from the bounds of one Association to another, requests a transfer of his ministerial standing to the Association of his new residence. If engaged in other than the parish ministry, a minister has his standing in the Association where he resides. If he be engaged in a ministry requiring his prolonged absence from the United States, or one that does not permit him a fixed residence, he is entitled to have his standing in the Association of his choice. A minister under sixty-five years of age who withdraws from active full-time service in the ministry applies to his Association for leave of absence. His Association may grant him such leave for one year at a time. Except in special cases leave is not granted for more than five years in succession. A minister retiring from active service by reason of age or disability retains his ministerial standing in the Association of his choice. A minister of the United Church of Christ serving a local church not affiliated with the United Church of Christ retains ministerial standing in the United Church of Christ so long as his Association approves. (This provision permits fruitful interdenominational arrangements.) A pastor's church membership is normally in the local church which he serves (though, as we have said, churches with Reformed background are likely to let the minister's standing in his Association serve as a substitute for his standing as a member of the local church). The discipline of a minister is the responsibility of the Association in which he holds his standing.

The Call of a minister to a pastorate establishes a covenant relationship between the minister and the local church. This relationship is also a concern of the Church at large as represented by an Association and a Conference.

So the Constitution. The covenant here spoken of is not the Covenant of Grace, to which we have so often referred, but it is part of it. God is also the prime mover in this relationship; and the spiritual life which he imparts to the minister is by him passed on to his church, as that given by God to the church is made available to him. At the point where these two streams of divinely inspired affection meet, the covenant relationship between church and minister comes alive. That this relationship is a concern of the church at large is obvious.

The whole process of calling a minister to a congregation is set forth in brief in the By-Laws of the church. It is the responsibility of a committee of the local church to seek a candidate for a vacancy in the office of pastor. In filling this vacancy or in securing supply ministers during the period of its duration, the committee of the local church, through its Conference executive, seeks the counsel of the placement committee, which consists of the Conference executive and other officers elected or appointed by the Conference. The committee of a local church requests the Conference executive to secure relevant information about any minister whom it wishes to consider for the vacancy. Any minister may confer with the Conference executive concerning a pastoral vacancy. At any minister's request, his name is submitted by the Conference executive for consideration by the committee of any local church where there is a pastoral vacancy. All vacancies within the Conference are reported promptly by the Conference executive to the Secretary of the United

Church of Christ for publication. The committee of the local church presents to the church the name of a candidate it recommends to fill the vacancy, and the local church determines whether or not it wishes to call the person recommended.

An ordained minister of another denomination who desires to enter the ministry of the United Church of Christ applies for *Privilege of Call* to the Association within whose bounds he resides. The Committees on the Ministry of the Conference and Association co-operate in examining the applicant as to his abilities, his reasons for desiring to enter the ministry of the United Church, his educational and theological attainments, his knowledge of the history, polity, and practices of the United Church of Christ, and his Christian faith and experience. If he is found to be qualified, the Association grants him *Privilege of Call*, thereby commending him for placement in the United Church of Christ. After he has accepted a call, he applies for ministerial standing in the United Church of Christ to the Association of which the local church extending the call is a part.

The Constitution concludes its article on the ministry by a brief description of two other kinds of workers, unordained:

A *Commissioned Worker* of the United Church of Christ is one of its unordained members who has been called of God and commissioned by his Association for a specific full-time church-related service.

A *Lay Minister* of the United Church of Christ is one of its unordained members who has been called of God and authorized by an Association to perform duties, mainly preaching and conducting services of worship, within that Association and under its guidance.

A person desiring recognition as a Commissioned Worker applies for that status to his Association. Often his local church requests it for him. His work involves his full time, but it is a specialized kind other than the pastorate of a church. It includes, for instance, the directorship of religious education, the profession of the deaconess in a hospital or charitable institution, that of the parish worker, of the minister of music, or of a teacher or officer of an educational institution related to the church. The Committees on the Ministry of an applicant's Conference and Association co-operate in examining him concerning his Christian faith, his character, his ability to do the work expected of him, and his education and training to meet the responsibilities of the office he seeks to fill. If he is found to be qualified, his Association commissions him.

The title Lay Minister seems a contradiction in terms, but it may be understood as a combination of them, signifying a kind of halfway station between two statuses. In various parts of the country are found churches that require chiefly preaching and the conduct of public worship, and in these churches dedicated laymen of special abilities can do a useful work, ordinarily not outside their own Association. Application for the status of Lay Minister is made through the local church to the Association. The Committees on the Ministry of the applicant's Conference and Association co-operate in examining him concerning his Christian faith, his character, his ability to do the work expected of him, and his knowledge of the history, polity, and practices of the United Church of Christ. If he is found qualified, his Association formally recognizes him as a Lay Minister, and as such his name is listed separately on the roll of his Association. He is not considered a ministerial member.

CHAPTER XI

STATE AND COUNTY GROUPS

Now THE CONSTITUTION MOVES INTO THE AREA OF DENOMINA-
tional organization, beginning with a paragraph on procedure
during the transition of the two denominations into the one
United Church of Christ:

Article VI.   Associations and Conferences
Pending their reorganization on a territorial basis, Synods, Conferences, Conventions and Associations in existence at the time
this Constitution is declared to be in force may act as Conferences
and Associations of the United Church of Christ and may perform
the functions thereof in accordance with the provisions of this
Constitution and the By-Laws of the United Church of Christ
with regard to such responsibilities as they may have heretofore
discharged. The Synods, Conferences, Conventions and Associations, with the counsel and confirmation of the General Synod,
shall take the initiative in their reorganization which shall proceed
with utmost dispatch.

The divisions within the Congregational Christian denomination—that is, the Associations and Conferences there—generally followed state lines for the latter, and county lines or
something roughly equivalent for the former. In the Evangelical and Reformed Church, however, the local Synods—in
size smaller than the Congregational Christian Conferences

and larger than the Associations, and doing the work of both
—had few parallels with the political divisions of the country;
they were churches grouped for ease and efficiency of common administration, often on two sides of a state border. One
of the first questions to confront the United Church General
Synod was as to what advice to give the churches as they
drew the lines of the new Associations and Conferences. At
the present writing, it is too early to know what shape the
new groupings will take, but with the union the distribution
of churches is so much more general and even than before,
that geography no longer presents serious difficulties to administration in most parts of the country, and it is likely that
for Conferences at least attention will be paid to political
(that is, state) divisions.

The term "Convention" (we may say parenthetically) is
the name used in some Congregational Christian areas for
what is generally known as a Conference.

For the interim the old Congregational Christian Conferences and Associations have, in general, respectively accepted
the status of acting Conferences and Associations of the
United Church of Christ, while the old Evangelical and Reformed Synods each serve both as acting Conferences and as
acting Associations. This status gives them the ready authority to unite or divide themselves into permanent divisions of
the church at an early date.

Now a Constitutional definition and a description of the
functions of:

Associations

An Association is that body within a Conference of the United
Church of Christ which is composed of all local churches in a
geographical area and of all ministers who have standing in that
Association.

There is one little word in this definition that might be
missed by many unfamiliar with the history of the churches

of this country—a word which seems as innocuous as the shadow of a summer cloud on the landscape, a mere adjective —but like the shadow of some clouds it does presage the possibility of storm. The word is *geographical*. Its dynamic significance lies in what it does not mean: specifically, it does not mean *racial*. The churches are divided into groups according to their geographical location, not according to the races that might make them up. In theory every local church of the United Church of Christ is as free from segregation as it is from any other disease of society, but in fact the churches in general parallel the morality of the communities in which they are located. There are today many United Church congregations which are indeed integrated in fact as in theory, and the number is increasing; and the denomination as a whole is aiding in the increase by writing it into the Constitution that the Associations—and, as we shall see, the Conferences as well—shall be simply the churches in given geographical areas, without regard to racial composition.

Subsequent to the initial reorganization of Associations in the United Church of Christ, the boundaries of any new Association, or any adjustment of boundaries between Associations shall be determined by the Associations concerned with the approval of the Conference or Conferences involved. The standing of an Association as a body of the United Church of Christ is determined by the Conference in which it is located.
An Association is that body which determines, confers and certifies to the standing of the local churches of the United Church of Christ within its area.
An Association is that body which determines, confers and certifies to ministerial standing in the United Church of Christ.

No comment is needed on these paragraphs save the observation that just as the local church holds the membership of individuals, the Association holds that of local churches and of ministers as ministers, and the Conferences that of the

Associations. It is this tenure which gives them severally standing in the United Church of Christ.

An Association may retain or secure its own charter, and adopts its own constitution, by-laws and other rules which it deems essential to its own welfare and not inconsistent with this Constitution and the By-Laws of the United Church of Christ.

This illustrates the freedom which pervades the United Church of Christ. One might guess that the largeness of this liberty, freely accorded the parts of the church, would result in a pluralism bordering on chaos. This, however, is far from the case: because the freedom is in Christ, that is, because it is directed to a common end informed by his own purpose, a symphony or, better, synergy (if we may borrow the word the physiologist uses for the working together of bodily organs) results. On the other hand, if an Association desires to make a new departure in Christian ministry, there is no Constitutional rigidity to say it nay.

An Association elects its own officers, and it elects or appoints such committees as it deems necessary for the transaction of its business and the correlation of its work with that of the Conference and the General Synod. It determines its own method for securing financial support. It is concerned with the welfare of all local churches within its boundaries, and seeks ways and means to assist them when they are undergoing unusual difficulties requiring help beyond their own resources. It offers encouragement, guidance, and assistance in the organization of new local churches and, with the counsel of the Conference, receives local churches into the United Church of Christ.

As we have noted, an Association receives under its care students for the ministry and extends to them fellowship, counsel, and assistance during their academic preparation; it grants licensure, ordains qualified applicants, and installs ministers; and in general, it serves the ministry as the local medical association serves physicians or the local bar association its lawyers. It receives and acts upon business referred to it by its local churches, its Conference, the General Synod and other bodies, and in turn, may petition and overture its Conference or the General Synod, and advise its local churches.

An Association is related to the General Synod through its Conference.

Though the Association has no direct representation in the General Synod, the wise Conference apportions its own choice of delegates to that body in such wise that all of its Associations are represented and, if necessary by some system of rotation, also sees to it that the ministry and the laity, both men and women, have their due opportunity to attend and participate in the meetings of the national body. Similarly, the wise Association draws up a schedule whereby its various churches have their opportunity to be personally (though not officially) represented on the General Synod.

When an Association meets, its voting membership consists of the ordained ministers holding standing therein and of lay delegates selected by and representing the local churches of that Association.

It should be noticed that the Association has two types of membership. Basically it is composed, as has already been recited, of the local churches and ministers in a given area, which is to say that its basic members are those churches and those ministers. Obviously, however, whole churches cannot get together to transact business; nor do the churches, although they constitute the foundation memberships, have the privilege of voting as churches. Any church may of course instruct its representative to vote as it requires at an Association meeting, but this is considered disorderly practice in Reformed circles, whether Congregational or Presbyterial, for it means that the representative does not subject himself at the meeting to the force of the arguments of the other representatives or to the personal guidance of the Holy Spirit. It contravenes the Golden Rule of our Lord; if all representatives came thus instructed, the meeting would be a waste of time for all. The Association therefore, besides its primary membership, has a voting membership, that is, its ordained ministers and the lay delegates appointed by its churches. These alone can vote at an "Association" meeting.

Meetings of the Association are held annually and at such other times as may be necessary for the discharge of its responsibilities.

Actually, most Associations meet semiannually and many quarterly. All depends upon how much they have to do—and even in the smallest Associations the tasks are not minimal.

Now follow similar descriptions of the work of

Conferences

A Conference is that body of the United Church of Christ which is composed of all local churches in a geographical area and of all ministers who have standing in the Associations of that Conference or in the Conference itself.

Note once more the all-important overtones of the word *geographical*.

A Conference, in the interest of the local churches, discharges those duties and provides those services which will strengthen the witness of the United Church of Christ. It coordinates the work and witness of the local churches and Associations; it gives counsel to local churches and ministers in situations calling for help beyond their own capacities; it renders an advisory service to local churches and to ministers with reference to pastoral placement; it establishes and maintains Conference offices, Conference centers, institutions, and other agencies needful to its growth and welfare;

it sponsors in–service training for ministers, and conducts conferences, retreats, clinics, and workshops.

Of the office-bearers of the Conference, none is more important than the President or Superintendent or Minister of the Conference, as he is variously called. As we have already suggested, he is the bishop of the diocese, though there is no episcopal succession involved. His consecration comes not through others who have occupied his office but through the churches whose representatives have elected and called him. He is *the* minister in the Conference: and this not only because he must have had experience and knowledge of the ministry, having preached and taught the Gospel in the local church, having immersed himself in the meaning and power of the church's sacraments and rites, and having known the pathos and joy of pastoral care and leadership, but also because he is the minister of the ministers, the Christian servant of all the churches. What he is, is more important than what he does: his work is to be to the Conference what the devoted pastor is to his congregation, a shepherd and bishop of souls.

Subsequent to the initial reorganization of Conferences in the United Church of Christ, the boundaries of any new Conference, or any adjustment of boundaries between Conferences, shall be determined by the Conferences concerned with the approval of the General Synod. The standing of a Conference as a body of the United Church of Christ is determined by the General Synod.

To the chain of holdings we now add another link: the local church holds the membership of individuals, the Association that of the local churches and their ministers, the Conference that of the Associations, and now it is indicated that the General Synod holds that of the Conferences. This means that the United Church of Christ accepts the decisions of the General Synod as to what are to be recognized as Conferences. This is of course a reciprocal decision, since no Conference takes standing in the United Church except by its own vote. This is corollary to the next provision:

A Conference may retain or secure its own charter, and adopts its own constitution, by-laws and other rules which it deems essential to its own welfare and not inconsistent with this Constitution and the By-Laws of the United Church of Christ.
A Conference is related to the General Synod as described in the By-Laws of the United Church of Christ.

This is to say that a Conference elects its officers, and elects or appoints such committees as it deems necessary for the transaction of its business and the correlation of its work with that of the General Synod; it receives and acts upon business, requests, counsel, and references from local churches, Associations, the General Synod and other bodies; it may petition and overture the General Synod; and it elects delegates and alternate delegates to the General Synod.

When a Conference meets, its voting membership consists of the ordained ministers holding standing in its Associations or in the Conference itself, and of lay delegates selected by and representing the local churches of that Conference.

Here again there is a distinction between primary membership and voting membership. The former consists of the local churches and ministers of the area of the Conference, but the latter only of the ministers and lay appointees of the churches.

Meetings of the Conference are held annually and at such other times as may be necessary for the discharge of its responsibilities.

Such meetings are seldom held more than twice a year.

The Constitution concludes its article on Associations and Conferences by a reference to the exceptional circumstance of

Conferences Acting as Associations
A Conference may exercise the functions of an Association when

they are delegated to it by an Association or where no Association exists.

This occurs in certain areas of the country where the United Church population is so thin that the Associations feel their work can best be done by the Conferences on which they are represented.

CHAPTER XII

THE NATIONAL BODY

WE COME NOW TO CONSTITUTIONAL REGULATIONS REGARDING
the national gathering of the United Church of Christ:

Article VII. The General Synod
The General Synod is the representative body of the United
Church of Christ. . . .

Note the definite article: this is *the* representative body.
It is the only such body. There are many Conferences and
more Associations, to say nothing of the local churches, but
there is only one General Synod and it is surrounded by a
unique cluster of "instrumentalities," as the various boards
and other national agencies of the church are called.

Because the General Synod is one and only one, it becomes,
as we have said, the symbol and expression of the church's
unity. It and its aiding instrumentalities are perfectly designed to speak and carry out the whole church's one will.
Not so the parts—the Conferences, for instance. They are several, and cannot possibly be or express a firm unity, simply
because they are not numerically one. They might express a
kind of unity if they were the mere arms of a higher national
body without any will or imagination of their own, but the
United Church of Christ believes that subordination of this

177

sort is repugnant to the freedom which is in Christ. They therefore, in their severalty, become the symbols and artificers of responsible freedom in the church, whereas the General Synod is the symbol and implement of the church's unity.

The General Synod, therefore, has one set of rules for itself. These may be amended, to be sure, as we have said, but only by orderly process. They are not subject to unauthorized substitutions. There is no quality of pluralism about them: they can change and grow but they cannot cease to be one and definitive.

But to go on with the constitutional notations:

The General Synod . . . is composed of delegates chosen by the Conferences, and of ex officio delegates; these shall constitute the *voting delegates*.

The ex officio delegates are the elected officers of the United Church of Christ, members of the Executive Council (of which more anon), and the Moderator and Assistant Moderators (of whom also we shall be saying more presently).

Now follow rules and regulations for the General Synod which are so much like those which govern other similar bodies there will be little occasion to amplify them by comment except in three or four instances, notably that which introduces the all-important subject of ecumenicity.

There shall not be fewer than three delegates allocated to each Conference. A quorum for the conduct of business shall consist of one-third of the voting delegates, provided that in this number at least two-thirds of the Conferences are represented by at least one delegate each. There shall also be *associate delegates*, without vote.

Powers

The General Synod has the following powers, provided, however, that no power vested in the General Synod shall invade the autonomy of Conferences, Associations, and local churches, or impair their right to acquire, own, manage and dispose of property and funds:

    a. To carry on, directly and through its Executive Council, instrumentalities and other bodies, the work of the United Church of Christ, and to provide for the financial support of this work;

    b. To organize as required for the transaction of business;

    c. To nominate and elect officers of the United Church of Christ who shall be chosen from the membership of the United Church of Christ and who with the Moderators shall serve as officers of the General Synod;

The Moderator is a kind of tribune of the people. He is elected by the General Synod on nomination from the floor. The office is filled alternately by lay persons and ministers. He presides at the sessions of the General Synod, and between sessions, as a representative of the entire fellowship of the United Church, often visits and addresses groups in various parts of the country. As a member of the Executive Council, though without vote, he is close to the point where important decisions are made between meetings of the General Synod, and so is enabled to speak to the people from a background of intimate knowledge of denominational events.

There are two Assistant Moderators of the General Synod, also elected on nomination from the floor, who assist the Moderator in presiding at the sessions of the Synod. The three moderators always include a minister, a layman, and a laywoman.

But to go on with the recital of the General Synod's powers. It is authorized:

    d. To nominate and elect those members of instrumentalities whose election is vested in the General Synod;

We shall have more to say about this when we treat in detail of the instrumentalities.

The Executive Council has many of the powers of the General Synod between sessions. The General Synod is empowered:

> e. To nominate and elect an Executive Council to act for the General Synod ad interim.

The Council consists of twenty-one voting members, not more than one of whom is from any one Conference. The President, the Secretary, and the Treasurer of the United Church, and, as we have said, the Moderator of the General Synod are members without vote. This Council submits to the General Synod any recommendation it may deem useful for the development of the effectiveness of the work of the United Church, and on critical occasions it itself makes decisions as to the organization and ministry of the communion in the expectancy that its action will be ratified when the General Synod next meets. It submits a report of its work at every meeting of the Synod.

Though publications in general are in the hands of the Board for Homeland Ministries—of which more presently—the editor of the *United Church Herald* is appointed by the Executive Council, as is also the editor of the *Reformatusok Lapja,* which is published for Hungarian congregations whose members have entered the country within the contemporary generation and do not yet read English easily. The latter are just short of being ten thousand strong in the United Church. The *Herald* is the organ of the denomination, though its editorial policy, expressing the individuality in fellowship that runs all through the United Church, is wholly in the hands of the editor. He, like the editor of the Magyar magazine, is supplied by the Executive Council with a committee with whose members he develops policy.

The *United Church Herald* has a distinguished history. It unites the Evangelical and Reformed *Messenger* and the Congregational Christian *Advance;* and behind each of these are worthy forebears, both English and German. The most interesting ancestor of the *Herald* is the magazine of a similar, though longer, title, *The Herald of Gospel Liberty,* which was the first religious newspaper published in this country. This was the product of the intelligence and energy of the Rev. Elias Smith, who was a northern New Englander associated for part of his life with the Rev. Abner Jones. He was a tireless organizer of Free Christian Churches, which later became members of the Christian Church, which in turn united with the Congregational Churches in 1931. The first issue of his paper saw the light on the first day of September, 1808.

The list of powers goes on. The General Synod has the authority:

f. To establish and maintain national headquarters for the United Church of Christ;

g. To establish a central treasury which shall receive funds contributed to the General Synod for the support of the United Church of Christ and for its instrumentalities;

h. To determine the relationships of the United Church of Christ with ecumenical organizations, world confessional bodies, and other interdenominational agencies;

The ecumenical organizations to which the United Church of Christ belongs are the National Council of the Churches of Christ in the United States of America, and the World Council of Churches. Since Congregational Christian Churches and the Evangelical and Reformed Church both had a hand in founding these councils, it is scarcely strange that the United Church of Christ should maintain an active interest in them and in every way possible seek to enhance their well-being. They are the largest organs of non-Roman Christianity respectively in the nation and in the world. The churches that compose them give each other fuller recognition than is yet possible between Roman and non-Roman churches, where the relationship takes the form only of "conversations" and never of councils, but the recognition here is only for purposes of collaboration: each church remains severely itself, retaining its own autonomy within the councils. This kind of co-operation among the various sectors of Christ's church is one in which the United Church of Christ rejoices. Into it, it throws its resources without stint or limit as the Lord gives it opportunity; but until co-operation has blossomed into union—permitting every part of the church to recognize every other part fully—it will feel that the goal on the road of unity has not been reached. It prays for a united rather than a co-operative church of Christ, far vaster and more inclusive than it is itself, but it supports co-operation among the churches not only because it is good in itself but because it makes toward something better.

In its relation not only to the other members of these councils but to the Roman Church as well, the United Church of Christ tries to err on the generous side, if it has to err at all, in the matter of recognition. It recognizes the ministries of other denominations, Catholic and Protestant, as true church ministries, and the members of those churches as true church members. It has no canon on its books calling for the reordination or reconfirmation of ministers or members that come to it from other communions. Without waiting for concordats with other denominations, it unilaterally (if need be) admits their members to the Lord's Table and hopes some day to crown this liturgical hospitality with an act of union with them.

The world confessional bodies with which the United Church of Christ is affiliated are the Alliance of Reformed

Churches Throughout the World Holding the Presbyterian Order, and the International Congregational Council. The Evangelical and Reformed Church has long been a member of the former and the Congregational Christian Churches of the latter; it is natural that these relationships should continue unbroken. As a matter of fact, churches of the Congregational and of the Presbyterian type have united in many countries of the world; on the Continent of Europe, as will be recalled, they have never separated. The emergence of the United Church of Christ will furnish one more line of connection to draw these two world bodies together.

There are other interdenominational bodies through which the United Church co-operates with its sister denominations in this country. These organizations, outside the World Council of Churches and the National Council, are generally engaged in highly specialized functions, as is the American Bible Society, which is one of them.

Now we come to the matter of ecumenicity, which for the United Church of Christ is cardinal to Christ's church. (Perhaps we should stop long enough to note that this polysyllable and its cognates like *ecumenics* and *ecumenical* are doing heavy duty today to describe the amazing movement of our times in which the various communions of Christendom, instead of breaking into ever smaller groups, are now drawing closer to each other in co-operation and organic union.) The United Church of Christ regards itself as having a special call from God in this field. The General Synod is given power:

i. To encourage conversations with other communions and when appropriate to authorize and guide negotiations with them looking toward formal union;

As proof that it wears the amice gray of the pilgrims on the ecumenical road, the United Church of Christ, having been apprised that the International Convention of the Disciples of Christ, and the Council of Community Churches, were interested in entering upon negotiations looking toward union with the United Church as soon as the constitution of the latter was adopted and its representative committees appointed, invited delegates from those two bodies to sit with its two ranking commissions—the Commission to Prepare a Constitution and the Commission to Prepare a Statement of Faith. Both the Disciples of Christ and the Community Churches responded by sending to the meetings of the commissions men who not only contributed wisdom in the creation of the Constitution and the Statement of Faith but by the very experience prepared themselves as liaison personalities, knowing both their own denominations and the mind of United Church leaders, to serve in the negotiations yet to come. It is probable that this was the first time in history when the union of two Christian groups was aided by representatives of third groups in an anticipated chain reaction.

If the United Church of Christ goes on to join forces with other Christian groups like the Disciples of Christ and the Community Churches, as it fully expects to, the name which it carries will doubtless be changed, not only because it would be confusing legally and generally for a church to have the same name both before and after it entered into a new union but also because the new name would symbolize a new creation, in which the new partner (or partners) would have as much place, and to which they would have brought as much, as the United Church.

In a further union, borrowings would doubtless be made from the procedures of all the uniting bodies, but the United Church would have one gift to impart which is hardly to be matched by any other church in existence. The gift of the United Church to ecumenicity, if we may anticipate the judgment of church historians of a century hence, is the Constitution of the United Church itself, or rather the principles on which the Constitution is based. It itself is an ecumenical document, and could be taken over as it is by an ecumenical church to a degree to which, so far as I know, no other church constitution would be susceptible.

But before we look into the future, it may pay us to glance back at the past. The United Church of Christ, drawing its life both from the churches of the Continent and those of Great Britain, naturally takes on the character of both, but this makes it different from either. It has often been remarked that the struggles of the church on the Continent during the centuries since the Renaissance have pivoted on questions of *faith*, whereas those of England have for the most part concerned themselves with issues of *order*.

The break between the curia and Martin Luther was occasioned by a division of opinion on the sale of indulgences, with deeper undertones as to whether faith justified a man in the sight of God. The unfortunate cleavage between Lutherans and Calvinists had nothing, or at least very little, to do with the manner in which the church was to be governed; it took place at the communion table, where those who believed that Christ was present consubstantially—that is, substantially present in the bread and wine, though not magically conjured there by the priest's words—differed with those who held that he was only spiritually there. The idea of government in the Lutheran was not different from that in the Reformed Church. Continental discussions all had to do with matters of faith.

When the historian looks across the Channel, however, he sees the breaks in the life of the church following quite different lines. Henry VIII and Pope Clement VII probably had the same views on all matters of faith, both of them orthodox to a fault; but they had diametrically opposing views as to who should be the worldly ruler of the Church of England. Later, when the Puritans began to ask for something better in the church than oppressive bishops and illiterate clergy, the battle was joined over points not of belief (though these were secondarily in evidence) but of authority. As we have pointed out, the very names of the best-known church divisions in the English-speaking world of the seventeenth century—Episcopal, Presbyterian, and Congregational—reveal differences not in the essentials of the faith but in modes of government. When, later, John Wesley entered the scene, he had no contest with the Anglican authorities on the fundamental means of salvation; he expected to meet in heaven the very bishops who warned him that if he, a priest, ordained ministers to service in the church, the act would be equivalent to separating himself from the church. Here again the controversy resolved itself into a matter of order; and just as truly as the Continentals have allowed for the possibility of several forms of government within a church of one faith, so the English have tended to allow several forms of faith— witness the theological extremes within today's Church of England and all other larger churches having English roots— under the one type of church government.

What then has the United Church of Christ inherited from these two parents, Europe and Britain? Positively, it is heir to the belief that both faith and order—that is, the forms of each—are important. But negatively from the Continent it has learned that it is not necessary to apotheosize orders, and from Britain that it is equally unnecessary to exalt any particular formulation of faith. It is essential that there be order, so that the grace of Christ may be apprehended and communicated by the great church to its members and by its members to the church; it is equally essential that this grace should be understood by the mind as truth, but the basic order that permits the passage of grace is not the same as any particular order, as faith is not the same as any particular systematization of it. The one essence is available to many forms: a particular historization (to use a word beloved of theologians) partakes of but is not the same as the eternal word of God it seeks to clothe in form. The United Church of Christ takes from Europe the knowledge that there is no sacrosanct order of government in the church, and from Britain a similar knowledge about extended formularies of faith, with the result that it dares to produce a Constitution that leaves room for orderly and consecrated diversity at both of these points and so opens itself to ecumenical uses.

The basic form of that Constitution has already been described. It provides, in the General Synod, a point of entrance for the Word of God to come to the whole church and thence to be disseminated to all the parts. Every means is used to keep this central area protected as a symbol and instance of the church in its wholeness. The General Synod in the United Church of Christ (we venture to repeat) is one and unique: it has no duplicate or substitute. It is catholic; it represents and, so far as is consistent with the freedom of the parts, speaks for the whole church. It is holy: standing like a priest between God and the total church, it has its godward side, mediating the blessing of God to that church and making possible its worship of him. It is apostolic: it has its manward side, being sent of God to carry the Gospel to all within the church and through them to the whole world. This is one pole of the church's life, the pole of its wholeness —and this or its equivalent is provided in almost every denomination of Christians.

The other pole—the individual pole through which the currents of God pass in equal measure, through which individuals and individual groups take from God and give to the church and reciprocally, enjoying the things of the total church, give thanks to God in worship—is also protected by the United Church of Christ to a degree which makes it, I think, unusual among the denominations. The church as a whole asks of its members only—but this is everything—that they maintain their touch with the waters of eternal life which spring from God in Jesus Christ. Beyond that, the individual churches create their own forms of worship (though the great church is ready to supply them with the time-honored precedents of its tradition); they set up their own government (though the communion will lend a hand if desired); and in general (though the influence of Christ pervading the whole church dictates harmony rather than harsh individualism) they make their own interpretation of the demands of Christ. It will be seen at a glance that a Constitution with such provisions offers a framework for the ecumenical church of the future (if ever it comes to be) which denominations that require (rather than recommend) uniform prayer books or uniform congregational government can hardly give.

I know no better description of the constitutional principles of the United Church of Christ than is to be found in the statement on the nature of the unity sought for the churches by the Commission on Faith and Order of the World Council of Churches, as published in the minutes of the Central Committee meeting in 1960: it understands that:

> . . . the unity which is both God's will and his gift to his Church is one which brings all in each place who confess Christ Jesus as Lord into a fully committed fellowship with one another through one baptism into him, holding the one apostolic faith, preaching the one Gospel, and breaking the one bread, and having a corporate life reaching out in witness and service to all; and which at the same time unites them with the whole Christian fellowship in all places and in all ages in such wise that ministry and members are acknowledged by all, and that all can act and speak together as occasion requires for the tasks to which God calls the Church. . . .
>
> *In particular we would state emphatically that the unity we seek is not one of uniformity.* . . .

I have ventured to italicize the last sentence because of its pertinence here. Constitutionally, the United Church of Christ is already in principle an ecumenical church.

Can a truly ecumenical church operate under any other type of constitution than this? One of the truths now printed on the minds of all who have participated in the ecumenical movement—which might have been guessed in advance but does not seem to have been, fully—is that members of the various communions do love their communions. They like the relationships within them. The average Methodist minister takes deep joy in his Methodism, as does the average Episcopalian in his Episcopalianism, the average Presbyterian in his Presbyterianism, and the others in their own communions and communion ways. This fine loyalty is, as a matter of fact, one of the most beautiful features of the life of any communion, even though it must be said that it sometimes seems to make the ecumenical hope more difficult. If Christ were not at the center of every church, attracting to himself its members there but also attracting to himself a larger company beyond any denomination, there would be no hope—but there he is. Part of the love of any member for his denomination, if he be a good churchman, is his love for its manner of doing things, the order it establishes and offers to him, the relationships, finely human albeit ecclesiastical, in which it comfortably enmeshes him. He will never unite with an ecumenical church unless he can find these there.

No plan of organic union of the churches, on a broad scale or a small one, can have any chance of success if it does not take account of every churchman's love of the ancestral ways of his church. The Faith and Order leaders, contemplating something like a universal church of the future, are therefore quite right in saying that in that church there must be episcopacy, there must be presbyterianism, and there must be congregationalism—to name the three classical types of polity other than papacy. There must also be Lutheranism, Calvinism, Pentecostalism, and all the other major formulations of faith. There must in fact be freedom of form in every aspect of the church's life.

This is the fact which the United Church of Christ has taken seriously, and woven, in principle, into its Constitution. The United Church of Christ is:

Presbyterian in its *legislative* functions, since it works through representatives or presbyters,

Episcopal in its *administrative* system, since here it works through superintendents or episcopi, and

Congregational in its *judicial* branch, since the congregations and several groupings make their own decisions and have no judge over them but Christ and the decent respect they have for all their brethren in Christ.

If some part of the United Church wishes to make itself presbyterian not only in its legislative but in its other functions, it could do so, provided this action did not prevent other parts of the church from being nonpresbyterian. One of the Conferences of the United Church of Christ is, in fact, already presbyterian in its general features: in the Southern Convention no property of a local church can be disposed of without consent of the Conference (the name used in that part of the country for the unit roughly comparable to a presbytery); it is the duty of every church to comply with the requests made of it by the Conference; and Conferences on their part have the full right of carrying any controversies by appeal to the Convention (which is the name given to what is known elsewhere as a Conference), whose decision is final. Any other part of the church could follow this example of presbyterianism if it wished.

Any part of the church might conceivably in parallel fashion make itself episcopalian in all its functions. There is nothing in the Constitution to prevent it.

The Constitution does, however, as we have stated, prevent any part of the church from using its freedom to deprive any other part of the like freedom. Suppose, for example, that ninety-nine churches in an Association of one hundred churches wanted to adopt a Methodist style of ministerial placement, whereby each church would be assured by the bishop or superintendent, or the episcopal or superintending committee, that a minister would be assigned to it, and the ministers on the other hand assured that not one of them would be without a pastorate; and further suppose that one church in the group felt strongly against this system and desired to have the privilege of calling its own pastor without recourse to bishop, superintendent, or committee—could that church be deprived of this privilege? No. It would not in fact be difficult to work out a plan whereby the majority could have its will at the same time that the exception was permitted. This principle is universal throughout the United Church of Christ: its freedom is complete in Christ—but the freedom of one Christian body which is used to take away freedom from another is not freedom in Christ.

The United Church of Christ could be hospitable to—and indeed provide the blueprint for—an ecumenical plan which, in Archbishop Fisher's phrase, ". . . took episcopacy into its system," but would be equally hostile to any such plan that drove nonepiscopacy out. The United Church of Christ permits the kind of episcopacy which itself permits presbyterianism and congregationalism, as it allows the kind of presbyterianism which in turn allows episcopacy and congregationalism, and the kind of congregationalism which does not shut out episcopacy or presbyterianism.

On this score the United Church of Christ believes that it may make a gift to the church of the future. There is indeed some ground for thinking it has already done so, for it has already set up a communion which is proving to the world of the church that unity and pluralism are not mutually exclusive, that the whole church may transmit the grace of Christ to each part of it while each part of it in freedom— real freedom to shape itself—devotes itself to the whole. The success of the United Church must give new assurance to negotiators for similar unions throughout the world that the end of their endeavors may be reached.

Now the list of powers of the General Synod concludes with the customary authorization to bodies of that sort:

j. To amend this Constitution as hereinafter provided; and
k. To adopt by-laws for the United Church of Christ and, as hereinafter provided, to amend them.

And then a word about

Meetings

The General Synod shall hold meetings at regular intervals as provided in the By-Laws of the United Church of Christ. Special meetings may be called in the manner provided in those By-Laws.

According to the By-Laws, regular meetings of the General Synod are held biennially at such places in the United States as are determined by the Executive Council.

Chapter XIII

THE ARMS OF THE CHURCH

Next to the last of the greater sections of the constitution is the important and exciting

Article VIII.   Instrumentalities

The United Church of Christ recognizes responsibilities at home and abroad for missions, fraternal aid and service, ecumenical relations, interchurch relations and Christian unity, education, publication, the ministry, ministerial pensions and relief, evangelism, stewardship, social action, health and welfare and any other appropriate area of need or concern.

The name *instrumentalities* is given to the boards and other organizations that serve as arms of the church. Theoretically, it would be possible for the General Synod to conduct its own missionary work in this country and beyond the seas but, practically, that kind of arrangement would be far too greatly overcentralized. It has been proved a better system in all denominations to separate the easily divisible functions of the church at the national level, and then assign each one to a particular group of interested people who will themselves learn all they can about the ends, ways, and means of the task, and promote interest in it throughout the communion. The division between homeland work and foreign work is a natural one. It is true, given the deterioration of the Christian atmosphere in the Western World, that the basic business of building the church is the same at home as abroad—the work of a church just outside the Loop of Chicago, for instance, being closely similar to that of a church not far from the Ginza in Tokyo—but there are other factors, such as that of language and of political government, which do differentiate the Christian task in this country from that elsewhere, and so the division is made.

The uniting denominations brought into the United Church of Christ mission boards and other agencies of Christian benefaction which already had had long histories of service. With the new consolidation of interests, however, new opportunities presented themselves, and so the church took a fresh look at its ministries to the world, and asked the General Synod, as the Constitution implies, to set up a well-balanced system of Christian benefactions by creating new instrumentalities or accepting old ones. It was a matter of

Establishment or Recognition

The General Synod shall establish or cause to be established boards, commissions, councils, offices, or other instrumentalities, temporary or permanent, incorporated or unincorporated, suitable for the discharge of its responsibilities. Such instrumentalities shall perform all their acts in accordance with this Constitution and the By-Laws of the United Church of Christ, and instructions given them from time to time by the General Synod.

The General Synod shall determine the conditions under which it will recognize an existing agency as an instrumentality of the United Church of Christ. Each instrumentality so recognized shall administer its own program and financial affairs, and establish its own by-laws and rules of procedure.

Though, as we shall see, the General Synod nominates and elects members to these recognized boards, the boards themselves are not mere puppets of the Synod. On the contrary, they are expected to take the initiative in Christian enterprise, making their own decisions within the general context of the fellowship of the whole church. Here again is a touch of the mutuality of freedom and fellowship in Christ found within the United Church.

Given the freedom of the instrumentalities to plan their own work and work their own plan, it is necessary for some single agency to keep all of their activities within its purview, both in their approach to their supporting congregations and in the fields in which they labor, and, when necessary, to help them to such combination of effort as would be needed to meet some unusual contingency. Accordingly the Constitution at this point has a paragraph on

Correlation

The General Synod and its Executive Council shall consider the programs of such instrumentalities with a view to correlating their work, publicity and promotion, preventing duplication and effecting economies of administration, so as to secure maximum effectiveness and efficiency through careful stewardship of personnel and financial resources. Due protection shall be given to all trust funds, including pension funds.

Chapter XIV

THE BOARD FOR WORLD MINISTRIES

Now we come to a description of the first great arm of the United Church of Christ which is engaged in

World Mission and Service

The General Synod recognizes the United Church Board for World Ministries as the instrumentality of the United Church of Christ for the planning and conduct of its program of mission and service abroad and of emergency relief anywhere. This Board continues the work previously carried on by the American Board of Commissioners for Foreign Missions, the Board of International Missions, the Commission on World Service and the Congregational Christian Service Committee.

This Board is based, vis-à-vis the state, on the charter granted by the Commonwealth of Massachusetts to the American Board of Commissioners for Foreign Missions in the year 1810. This makes it the oldest foreign-missionary board in the United States.

The General Synod nominates and elects the corporate members of the United Church Board for World Ministries. This Board shall report its program and finances annually to the Executive Council and to each regular meeting of the General Synod. It shall submit to the Budget Committee of the General Synod a detailed request for allocation from the budget to be recommended to the General Synod for the component parts of its program.

But why should we wait for a report of the Board at a meeting of the Executive Council or the General Synod? There seems no better time or place to recite its interesting reasons for being and ways of doing than here and now.

Up till now we have been talking about the United Church of Christ on its interior side. For analytical purposes we have abstracted it from the world. But, as William Temple once remarked, "God seems to be interested in a lot of things besides the Church." And the United Church of Christ is interested in a lot of things besides itself or, indeed, the whole church of Jesus Christ. A study of a board which is dedicated to carrying the Gospel beyond the pale of the church provides occasion for thinking of the relation of the church to the world—a subject which is occupying the minds of many in these days, and in consideration of which we may gain further insight into the United Church of Christ and its spirit.

So far as the United Church is concerned (if I read its thinkers correctly), the world is one. God sent his son into it not to show special favor to church people but that the whole race should be redeemed. He makes his sun rise on the evil and on the good, and sends rain on the just and on the unjust. We have said a good deal about the twin ways he has of bringing his grace to a person in the church—directly, by giving him immediate discernment of certain things; and indirectly, through the society in which he lives. But this is not a situation peculiar to the church, for God speaks in this dual way to everyone. He gives us each our individuality and our society, whether we recognize him as the giver or not. He treats us as one world.

The division between this one world is simply on the matter of our recognition of God's gifts. Part of the world sees his hand in them, and the other part does not. Actually, a great many more of the world's inventors and discoverers belong to the class of those who know that God has had a part in their work, than might be expected. The prophets of the Bible, the builders of the Catholic Church, many of the great poets—these all believed that God was working directly through them. So, we read, did Columbus as he voyaged westward; so did Dante, so did Handel, as they composed their masterpieces. But I take it that there are many others who simply take their own creativity for granted and never associate it with God at all. Did Roebling make any religious connection with his planning for the building of the Brooklyn Bridge? Do engineers in general conceive that they are helping God build his world? Or businessmen? Some of them do, I know, but if I may judge from appearances, some of them do not take time to reflect that they do not really own anything they work with, that all that they have and all that they are came from God, and that their most personal contributions to the world, without ceasing to be their own, have a divine mark upon them. As for the gifts we receive from our society, many of us know that our nation gives us protection and any number of other benefits, but only some of us think of God as using the nation as a medium of his own gracious interest in us. Many recognize that their breakfast table is made up of requisitions from all quarters of the globe—the coffee from Brazil, the sugar from Central America, the wood for the table itself perhaps from Africa, the salt-and-pepper shakers from Japan—but not all can conceive of God as standing behind the whole process of growing or manufacturing what they enjoy. The world seems to be divided into the recognizers and the nonrecognizers of God.

The United Church of Christ approaches the nonreligious world, therefore, not as a group who have some special God that others do not have, and who consequently have some special standing in the universe. Not at all. They are one people with all other people, having one God who treats them all alike. They, like the others, live now in decency and now in sin. They are one-part wisdom and one-part folly as the others are. But they do count themselves among those who, recognizing God, are conscious not only of him but of their shortcomings in relation to him—and consciousness, after all, is a form of life, the coefficient of abundant life.

The consciousness of having a loving God is an ebullient thing: it runs over. It is perfectly impossible for a man to have it without wanting to share it with others. It does not make one a better man morally or intellectually but it does add to him a new dimension of vitality. It is in this consciousness and not with any sense of human superiority that the United Church ministers to the nonreligious world. Its ministry is motivated by a love which, like that of the God who inspires it, goes out not merely to the people of the United Church, to other Christians, or to religious people as such, but to the whole of mankind, recognizing no limits within the family of man. Since its missionary work is the extension of a consciousness, it has no truck with the use of force. It never compels; it only attracts. It wants all men to come to know consciously that God has declared his love for them in Christ and so it acts toward the nonreligious world in such ways as will promote that consciousness of being loved.

Beginning with the proposition that the human family is one, the United Church of Christ argues that wherever there is need, in order to show the love of God and their own love, the privileged should be at work for the underprivileged. The statistics of the situation are that there are more physicians in the United States—indeed a very great many more—than in many countries of Africa and the Orient, and this means from the Christian point of view that the American church needs to be concerned about physicians in Africa and the Orient. It is because the consecrated missionary doctor feels he does not belong to a superior part of the human race that he offers his services in those parts of the world. If he thought that his race were intrinsically superior, he would follow in the Nazis' way (with their pride of Aryan blood) and build up barriers between his race on the one hand and the rest of mankind on the other. He would believe in the segregation of races as all those who think themselves racially superior do. But because he has a passion for humanity, articulated in the definite belief that God has made of one blood all nations of men, the whole world is his home; he builds no barriers in it, and he goes to the help of the needy wherever they are and of whatever race.

When I was younger than I am now, we used to hear a good deal of criticism of foreign missions on the ground that each nation had its own resources and should look after itself. That was before we knew that the best way to save America from the decimation left by Spanish influenza was to attack it at its beginnings in the slums of Madrid or wherever it began; before we realized that we could do better against Communism in this country by giving vital help to newly born African nations and teaching them the ways of democracy than by merely inveighing against the Marxian philosophy and making an arrest now and then here at home; before we learned the hard way that this is one world and that those who believe that any of its parts can be neglected by any other parts belong to an era that is as dead as the Chin Dynasty and as outmoded as its Chinese Wall. The Christian Church as a whole and the United Church of Christ as a part of it believe in foreign missions as a woodsman believes in the woods, as an eagle believes in the air—the whole world, and nothing less, is the medium and arena of its life. Nations to it are necessary and useful groupings of mankind, but when they erect partitions against each other so that mankind is broken and cannot be itself, then, in the eyes of the church they slip away from their own high destiny and lend themselves to evil. Internationalism is fostered by the church as the best background for a salutary nationalism, and within itself the church wages an unrelenting war against that ecclesiastical nationalism that "does not believe in foreign missions."

In the early days of foreign-missionary work there was apparently too close an association between the Gospel and the Western forms in which it was presented; even Western hymn tunes were copied, and the indigenous melodies of the foreign country, based on its own musical scale, were left unutilized. Even Western dress was affected, as the Mother Hubbard of some of the Pacific-island women today woefully testifies. The modern missionary of the United Church type, however, sees as clearly as unimpaired insight reveals it to him that the basic Gospel and the Western forms in which it is clothed are two distinctly different things, though related, and that what is needed for Asian or African peoples is the Gospel in forms drawn from Asia or from Africa. So services of worship in the villages of India are held in the way of all other village gatherings, the worshipers sitting on the floor or standing—without trying to balance themselves on Western chairs or pews. So some of the native Indian musical forms are used, though Western hymns have taken on, also— as potently, we may add, as has jazz in its own field.

But the missionaries go farther. Knowing the dangers of Western materialism at first hand, they are often the ones to act as conservers of the local culture in the path of the oncoming juggernaut of Westernization. In the less developed countries they and they alone have transformed the hitherto unwritten dialect into legibility on a written page, and so opened the door to the preservation of native prose and poetry as literature. No one can be a good missionary of Christ who does not love the people to whom he is sent— the people *and* their folkways. This is the reason that in instance after instance, especially among the more primitive peoples, it is the missionaries who have brought those among whom they labor to see the magnificence of the arts which they themselves have developed artlessly. The permanent culture of the world is richer because wise missionaries, with a love for humanity and a penchant for preserving the good ways of men, have done their work broadly and well.

Because the "foreign" missionaries of the church really regard no one as foreign to them and go out not as ambassadors from a particular nation but simply as emissaries wanting to lift the whole of mankind at home and abroad to the sense that God is concerned for them all, they become most effective agents of international peace. Of course the nations themselves must be depended upon in the last analysis to keep the peace, but they cannot do so unless there is a will to do so, and mission boards of the United Church type develop this will in two ways. In the first place they keep preaching the Gospel of Christ, which stands in unflinching contradiction to selfish nationalism. The ethics that flow from the fact that God is the God of the whole world, and not of the United States of America alone (as the professional patriot might think) or of any other particular nation on earth—these ethics teach that humanity comes first and that any nation that lifts itself up against the world's well-being stands condemned. The Gospel brooks no nonsense of the "America First" type except when this means America first in service to the world; and it knows full well that a nation is nothing but a gang—and a most dangerous gang at that, because it is so powerful—when it seeks its own way without respect for the total rights of the whole world. By preaching this kind of morality, oriented to the whole race of man and not to any particular part of it, the Christian Church at home and abroad instills the will to peace. But in the second place —and more importantly—the church creates an international society. One has only the highest praise for the peace societies of various kinds throughout the world—the city almanac of New York or Chicago or Los Angeles listing scores of them

—but which one of them can compare to the church itself?—
which not only talks peace but sends out its people to foreign
countries to live a life of brotherhood, becoming in effect
citizens of two countries. Their own persons become channels
through which good will is carried across international
boundaries. So the church covers the earth in a reticulation
of brotherhood which, being in human form, has no rival for
effectiveness. One can only regret that the church's outposts
of human understanding are relatively so few.

It is a delight to any lover of humanity that the nations
themselves, through the United Nations Educational, Scientific, and Cultural Organization, and by other means, are now
on an immensely expanded scale adopting the same sort of
purposes that the enlightened mission boards have pursued
for some time, and in some cases using the same techniques—
the planting of hospitals and educational institutions, the
inauguration of village rehabilitation programs, for instance.
The Peace Corps of our federal government, though it has
a national base, has, we believe, the same kind of deep international humanity-wide motivation; and it uses similar techniques. This is all as it should be and as it has been before—
the church at its best acting as a forerunner to enlarging
civilization. In the person of its missionaries—doctors, teachers, social workers, ministers—it has brought into being the
kind of human relationships which beget and nurture the
will to peace and are the promise (unless the world goes
crazy and finishes up by sprawling in the devastation wrought
by its own atom bomb) of the kind of world we shall have
tomorrow.

Missions, however, bring not only peace but, like Christ,
a sword. The United Church of Christ as part of the total
church must accept some of the responsibility for the revolution that is taking place in Asia and Africa. Some of the countries there are convulsed with disorder, and for that the
Christian Church should not be held responsible; but these

disorders are the outward and temporary manifestations of a deep change taking place in the peoples, of which the church is in part the cause. Those peoples are for the first time beginning to feel their worth as human beings.

Democracy has many facets, but one of them is surely the doctrine of the value of human individuals—and whence did that come from in contemporary history? Certainly we have seen it spread from the mind of the West to that of the East and of Africa—and the mind of the West has been formed, slowly but inevitably, in the matrix of Christianity. A religion which century after century tells the story of the lost coin, the lost sheep, and the lost son, will gradually suggest to humanity that the teachings of these tales avail in the political and economic realms as well as in the religious, and that the government which does not seek out the last citizen and give him his rights falls short of its responsibilities. This is at least the patent effect which the teachings of the Gospel have had upon the awakening peoples of today.

In villages in India, where for generations upon generations the people have been content to follow the seasons round without change, the advent of Christianity, with its teaching of God's interest in human life, his invasion of it, his desire for every part of it to be at its best, has been one of the reasons why the people now ask for schools, clinics, betterment all along the line.

In some cases the governments themselves have caught this spirit of amelioration, but have set themselves to reach their new goals by communistic methods. It is not exactly strange that they have done so, for they have not known Christian democracy. The organized Christianity which the most powerful of the communistic nations knew was that associated with the reactionary court of czarist Russia, and the democracy with which Asia and Africa were best acquainted was the kind which had been perverted into colonialism and exploitation. The new communistic governments, though they are in part the result of the leaven of the intelligent and forward-looking Christianity of Protestant missionaries, are neither Christian nor democratic. To some this seems an argument against foreign missions.

Not so to the United Church of Christ and other like-minded communions. In the long history of mankind they regard this as an intermediate phase of development. When young people first feel the freedom of the teens they often use the very liberty given them by their parents for activities which the parents would hardly condone, and even travel in antisocial gangs, but they are not from this circumstance to be judged incorrigibly beyond redemption by further education. So one can hope (indeed it is the only thing to hope) that the Christian education of the human race will not be given up; maintaining the impact of the Gospel on the nations of the world must finally bring them all—and this includes our own—to political organization in which freedom of a socially responsible sort is the primary fact. This summons the church to a foreign mission of a better, vaster, more relevant type than even the past has known—and to this the United Church of Christ is dedicated.

As proof that foreign missions are really a sharing of goods, witness the increasing number of persons who come from abroad under the auspices of the church to become, as it were, foreign missionaries to America. The United Church Board for World Ministries assigns a considerable part of its budget to the work of visitors from other countries to our own. So do interdenominational boards. So do Conferences, on occasion. A bishop from the Philippines, for instance, will move through the churches of Massachusetts; talk in public and private to the people; sit with the official boards of Conference, Association, local church; counsel with young people about their work, especially those who have some thought of going to the South Pacific; and in every way he will seek to bring the strength that he has found in his Visayan- or

Tagalog-speaking home to the homes he visits here. Or it may be a minister from Ceylon who has had amazing success in interpreting the Christian religion to his own Ceylonese people; when he comes to the United States, full of stories of the change the Gospel has made in the lives of people, he is most effective in bringing the meaning of the Christian life to those who do not know it in this country. The comments of a man of his skin pigment on the treatment of Negroes in some parts of this country are far more telling than any that white American churchmen can make, not because they are vicious or unkind, for they are not, but because, being himself a graduate of a distinguished British university and himself a representative of the earth's dark-skinned majority, by his person rather than his words he argues the necessity for receiving him and his like into the highest privileges we can give. This is the negative and merely moral side of the matter: the positive and Christian motives in his hearers are stimulated by his simple winsomeness. Others seeing the work of Christ in him can wish only to belong with him to Christ, and thus a sense of that Christian future where God rules and every man is a brother to all men is engendered.

Nor is it by relatively short visits only that the two-way movement of missions is maintained. Students are brought to this country for many years of study and while here they are invited to share the goods of their spirit with their fellow students. Men and women from the countries we used to call "missionary fields" who are masters of English have been called to this country to serve in church offices. This offers opportunity not only for a fruitful cross-pollination of ideas but does actually serve to show the world the kind of internationalism for which the church stands.

Given that the fundamental business of missions is to make all mankind conscious of the love of God, what is the attitude of the United Church of Christ to the other religions of the world? Granted that there is work to be done in breaking down iron, and other, curtains in order to establish a harmonious interpenetration of the cultures of men, would it not be better, when it comes to the matter of faith, for Christianity simply to regard itself as one religion among many and not try to make converts of good and regular devotees of other religions?

Here we must once more recall that the idea of God is the greatest thought that can occupy the human mind, and the idea that God is willing to give himself in order that man may know and enjoy his love, is the most powerful of thoughts. The latter is such that it cannot be contained; no man can settle down with it in selfish content, for it cannot be possessed unless it be shared. There can therefore be no expectation but that a Christian will, by word and deed, let the whole world know about this relationship which, thanks to God's initiative, can be established with God through Christ. It is a story which must be told; it is a consciousness which cannot be borne without expression. But the very theme of the story, the very content of the consciousness, being concerned with love, prevents its being told or communicated in an unlovely way. It cannot demand a hearing of anyone: every non-Christian has a right to his own privacy, and with it a right to his own religion. Thus, the missionary of the United Church ideal is one who is out to share his faith, but in the sharing of it he is never boorish, never inconsiderate, never unready to listen to the religious expressions of others, never unmindful of the strength for living that non-Christian religions have given their adherents, never without Christian love.

Often one hears it said that, after all, all religions are the same at heart, since all point toward God, and no one of them is better than the others. This belief that all beliefs are equally good is a philosophical proposition; it can be argued in one's mind pro or con: it is belief *that*. . . . Belief in God,

however, is not, first of all, belief *that*. . . . It is belief
in. . . . Belief in a God who has touched one is the remembered experience of a personal relationship. This is a piece
of reality—not a conjecture about reality, as the belief that
all beliefs are equally good is. You may think the latter, but
the former you know, in the intimate way of a religious insight. When a person comes to realize that God revealed
himself in Jesus Christ, he is no longer doubtful about God's
character; he knows that it is one of justice and unselfish
love, and this becomes a fact of his life. When now a Buddhist
enters the scene, or a Mohammedan, and describes the character of God from his point of view, the Christian cannot
accept this testimony with the same immediacy that he accepts his own experience of Christ, simply because he has
not known God through Gautama or through Mohammed as
he has through Christ. He does not question the testimony
of the other; it is only that he knows God directly through
Christ and only indirectly through the other—and there is
simply no comparison between the two types of knowledge.
The reason that the belief that all religions are equally good
tends to degrade one's faith is because it involves putting
one's own experience of God on a level with what has been
told one about God by a third party. The I-you relationship
is reduced to a mere he-him type. You know that your religion is good; it is only by indirection that the same can be
affirmed of the religion of others—and to classify them together is to remove your own experience of God from the
realm of fine incisive personal relationships to that of philosophical speculation. All religions may be equally good or
they may not be; that is a matter known to God and to be
thought about by man, but the hold that the Christian has
on reality tells him that God is love, no matter what other
religions may or may not say. This is primary.

Taking this point of view the United Church of Christ
seeks out the human race with its manifold of religions, but

always with the attitude of love. The religions of others it holds in the high regard that one holds the cherished possessions of one's friends. The United Church of Christ is glad to have the emissaries of other religions come to these shores, and whether here or abroad it is glad to enter into conversation with them. It looks with utmost approval upon the centers in various parts of the world where facilities for such conversations are now made available. Because of the absoluteness of its confidence in Christ's revelation it mingles freely with men and women of other religions who wish to hear the witness of Christianity and make their own. This attitude, as may be noted, is very different from operating upon a philosophy that all religions are equally good; it is to make the revelation in Christ the presupposition of all action, and to say of other religions that so far as they deny that God is a loving God, they are false; insofar as they only leave room for a loving God but do not proclaim him, they are inadequate, and insofar as they declare him, they are true. It is as simple as that: Christianity supplies a yardstick against which other religions may be measured. If it is suggested that other religions may supply a yardstick against which Christianity may be measured, the possibility is undeniable, and Christianity gladly exposes itself to any such test; but in the meantime it rests upon its knowledge, vouchsafed in Christ, that God is love and that no tests of any sort can disturb this fact. This is the source of the church's imperturbable serenity and, incidentally, its unremitting sense of falling short of its own high calling.

This attitude of the United Church of Christ, at once communicative and not aggressive, is simply one more indication of its fundamental character. So it is related to other denominations. So every member of it is related to every other member. It is an attitude not to be described as ecclesiastical *laissez faire;* it is not expressed in the dictum, Live and let live; the word is rather, Love and let love. The atmosphere

of combined independence and concern pervades the whole
United Church.

The United Church of Christ in the World

The mere listing and brief description of the enterprises
of the Board for World Ministries is sufficient to demonstrate
the dimensions of the undertaking, the boldness of it, the
idealism of it, the blessing of it for the entire world.

It was in 1869 that the first missionaries of the American
Board arrived in Japan. Their efforts, and those of the first
emissaries of the Evangelical and Reformed Church Board
were concentrated on giving the communities in Japan to
which they ministered education of a broad Christian kind.
The first arrival was only fifteen years after the famous visit
of Commodore Perry, which had opened the doors of the
island empire to foreign intercourse, and was almost precisely
synchronous with the abolition of feudalism and the beginning of the enlightened Meiji period. No type of work could
have been better adapted to the awakening spirit of that
remarkable people: the Gospel's call for a better Japan and
a better world evoked a most positive response from some of
Japan's nobler souls. The young Neesima, for instance, established the Doshisha University in Kyoto, which presently
became the largest nongovernmental institution of its sort,
and poured into the life of the country qualified leadership in
many fields.

Given the ecumenical bent of both Congregational Christians and Evangelical and Reformed Churchmen, it is not
strange that the churches they formed in Japan were in the
forefront of the movement to create out of the many denominations in that country a single "United Church of Christ in
Japan." It is true that the government in 1941, when this
occurred, was advising all groups in the country similar to

one another to get together so that, as in Hitler's Germany, there might be a harmony or *Gleichschaltung* throughout the nation, but it is not true, as some who were not close to the situation have said, that the government's policy was the effectual cause of the uniting: it was the occasion for carrying out a union which had long been desired by the less self-centered of the denominations.

There is no United Church Mission to Japan in the technical sense; that is, there is no work in Japan being carried on under the auspices of the United Church of Christ. The United Church provides missionary personnel and financial aid to the United Church of Japan but ties no strings to its contributions; these are all subject to the control of the Japanese Church. The United Church of Christ joins with six other American denominations in providing this kind of assistance to the United Church in Japan—the kind of aid that adults give to adults.

Christian leaders are everywhere in demand in Japan, and there (as in every country) nothing less than leaders with good training will really do. This fact has maintained the emphasis upon education; and there is developing in Japan a system of Christian education which is crowned by the International Christian University outside of Tokyo, whose first president, Dr. Hachiro Yuasa, was as much at home in the United Church of Christ here in this country as in the United Church of Japan, for it was under the auspices of the American Board that he received his early education.

One of the new instruments in evangelism is illustrated in the work of United Church missionaries in Japan who are trained and experienced experts in audio-visual materials. The greatest obstacle Christianity has to overcome in the Eastern part of the world, as we have hinted, is its association with the West. Jesus himself actually was not a Westerner, having lived and died in the Near East, having never seen Europe or dreamed that an American continent lay hidden on the other side of an ocean many, many times the size of the Great Sea which washed the sands of his Galilee; but still the West has tried to make him its possession. To free him from the West and give him to the world, one method is to have the Gospel set forth in pictures, which are a universal language, and with a sound track in a dialect as indigenous to each locality as the exclamations of the audience.

I never realized this completely until, years ago, I sat in the midst of an Egyptian audience viewing the life of Christ in motion picture, with the speeches in Egyptian-Arabic. As scene followed scene, the men and women around me grew ever more animated. The crowd shown on the screen and the crowd about me—dressed strangely alike after nineteen centuries—seemed one. They mingled their shouts; all stood; all shook their fists. The only difference was that the people on the screen were for crucifying their victim; those about me were for saving him. The latter fairly screamed their denials of the others' accusations and roared their warnings to Jesus when his enemies seemed to be closing in on him. When (on the screen) on the first Easter morning, Jesus made his appearance as the Risen Lord, the people about me were beside themselves in the enthusiasm of victory; the man to whom they had all been drawn in the early scenes of the film, had now defeated not only his human enemies but even the dreadful cross. I had never before felt so fully the meaning of the "When thou hadst overcome the sharpness of death, thou didst open the Kingdom of Heaven to all believers." In Japan, in Egypt, and in many other places on the planet, foreign missionaries of the United Church and other churches utilize the new instruments which the audio-visual sciences have placed in their hands.

Christianity is the religion of a book. Like all of the surviving religions of the world, it utilizes the written or printed page as a medium of transmitting and interpreting its teachings, and one of the by-products of this method has been the need for missionaries (and their native helpers) to translate not only the Bible but other books of spiritual power from their own tongue into that of the land where they work. Japan, with its own rich literary tradition, has seen a great many such translations into Japanese of high excellence. Mrs. Gilbert W. Schroer and Mr. Isamu Morikasa, for instance, have translated Nevin Harner's *I Believe* into Japanese, and by way of interpreting Japan to the United States, the Rev. Philip E. Williams has written a book describing his first term in Japan, entitled *Journey Into Mission.*

In the Philippine Islands, as in Japan, there is no missionary work under the direct control of the United Church of Christ in the United States, because all of that church's work is channeled through and is conducted under the auspices of the United Church of Christ in the Philippines, a communion of 110,000 members, made up of the adherents of the former Congregational, Disciples', Methodist, and Presbyterian Churches, which gave up their denominational approach to become a strong unified body.

During World War II, when American forces were occupying various islands of Micronesia in their advance on Japan, they had many a surprise, for the missionaries of the nineteenth century had, in some cases, preceded them. One chaplain whom I met shortly after he had had the experience told me that he had gone ashore with his unit because he alone could speak a few sentences of Marshallese (which he had learned out of a book he had found in the Honolulu library) and that as he and some of the men were moving up on the possible enemy from cover to cover, they spied three natives walking toward them on the beach. When the Marshallese were opposite them, the chaplain called out to them in their native language—whereupon one of the three called back, in pure Oxford English, "We've been expecting you. The whole village is assembled on the green." With this introduction all the invaders came out of hiding and marched to the center of the village. There the native men and women were all dressed in their best, and the man with the Oxford education made a speech, in the course of which he referred to the fact that the Americans were undoubtedly, for the most part, Christians like themselves. The chaplain later told me, "When I heard that, I looked around at my men, all of them carrying Tommy guns and other weapons of destruction, and wondered."

It is of note that more than one missionary in a remote part of the world today, learned of the needs of the country to which he has gone while serving in the Armed Forces of the United States. Until they had gone out from the comfortable but sequestered village or town or city of their own home, they had never realized that such poverty, ignorance, and disease existed elsewhere—but once they saw the terrible evidence of these human scourges, they did something about it by enlisting in the service of the church and asking to be sent as missioners of peace to the territories they had entered as soldiers, sailors, marines, or airmen.

For many years the church and school work in Micronesia were knit together by the visits of an American Board missionary who found his way from island to island on a ship which he captained called *Morning Star*. During the last three generations there have been six *Morning Stars*—and not the least intrepid of those in charge has been Eleanor Wilson of *Morning Star VI*. Maribelle Cormack's *The Lady Was a Skipper* is the book which tells her story. She ventured with the craft through thousand of miles of open sea, taking the thunder and the sunshine with the frolic welcome of Ulysses. Of such stuff are missionaries made.

It must not be thought that with the Communist conquest of China the Christian Church there has been brought to naught. Within an environment often hostile the congregations maintain themselves and are now (this good having been blown to them by an ill wind) demonstrating to their neighbors that Christianity is as Chinese as it is non-Chinese. If they are not yet allowed to demonstrate that it is a world religion, the day will come when they can do so if their courage does not fail—and there is no sign that it does. Young people have been known to write at the end of an ideologically correct answer in an examination: "This is what I have been taught but my Christian faith gives a different answer." It is to be hoped that the Christian "remnant" which is ever a potent force, will be a leaven in the lump, lay hold on all that is good in the Communistic regimen, and restrain and overcome the evil.

It almost takes a visit to Eastern Asia to make one realize that the closing of doors to missionaries into China by no means arrests direct missionary work among the Chinese people, for there are millions of Chinese—some of the most enterprising of their race—who have overflowed into many countries of Southeast Asia. In crowded Hong Kong, which numbers five times as many people as it did fifteen years ago, the United Church of Christ serves within the Hong Kong Council of the Church of Christ in China, with teachers, relief workers, rehabilitation personnel, doctors, and nurses. There is an interdenominational college for Chinese there, and also one in Taiwan, where leaders are trained—and in Taiwan also, a theological seminary.

Since 1956 the Evangelical and Reformed Church, and now the United Church of Christ, have been engaged in a growing program of co-operation with the National Council of Churches in Indonesia, which represents over 2,700,000 Protestants on the 3,000 islands of the young nation. Participation began with grants of money for special projects, but in 1960 an advance step was taken in the sending of a missionary couple, the man to teach at the Union Theological School, his wife to help also in the training of ministers to meet the critical shortage in the relatively large Protestant population.

The churches of Okinawa suffered when Japanese leadership was withdrawn from them at the close of World War II, but they have done their best and have done well to meet the opportunities that have come to them. The Board of International Missions, and now the United Church Board for World Ministries, supports the United Church of Okinawa (which itself unites several denominations) in rural-center programs, medical ministries, and student work in the metropolitan area.

Korea has traditionally been the field of Presbyterian and Methodist endeavor, but in these days when co-operation is the keyword in all but the highly denominationalized missions, the United Church is ready to send helpers wherever they will count most, and in this impoverished land pays the salary of one nurse and relief worker.

The work of the United Church in India is the oldest, the most widely spread in many ways, and the most fruitful of all its missionary enterprises. Evangelical and Reformed work was begun in the Chhattisgarh region of the Central Provinces in 1868. The Christians in this part of India now number eleven thousand and are sufficiently matured to provide leadership from among their own number and even maintain their own missionary work.

At Madurai, the ancient political, religious, and cultural capital of the Tamil people, the American Board, one of the United Church Board's predecessors, began its mission in 1834. Here, as elsewhere in the older missions, Americans and their Indian colleagues work side by side. Responsibility for the entire program of worship and work is in the hands of the Church of South India, which combines episcopal, presbyterian, and congregational elements in one of the first great unions of its kind in the world. Representatives of the United Church of Christ in the United States receive their appointment and assignment not by a mission board in faraway Boston, New York, Philadelphia, or St. Louis, but by the Church of South India itself.

The first foreign mission anywhere in the world set up by an American board was that founded in western India in 1813. This today is the Marathi Mission of the United Church Board for World Ministries. The Nagpada Neighborhood House in Bombay is the center of a social-service enterprise in one of the most densely populated areas of the whole world. The demonstration farm in Vadala has had a wide influence. Ahmednagar College helps to combat ignorance, and the leprosy and tuberculosis control programs arrest the ravages of those dreadful diseases. For a generation the churches of the Congregational and Presbyterian persuasion have been joined in the United Church of North India, and in less than a decade it is expected that this body will have entered into a communion, drawing upon as many different denominations as the Church of South India itself, to be called the Church of North India.

Christianity being a spiritual faith which does not consider its work done until it has embodied itself in all the relationships of mankind, even the most material, it is not strange that the mission in Ahmednagar is sometimes known for its development of the sisal industry. Sisal is a great shrub, looking something like a giant century plant, which grows abundantly in that somewhat arid area. So far as is known, it has always grown there—in the midst of villages where people have struggled for existence at a subsubsistence level. Then a missionary woman, seeing the opportunity to help the people help themselves, developed a method for drawing the fibers out of the long leaves, dyeing them, and weaving them into handbags and innumerable other accessories which have a sale in the cities. By this means a whole population was lifted out of indigence into the dignity of a decent livelihood.

In Ceylon also, there is hope for the establishment of a Church of Ceylon—or the Church of Lanka, as it will be called, from the ancient name of the island—which, like the Church of South India, will unite most of the Christian forces of the country. The Christians on the island who are related to the United Church of Christ in the United States are strongly in favor of such a union. There are two hospitals, six elementary schools and junior colleges—and there is Jaffna College, a distinguished center for higher education, whose students take the examinations of the University of London for B.A. and B.Sc. degrees.

Now to fly over the Indian Ocean to the huge awakening continent of Africa and visit certain areas where the United Church of Christ in the United States has linked itself to the destiny of the African peoples. There is not a single country from Cape Town to Cairo which is not feeling the stir of the cry, "Africa for the Africans"; and some of them are seething with revolt. As we have said, the missionary must accept part of the responsibility for the new day, for the teaching of the Gospel makes plainly in the direction of the dignity of man and against that type of colonialism which is a cover for human exploitation. It is of some significance that in the Congo, which was once the personal holding of Leopold, King of the Belgians, there was a grim determination on the part of his entrepreneurs to keep Protestant missionaries out of the area. They realized that what they themselves were doing to the people and what the missionary forces would do for them if they had the chance, were poles apart. The missionaries would have brought with them education and the sense of Christian responsibility, along with the passion for freedom; but when finally the passion for freedom came, seeping across the border from neighboring countries, the educational program and the sense of social responsibility fostered by the colonial government were discovered to have been so weak that the nation had no intrinsic strength.

In Ghana, in contrast, a different type of colonialism, which permitted Protestant missions and fostered the development of socially concerned leaders, had been of late decades instituted by Britain, and when Ghana achieved its freedom, it had indigenous leadership at hand to serve it. If the missionary movement in the vast continent had had its full way, it would have brought with the general awakening: education, the elimination of race prejudice, equality of opportunity for blacks and whites alike, and, above all, a sense of brotherhood in the facing of common problems. Because these moral virtues are still more conspicuous in the breach than the observance, there is still need for the vigorous prosecution of Christian love, the kind for which the church (at least in its best and most characteristic moments) stands.

I say "in its best moments" because the kind of relationships which are being developed by some so-called Christian governments in Africa are not what the United Church of Christ would call the expression of Christian love. The policy of *apartheid*, which calls for political segregation of the races, but which leaves the white race dominant where it is outnumbered, is one which seems to have the connivance of some local white churches. If this is the case, it can be concluded only that this is the church not at its best. The government in South Africa with its steely policy, recognizing no exceptions, has taken over most of the schools operated under the auspices of the United Church, but some remain, segregated in fact by government order though not in spirit, and these are seed beds of new Christian endeavor. The United Church of Christ has not the slightest intention of withdrawing from this area.

When one moves north to Rhodesia, he still finds electronic tensions in the air which may at any time become lethal, but they do not begin to have the intensity of those in South Africa. There is still hope that Rhodesia, feeling the influence of the churches, will be able to establish a multiracial society held together by mutual respect and trust; but Satan is at work in his familiar guise as the bringer of the blessings of white supremacy, and no one knows what the future will bring forth.

Moving over to the west coast of the continent, one reaches Angola and the various missions there. Here the work of the United Church of Christ was established in 1880, in the central highlands, where the vigorous tribes of the Ovimbundu live and where the primary language is Umbundu and the secondary one Portuguese, since the country has long been a colony of Portugal. One of the best known studies of Umbundu culture is that of the Rev. Gladwin M. Childs, a missionary of the United Church of Christ in Nova Lisboa, entitled *Umbundu Kinship and Character* (Oxford, 1949). Here, too, the humane spirit of the church often finds itself at odds with that of the repressive colonialism of some government officials.

To refer briefly to Ghana again—in recent years whenever the name of that country has been mentioned in any gathering of Africans, the psychological voltage has gone up as from a shaft of lightning, for Ghana was the first free decolonialized African state and, therefore, in the mind of Africa, the promise of the future. Other states now share with Ghana the advantages of freedom, but Ghana at least at its start was the Abraham that led into the Promised Land. Here the opportunities for missionary usefulness not only to Ghana but through Ghana to the whole of Africa are, almost literally, unlimited. The work in parts of this country —then the Gold Coast—was turned over to the Evangelical and Reformed Church in 1945. Beginning with two workers, this mission has increased its staff to 35—and more, if wives be counted, who also serve—all under the Evangelical Presbyterian Church of Ghana, chiefly in educational, medical, and women's work. It is to be hoped that Ghana will fulfill its promise. The mission will lend it incentive to do so.

Crossing the Atlantic on the equator and proceeding as far as the west coast of South America, we come to Ecuador, where a most interesting missionary project is in progress, in which the United Church of Christ has a part as a result of the work of the Board of International Missions. In 1945, a careful sociological study was made of the Indian life of the Andean highlands, and as a result four denominations together set up the United Andean Indian Mission, which ministers to a rural people in circumstances of destitution that beggar description. The fourfold program centers in church, agricultural, educational, and medical ministries.

Further north in Central America, where missionary work was begun in Honduras in 1921, the main emphasis is given to evangelism, education, and the ministry of healing. When one considers that the eighteen congregations now constituting the mission there are made up in no small part of people who a short time ago could not read or write a single word, and that today they have their own trained teachers, it becomes evident that missionary work is one of the world's main hopes.

The Rev. H. N. Auler, Jr. is one of those indispensable on the frontier who can turn his hand to things mechanical without turning his head away from things intellectual and his heart from things human. As a licensed amateur radio operator, he has set up a short-wave system that connects the mission stations and thereby the various rural communities with one another. A similar installation in the outback of Australia inaugurated by British missionaries has proved so indispensable that the government has now taken it over.

Protestantism in Mexico has had hard sledding. It not only had to endure the antireligious feeling that seized the country for a number of years a generation ago but throughout its history it has had to face the often thoughtless and always unrelenting hostility of the Mexican Catholic Church. In spite of all vicissitudes, however, the native church is coming into its own. The mission there has developed centers of work in Guadalajara and other west-coast communities, as well as the Union Theological Seminary and Union Publishing House in Mexico City in the support of which it pools its contributions with other denominational boards.

Now we move back across the Atlantic to southeastern Europe and the Near East. In 1820, the American board began the work in Bible lands, which it turned over to the Board for World Ministries of the United Church as its successor.

The United Church Board for World Ministries combines not only the American Board of Commissioners for Foreign Missions (Congregational Christian) and the Board of International Missions (Evangelical and Reformed) but also the Congregational Christian Service Committee and the Evangelical and Reformed Commission on World Service; the latter two being concerned more with relief of temporary crises than with long-term problems of disease, ignorance, and oppressive conditions which can be met only by continuing institutions. The line is sometimes hard to draw between the two types of ministry, however, and in Greece one finds them both. The Fellowship House in Athens is a social-service depot for the pathetically poor in one of the deteriorated districts of the city, which was started as a relief station shortly after the last war, but it has become such a seed-ground for the training of permanent social workers that it now appears as a ministry that will go into the future; and it has indeed extended its operations into the city of Thessalonica and strategically located villages in northern Greece. Pierce College, on the other hand, from the beginning was intended by the Board as a standing contribution to the life of Greece. It is now an independent institution, but with the same permanent purpose. Those who have come in by air to the port in Elleniko may recall the beautiful campus just adjacent where, for many years, at the edge of the blue Aegean, young

Greek womanhood has been receiving education of highest quality. It is, in fact, the necessity for lengthening the runways of the field to accommodate jet planes that has compelled the removal of the college to an equally lovely site on the slope of Mount Penteli, one of the guardian mountains of the city. Anatolia College, another institution of superior grade, is located at Thessalonica. It also is independent today.

The major responsibility of the Board for World Ministries in the Near East is in Turkey, where a comparatively new nation is in process of coming to itself. When, years ago, at the time of the revolution, it was decreed that no religious doctrine could be taught in the schools of the country without certain permissions which were not available to the schools of the Board, the question was whether these schools should be continued or not. Some missions, in face of this obstacle, closed their doors and left Turkey, but the American Board, in the belief that life is more than doctrine and that immense contributions could be made to Turkey even under this governmental restriction, stayed on; and it now represents western Protestantism in the country.

All through the land, as in other parts of the Near East, representatives of the United Church are renewing their study of Islam, in the hope of building better bridges of understanding between the adherents of the two religions.

In Lebanon the United Church Board and that of the United Presbyterian Church support the Near East School of Theology, which is a center for the training of workers in Beirut and all the region round about. Beirut also is the center for the service of the Board to Arab refugees from Palestine now in that locality.

Crossing the border into Syria one finds in Aleppo, the largest city of the country, the well-known institution of Aleppo College, with its boys' and girls' divisions. Here the sponsors are the same as those who preside over the work in Beirut, the two American boards and the two groups of local

Protestant Churches, the Arab Synod and the Armenian Union.

The situation in Iraq today illustrates one of the greatly needed missionary virtues, for, in 1959, the then anti-Western and pro-communist government requested all missionaries to leave the country. In the absence of the missionaries the local churches, Arab, Assyrian, and Armenian, have been carrying on, and the formation of a Synod of Protestant Churches seems imminent. The missionaries, in the meantime, are waiting to return, studying Arabic and Islamics, and in many ways utilizing the opportunity to improve their skills. The virtue needed is patience—but Christian love, as St. Paul said long ago, possesses this to a full degree.

It was only with the last Great War that "missionary" work in Europe began—but since the aim of the missionary enterprise is simply to share one's best with others there seemed no reason not to throw out lines of brotherhood to the "Christian" countries of the Continent as well as to the "non-Christian" countries elsewhere. The Lutheran denominations have been especially praiseworthy in their giving here, but all American communions have participated. The United Church Board for World Ministries in Europe co-operates in the program of the Department of Interchurch Aid of the World Council of Churches, which unites all the ranking non-Roman denominations of the world.

There is the Fellowship Center in Chambon-sur-Lignon in France, which is used not only as a center by the College Cevenol, also located there, and by the local church and community, but also for international groups dedicated to building up better relations among the nations of Europe. Every year, for instance, chosen German and French pastors gather there to learn of each other's problems and help each other spiritually; and through them a little stream of reconciliation begins to flow through the arid no-man's land of international hatred which has so long divided the countries. In Germany the Board for World Ministries assists in church work among the laboring classes and in the production of Christian literature for youth. In Naples the board helps in the pioneering social work of Casa Mia, founded in 1952 under the brave leadership of Dr. Teofilo Santi. In Sardinia it is the Homeless European Land Project to which the board contributes funds and trained personnel. Here a nucleus of small businesses and industries as well as homes is being built up to fight and conquer the poverty which has dogged the refugees; and being a pilot undertaking, it is already proving to governments and the United Nations that persons formerly barred from emigration because of health and like reasons are still capable of helping themselves.

All this work done around the world seems little enough when one considers the globe's total population and its needs, but from another angle it merits descriptive adjectives of superlative meaning, because of its essential rightness. The world of missionary largesse, those who can sharing their goods with others to the end of creating a brotherly human community under God, is the kind of world to which the United Church of Christ is dedicated. It believes this to be the only kind of world in which peace and prosperity can find a final home.

Chapter XV

THE BOARD FOR HOMELAND MINISTRIES

Missions are as important in the home field as in the foreign, and to see that these are carried out for the United Church, the Board for Homeland Ministries works around the clock. Because it is in the home field, it is always in collaboration with the home churches, doing for them what single churches cannot themselves do alone, both inside and outside the established parishes. It tries to keep its ministry flexible, adapting its program to meet the changing needs of American life. The almost infinite variety of the work of the board can in part be understood by glancing at the main phases of it.

The Constitution in briefest outline sets forth services of

Homeland Mission and Service

The General Synod recognizes the United Church Board for Homeland Ministries as the instrumentality of the United Church of Christ for the planning and conduct of the homeland mission not otherwise assigned.

The United Church Board for Homeland Ministries continues the work of, and acts as agent for, the following corporations during the life of agreements as executed by them:

Board of National Missions	The American Missionary Association
Board of Christian Education and Publication	Congregational Church Building Society
Board of Business Management	Congregational Education Society
Board of Home Missions of the Reformed Church in the U. S.	Congregational Home Missionary Society
	Congregational Publishing Society
	The Congregational Sunday School Extension Society
	The Congregational Woman's Home Missionary Federation

The functions of the organizations named in the first column were united at the time of the formation of the United Church of Christ. Those of the second column have been united since 1925.

The functions of the Board for Homeland Ministries are as broad as the United States of America is broad. Says the Constitution:

The United Church Board for Homeland Ministries is responsible for evangelism in the United Church of Christ.

At the heart of all Homeland Ministries is evangelism—the attempt to bring all people into acquaintance with God as he reveals himself in Christ. In the case of the United Church of Christ, do not associate this word too narrowly with the procedures of professional evangelists who hold meetings at which, in the midst of an atmosphere surcharged with religious emotion, they strive for a mass effect which will carry the susceptible into a state of conviction about God. There is nothing in the theology of the United Church which rules out such meetings as beyond the pale of decent Christianity. One must remember that if Dwight L. Moody (who would have been a member of the United Church, were he alive today) had not in this way reached a young medical man by the name of Wilfred Grenfell, there would have been no such magnificent work for Labrador's needy as Sir Wilfred later administered. But new occasions teach new duties: when Dr. Billy Graham was arranging for his meetings in New York City, members of the United Church, that is, men who were to become members when the church was formed, with others waited upon the committee making the preparations in order to suggest that the evangelist surround himself with some devoted psychiatrists, social workers, and others trained to understand and give aid to people in difficult situations, but the committee was apparently predisposed to the out-moded idea that the only thing people require in order to live useful and healthy lives is the will to be what God designed them to be. That such a will is essential all wise men know, but if evangelism leaves off at that point, it is comparable to swimming instruction that takes the pupil to the water and no further.

The United Church of Christ believes in the evangelization of the whole man and his whole environment and without minimizing the crucial part that the right attitude to God and man must play, goes on to help the person understand what the good life is for him and how he may live it, calling upon every agency of education and the representatives of every profession—and of business and industry, too, for that matter —to assist him by teaching and demonstrating what that good life should be.

This philosophy is behind the aid that the Board for Home-land Ministries makes available to every local church. It seeks to help the churches resist that sclerosis of the mental processes which attacks parishes and keeps them from re-newing their youth. It suggests to local churches that they make a special effort at appropriate times in a teaching, reaching, preaching mission, which aims at renewing the life of the church by deepening it—specifically by getting the people to come to a personal encounter with God.

Trained sociologists are continuously at work behind the scene in the total work of evangelism in the United Church of Christ. Recently, for instance, a new study of the evolution of the attitudes of the city dweller was completed, confirming some guesses that had already been made, confuting others, and in many ways discovering why the approach of the church to its neighborhood has been weak and where new opportunities lie. The members of the churches themselves were studied. One third were discovered to be "nominal" with little understanding of the Christian faith, another third, though active, were found to be actually captured far more securely by the secular culture round about them than by the Gospel—and only two per cent had a full perception of the meaning of churchmanship in terms of worship and human relations. This is only one of many surveys already undertaken and to be undertaken, such as the testing of the new United Church School Curriculum, and the research made in connection with the placing of the permanent headquarters of the United Church of Christ. By research the great industries constantly seek to improve their product and make it more salable; by research the United Church of Christ constantly seeks to know how it can be more faithful and obedient to the Gospel of Christ.

As the church seeks to minister to the needs of people in this period of population expansion and unprecedented mobility in the United States, it is constantly called upon to form new congregations in new areas of development. The ministers and people who gather together to initiate these enterprises are of the pioneer type and often have to put up with pioneer conditions. Beginning to worship in a home, a school building, a community center, they need almost all the equip-

ment that an ordinary established church takes for granted—
and there is the Board for Homeland Ministries to help them.
These churches are fostered by the Board where they will do
the most good: some are spearheading crusades against racial segregation; some are trying to meet the needs of a
bulging faculty and student population on the edge of a
growing university; some in the Southland, originally placed
there at the request of the retired, now find their accommodations overflowing not only with senior citizens but with
younger people who see a future in the area and have come
to live there permanently. Some of the new churches are
strategically located to sponsor incoming refugees from
abroad, helping them settle, finding jobs for them, and always opening to them their hearts and homes in Christian
fellowship. To bear its share in the building of new churches,
the United Church of Christ, which considers that its proportion of Protestant responsibility, statistically speaking, is
about four per cent of the total, should be dedicating two
hundred new churches a year. In its first three years it started
new churches at the rate of a little more than four a month,
but it will hope for acceleration.

In spite of the wholesale migration to the city which recent
censuses of our population have revealed, town and country
remain indispensable elements in the foundations of our society, and if the church picks up its own goods and chattels
and rushes to the city also, leaving only second-rate leadership behind at the grass roots, it weakens both itself and the
country. Because the United Church has this clearly in mind,
it directs its Board for Homeland Missions to seek out men
in the midst of their seminary training who will commit themselves to the rural pastorate, to help the lay people of the
rural churches come alive to the need for new methods of
churchmanship just as they have accepted the advantages of
new methods of agriculture; and above all to bring to each
town and village the spirit of ecumenicity, since the old de-

nominationalism has proved that it is an unfit instrument to keep the spiritual life of a rural community in good health.

The United Church in any town stands for a united Christian approach to town problems and attempts in every way to woo the other churches there (if they need wooing) to take the same view. There are 20,000 villages in the United States without a resident pastor; it ill behooves the denominations to duplicate efforts in overchurched villages, or in any way to allow the shortsightedness induced by competition to blind them to general needs.

The "Pilgrim Circuit Rider," the Reverend Miss Leila Anderson, with her car stocked with all the essential literary needs of a small church, drives about the country visiting (on invitation and with careful plans made in advance) one church after another, helping in every way she can—meeting with women's groups and their leaders, men's groups similarly, youth groups, church schools, always with the intent to evangel-ize, that is, to bring the Gospel.

In places of special need—on the plains of Western Canada; in the Missouri Ozarks; on Madeline Island in Lake Superior; in the rich level land of southeastern Missouri which has been smitten by feuds between planters and sharecroppers and almost every kind of industrial difficulty, and until recently was destitute of churches, schools, or any kind of social institutions; on the beautiful Cumberland Mountain Plateau of Tennessee, where there have been similar social needs; and indeed in a thousand spots throughout the nation—the United Church of Christ, through institutions set up and sustained by its Board for Homeland Ministries and by other means, is seeking to respond to the call of the rural areas for intelligent spiritual planning.

By "other means" I have reference to the widespread work done by the Conferences. Being closer to the needs geographically than a national office can be, the many Conferences move into action in their own areas in somewhat the same way as the national Board. This decentralized phase of the work illustrates the kind of responsible leadership the United Church of Christ expects its parts, in their full freedom in Christ, to assume.

One of the most telling means of strengthening the churches of town and country has been the program of continuing education for ministers in service, which has been going on for many years. The Board of Home Missions (now part of the Board for Homeland Ministries) pioneered in setting up such summer schools as those at La Foret in Colorado, and Deering in New Hampshire, where ministers can take refresher courses of the highest grade. The same privileges have been offered by the Evangelical and Reformed seminaries, both for ministers and adequately prepared laymen. The United Church delegation at the Town and Country Leadership School held annually at Michigan State University has been for some years in excess of seventy-five pastors and wives. The churches to which these people return take a new lease on vitality with the new knowledge and new techniques brought back to them from the Leadership School.

No one can overemphasize the importance of the city in contemporary American church life. No age has seen cities grow so rapidly—nor decay so dismally. The United Church of Christ and its Board for Homeland Ministries feel the challenge, and accept it, but with no sense of being able to accomplish their ends alone. God himself must be called into the lists, and every agency for social planning and amelioration put into his hands as an instrument; and just now an urban renaissance in American seems to be a real possibility. To date, churches for the most part seem to have fled from the city's dried-out interior to the lush suburbs where a million acres are being taken over by new homemakers every year—but the United Church Board is one of those which does not intend to desert the massed populations of the city proper. It is said that by 1970 America will have thirty-one metropolitan areas with more than a million persons each; and if the past is any guide to the future, these centers are likely to be the creative matrices of our culture. If that culture is to have the lineaments of Christianity, the church must be there.

To this end the board enlists students and ministers who will devote themselves to the betterment of the inner life of the city, as others have dedicated themselves to the life of the country. Training is made available for ministers already at work "where cross the crowded ways," both in summer school and winter classes. Conferences are held on specific phases of urban work, and groups of churches in city situations are aided in making self-studies. All along the line preventive therapy is instituted to keep strong churches within the vortex of the city's life from becoming weak and losing their hold.

In Cincinnati, for instance, a church which was faced with the downtown problem—a so-called white church which found itself in a Negro neighborhood—voted that "a Christian church does not a have the right to determine who can or cannot participate in its life. That was decided long ago by our Lord, who gave his life for all peoples." Today, fully integrated, this church pours its spiritual strength into the heart of the West End (the opposite, in point of fashionableness, from London's West End).

In Louisville, the church which had been host to a workshop on the city church, decided to hold its ground in the inner city but also to create a mission extension in a new section of the city needing a church. Today, the one congregation keeps itself responsible for the two centers of worship and service.

A predominantly Negro church in Brooklyn, New York, has been selected as the center for a pilot experiment which, if successful, will be extended to other large cities. The work will be conducted on several battlelines. Storefronts, a type of depot for religious work with which the neighborhood is familiar, will be rented as halfway houses—half way between the completely secularized community and the church. A street worker will mingle with the teen-agers who do not yet belong to fighting gangs but are potential delinquents. An evangelist will work in the homes of the community in a "house-party" system, starting in the homes of those who are already church members and branching out as the group increases. A community rebuilding co-ordinator will help the overcrowded residents of the area solve their housing problems, making the halfway houses meeting places for community planning, always co-operating with other agencies interested in housing improvement. A Puerto Rican minister will work with the Spanish-speaking families who, in great numbers, are making an irruption in the neighborhood.

In a deteriorated area of Chicago, the Board assists the local church in its church-school services to the children of the neighborhood, its nursery school for the children of families in which the parents both work, its vast program for boys and girls of school age, and its program of general church work among and for the adults—with special and never-ceasing emphasis on counseling.

On the West Side of New York City, an Evangelical and Reformed church and a Congregational Christian church have united their forces to set up a community center for the Puerto Ricans and others crowded into the locality. Here, there are made available housing clinics, legal-aid clinics, and trained personal counseling, as well as a complete social-service program—all built around the congregation of worshipers, slowly increasing in numbers and serving as a warm focus of inspiration. Behind this stands the Board.

The work of the East Harlem parish, which has been featured in *Life*, many newspapers, and denominational journals, is well known. Equally significant, and of the same all-round religious, economic, social, and individual character, is the

Inner City Protestant Parish of Cleveland. The Board of
Home Missions (now part of the United Church Board) was
in at the start of both of these interdenominational projects.

No city has been better served city-missionwise than has
St. Louis by the Evangelical and Reformed Churches. A
chaplain visits the hospitals, conducts services for those able
to attend, performs the infinitely welcome offices of the minister at the bedside of the sick, and keeps the churches of the
city alive to their responsibilities to the bedridden. Neighborhood centers are sustained, where service to families and
Christian education for individuals and groups are supported,
along with projects for the good of the community too numerous to mention. This is the kind of enterprise the United
Church Board for Homeland Ministries encourages: the
churches of an entire city, rich and poor, combine to face
their common tasks, each giving what it can to make the
city a better one and not retreating from impoverished neighborhoods. Only by such means can the Christian Church influence the surrounding culture and save itself from becoming
its creature.

When the church is alive and growing, new church buildings have to be built. In new communities the new building
has to be conceived and constructed from the ground up, and
in old communities the churches often require new wings or
refurbishing or complete rebuilding. Usually in the former
case and often in the latter the denomination as such has to
come to the aid of the local community with loans or grants
of money for construction, and technical wisdom—born out of
long experience. Questions as to the size of the main place
of worship, the organization of church schoolrooms, the type
of parish hall required—these and a score of others, including
the all-important matter of general architecture—come to the
fore when building blueprints are on the table; and it is at
that time that the seasoned advice of those who have built
church after church and studied the effects of this arrange-

ment or that, is welcome. By and large, the congregation that realizes that a church building is basically a place to provide public worship for the community and that all its other parish activities are ancillary to that, will put up the best structure and, indeed, if it understands the meaning of worship, it will design its sanctuary with the most becoming lines, masses, and color.

The rate of growth in resident membership in the United Church of Christ exceeds that of the population; and now we are told by the sociologists that our American cities will expand as much in the coming decade as they did during the entire period from 1630 to 1900—a period of almost three centuries. One architect recently said, "Before they reach middle age, the children born this year will see the building of the equivalent of another United States." This means that all the money used to build churches is as a drop in the bucket in relation to the coming need.

One phase of the work of the Board for Homeland Ministries which deserves more than passing mention is really misrepresented in the name by which it is usually known—Church Finance Advisory Service. It is actually an organ for the teaching of stewardship among individual members of the churches. Men who are especially gifted in helping people to see that their covenant relation to God and their fellow man means real sharing of their substance are sent to churches on invitation, where, for the period of a week or more, they talk with the leaders and others simply about the implications that church membership has for the use of personal income. Most Americans have been bred to a generous attitude toward the needs of their community, but in the midst of the general inflation of the last decades they have lagged in increasing their benevolent giving to meet the increased expenses of the charitable institutions they support. The men of the Church Finance Advisory Service lay no external pressure upon their hearers to give more; they only ask each person to reconsider his budget of benevolences and readjust it according to his conscience. The changes that this practice effects in a parish are usually little short of miraculous.

Ninety-four campus ministries in colleges and universities are supported by the United Church Board for Homeland Ministries. In addition, fifty part-time ministries are carried on by local churches or Conferences. It is hard to overemphasize the importance of this work, for by this means the church is able to become acquainted with the leading members of its student world, who are bound to assume leadership in the communities to which they go. Before some of them who seem appropriately gifted, the claims of the ministry are laid; to all of them is given the call to Christian service, whatever be the profession they may enter. It is notorious that student groups led or inspired by persons not on the faculty and responsible to organizations outside the college or university may become, in certain circumstances, a most magnificent nuisance to the administration of the institution—aggravated by the fact that, if they are several, they enter into competition with one another. For the United Church campus ministry it may be said, in contradistinction to those which are highly denominational, that it is ecumenical in spirit, having already been instrumental in creating a student fellowship which unites other denominations with its own; and that it recognizes from the start that it has, toward the administration of each institution in whose environs it works, the responsibilities of a guest, however important a guest it may consider itself.

No denomination has done more in the past to break down the barriers between the races in this country, and none devotes a larger portion of its budget to this end today. The United Church hails with gratitude the Negroes' discovery of Gandhi's technique of nonviolent resistance to achieve the ends of justice and fair play, which has now advanced desegregation in public places in an unprecedented degree and, because of its turn-the-other-cheek philosophy, has given no justified occasion for hostility. The Board for Homeland Ministries, standing behind the local churches, seeks first of all to discover the facts in any local situation; then, within the white communities and the Negro communities where feelings run high, it attempts a task of interpretation in the light of the facts; and through its staff and dedicated church leaders on both sides it seeks ways of reconciliation and co-operation.

The facts are often gathered by the forward-looking leaders of the communities themselves. Take the instance of Baltimore, Maryland. This is the sixth-largest city in the United States, with Negroes numbering about a fourth of its population. For years the traditional practice of segregation in housing, public accommodations, public education, and social welfare characterized the life of the city—until a group of leading citizens decided to make a factual inventory of racial practices from which to chart a plan for change. This was Baltimore's "Community Self-Survey of Inter-group Relations." Advice and help were sought from the United Church department (actually the Race Relations Department of the Board of Home Missions, before this became part of the United Church Ministries) which had invented this useful instrument of social engineering and possessed the broadest experience in its use; three members of the staff gave leadership to the committees for over a year—and the total result has been such a change in the racial atmosphere of the city that none of the outbreaks that have defaced the reputation of other cities similarly situated have taken place there. On the contrary, the new freedom from segregation has given the city a strength it has never known before.

Up and down the Southland, especially where the tensions are greatest, move emissaries of the United Church of Christ to lend their hand in any way they can to the forces of reconciliation. They work quietly with Negro pastors and churches and with white pastors and churches and with both together when possible. Experienced in the gentle but exquisitely difficult art of reconciliation, and in touch with all the forces which create the tensions, these unobtrusive missionaries go where they are needed, setting up small but influential interracial committees to maintain permanent watch on the situation, to the end of developing a permanent cure and in some way providing for a Christian way out of a social illness sometimes called falsely a way of life. These people are not accompanied by trumpets and fanfares; many do not know of their work, but there is no secret about them. Their names appear on the list of workers for the United Church Board for Homeland Ministries and they are openly trying to do the work of the church—creating and strengthening the bonds between God and man, and man and man.

Work toward the same great end, though not on the mainland, is that done in the Yuquiyu rural community in Puerto Rico. This consists of 250 families who live on small farms of three to seven acres. The director there, Mr. Oramel Greene, writes:

The idea of discovering and solving common problems by means of general community assemblies and study circles (now being utilized by the Government) was experimented in first in Yuquiyu (and some of the worst mistakes were made here!). Much has been accomplished in the field of agriculture, soil conservation, health, family relations, and recreation. However, if we have accomplished *only* this, we have done nothing, since there are many civic organizations which do the same. We don't organize co-ops for economic reasons only, but because they constitute one way to put into practice what Jesus taught about loving and helping one another.

The Ryder Memorial Hospital in Humacao, Puerto Rico, is another point at which the United Church of Christ is in league with the Puerto Rican church to make life better for the people of the island—but here, as all along the line in the vast social work of the Board for Homeland Ministries, the emphasis made by Mr. Greene, just quoted, must be borne in mind: all of the institutional work, all of the general work such as that which supports the improvement of economic and political relations between the races, all of the labors to achieve better man-to-man understandings, are predicated upon the fact that improvements in social relations depend upon changes in attitudes of heart. So the United Church of Christ, with all its many-sided interests in social amelioration, does not forget that it must finally penetrate to the inner core of men and women if fundamental good is to be done—and this is the area of religion. A man who believes that God hates racial discrimination, or poverty, or disease, is likely to be a more deeply committed enemy of these ills than another who believes only that they are untoward and have unhappy results. And so the United Church of Christ through its boards and churches, day in, day out, week in, week out, year in, year out, century in, century out, tries to make itself a means whereby this spirit may breathe upon men; anything less is to heal the hurt of the world's people slightly, temporarily, if at all; the church is most itself when it is dealing with human hearts.

The United Church Press is the name under which the United Church of Christ expects to do most of its publishing. The people of the United Church are people of books, and there is every expectation that the field to be covered will be a broad one. The press will do all it can to get the people of the pews to read—not to mention the people of the pulpit. When, sometimes, a minister in late middle life comes into the possession of what Charles Lamb called "the self-sufficiency of surpliced emptiness," it may usually be discovered that he has not read a book since graduation from his divinity school. The United Church Press is the enemy of the kind of piety which is intellectually vapid.

Of all the labors to which the United Church of Christ devotes itself, save that of worship itself, there is probably none more important than that of education. The task is not an easy one; since the essential characteristics of Christianity are not today taught in the average American home, the church in the United States has work comparable to that of the church in China—it has to teach within a cultural setting which is alien or at least neutral to the Gospel. And it has to teach all ages, both sexes, and all classes of society.

Children's work covers a span of twelve years, and involves the quick learner and the slow one, the city child, the suburban child and the rural one, the haves and the have-nots, the loved and wanted, and the unloved and unwanted. It requires in the teachers both the ability to help the children bridge the times between the Old and New Testaments and their own—so that they can identify the truths which are timeless—and the abilities that teachers in general must have, kept whetted and sharp by the reading of pedagogical materials. This tremendous task of bringing the two generations together so that the religious insights of the older may be communicated to the younger is part of the program of every local church, however small, but behind every congregation of the United Church, stands the whole communion which, through its Board for Homeland Ministries, supplies curriculum materials, supplementary literary aids, and magazines, all produced by experts in their fields.

The same colossal undergirding of the efforts of the local churches is supplied for work with youth, adults, and families.

The editorial work alone in the area of education for the whole church is staggering in its proportions, especially when, as now, a new curriculum has to be prepared—and this curriculum is designed to be as good as modern pedagogy, the best contemporary theology, and the latest discoveries in Biblical and later church history can make it.

Curriculum materials are only instruments to place in the hands of leaders. For this reason every effort is made to keep the stream of leadership at the flood in every church and throughout the nation. A specialized training school for Christian educators is held every summer. Workshops are held throughout the year and all through the country. There is constant search for persons who have an understanding for and are sensitive to other persons, who are faithful and informed members of the Christian community, and who know how to foster such relationships as will enfold others within the redemptive life of the fellowship.

Education, the Board for Homeland Ministries knows full well, is not a phase of production-line manufacturing. It is effective in proportion as it is tailored to the individual. This involves Christian training for exceptional children; literature and programs for young adults, married and unmarried; resource books for families to use in the Christian nurture of their children; specialized services for summer camps for work camps of young people; and for "caravaning," or visitations of parishes by groups of young leaders. Like Napoleon's army, it is concerned for every talent.

The United Church of Christ in the Nation

In the Constitution we find:

The United Church Board for Homeland Ministries coordinates the mission of the United Church of Christ in higher education and in health and welfare through the Councils hereinafter described for service in these fields.

We shall speak of those services at greater length under the constitutional paragraphs which deal with the Councils mentioned. The section on Homeland Ministries concludes with a series of notes on procedural matters:

The General Synod nominates and elects the corporate members of the United Church Board for Homeland Ministries. This Board shall report its program and finances annually to the Executive Council and to each regular meeting of the General Synod. Each organization related to the Board shall have a part in determining the program and budget of the Board. The Board shall submit to the Budget Committee of the General Synod a detailed request for allocation from the budget to be recommended to the General Synod for those parts of the Board's program not otherwise provided for in this Constitution and in the By-Laws of the United Church of Christ. Organizations related to the Board shall have free access to the Budget Committee of the General Synod.

Here, as in the case of the Board for World Ministries, nominations and elections are so distributed as to be equitably representative of ministers, laymen, and laywomen.

Pages more might be written of the varied work of the Board for Homeland Ministries, but space allows for the mention of only one other matter: the Board is the leading single agency within and on behalf of the communion to link together the Gospel and the fine arts. It is natural that this should be the case since the Board is more concerned with architecture (in the building of churches) and the graphic arts (in the publication of books) than any other organization in the United Church. It shares a great interest in the arts of worship, also, with the Commission on Worship and with all the local churches.

In the Puritan inheritance of the United Church of Christ, eager interest in the arts is not so conspicuously absent as is sometimes supposed. The Puritans are sometimes falsely held responsible for the destruction of the stained-glass windows and statuary in certain of the cathedrals in England— but it is now known that this was rather the work of irresponsible mobs who utilized the unrest of the times to vent their spleen on the property held by authorities they considered their enemies. Cromwell enjoyed paintings and was passionately fond of music. The chaste white churches of New England were not put up by people cold to loveliness. The Puritans boycotted the stage completely, to be sure, but the stage at the time was associated with moral corruption. They cannot, however, be said to have been promoters of the arts in the church or outside of it. They held that the church had depended too much upon its artistic symbols, allowing them to obscure rather than distinguish the holy realities to which they were supposed to point. Discouraging the use of any art that might become ornate, excessive, they often allowed themselves to worship with forms more notable for their plainness than their beauty. That was in the seventeenth century, whose spirit continued through the eighteenth and into the nineteenth, but when, in the twentieth century, Puritanism entered the United Church of Christ, it had matured.

Today the modern Puritan sees that the need for strict devotion to God—which he still gladly cherishes—cannot find its full fruition apart from forms of beauty. He sees that it is unchristian, when one has the choice between the two, to put ugliness instead of beauty into human life. His continuing preoccupation with God's sovereignty today does not prevent him from, but rather incites him to, using the arts as his vehicles. But always as vehicles, never as idols.

When now this full-blown Puritanism, which pursues standards in art as avidly as it has always pursued standards in morality, meets in the United Church a German stream of tradition in which the love of music, the bold use of color in architecture, and a Continental creativity in the decorative arts in general (which has never known a Puritan revolution), the issue cannot be predicted, but it is safe to say that that church will not be a stranger to the beauty of holiness or to the holiness of beauty. Though the arts of the Pennsylvania Dutch did not stem directly from the Reformed immigration, they were closely related to it and early appreciated and apprehended by it. The Mercersburg Movement brought treasures out of the past, some of them no less artistic than theological. Many of the older Evangelical Church buildings of the Middle West, though in a different manner from the Georgian churches of New England, testify to an aesthetic heritage. That this interpenetration of cultures will produce new interest in the arts is almost a foregone conclusion.

In fact the United Church of Christ may already be said to have become a patron of the arts within the church. Its new church buildings, largely influenced by the pre-Gothic vigor of Scandinavia and the genius of modern functionalism, all declare the meaning of God in human experience and aid in the human response to him in worship. It is noteworthy that the new Statement of Faith of the United Church of Christ had hardly been accepted by the General Synod before it was set to music. It can now be heard in a lovely anthem whose music is reminiscent of the Gregorian mode, or in the setting of a complete oratorio. At meetings of the General Synod the works of modern ecclesiastical artists have been exhibited. The solemn dance is to be witnessed in the church again—as seems natural and right, since it was in the church that it had its origin—and United Church youth who have participated in it are certain that this is a means of expressing oneself Christianly which no other form of devotion can supply. For pictorial illustrations in curriculum material for the church school, American denominations for a long time have been using hopelessly idealized Biblical scenes in which our Lord usually appears as an effeminate though bearded Nordic; but the United Church of Christ has broken with this tradition in favor of the down-to-earth productions of the modern artist, through which, as in the rugged events and figures of life itself, the enquiring spirit may discover God's revelations. Other communions, as well as the United Church, have welcomed the new expressions of art which the twentieth century has brought—and some of them in more striking ways than the United Church. It is to this part of Christendom that the United Church belongs—the group to which the arts are the handmaidens of worship and Christian concern, without which the church would seem sterile, and life intolerable and not understood—and to the Board for Homeland Ministries, more than to any other of its component organizations, the United Church looks to maintain this flame on its altars.

The Educated Christian

The Constitution now declares its way of caring for:

Higher Education

There shall be a Council for Higher Education with purposes and organization as described in the By-Laws of the United Church of Christ.

This Council is composed of the executive heads of the academies, colleges, and theological schools which indicate their desire to be recognized as related to the United Church of Christ and which are accepted by the Council as conforming to its standards, together with the members of the board of directors of the Board for Homeland Ministries assigned to the Council. It devotes itself to the general program of Christian higher education in the United Church of Christ, which includes the cultivation of close relations between the educational institutions and the church, the maintenance of the Christian religion in the institutions, and, with the Board for Homeland Ministries, the promotion of higher education as an integral part of the church's mission.

From the beginning of the Evangelical and Reformed and Congregational Christian denominations, which today constitute the United Church of Christ, there has been undeviating concern for higher education; and so it is today, for the communion has not lost its belief that a Christian must live up to his highest capacities. There are colleges which are definitely fostered by the United Church of Christ; over thirty of them belong to the United Church family—and as many more, like Harvard and Yale, owe their beginnings to ancestors of the United Church of Christ.

Besides the colleges and universities there are the theological schools. If leadership is nine-tenths of the success of any enterprise, the church cannot claim to be an exception. The country, as a matter of fact, is the graveyard of many a church that died for want of ministerial leadership—but when good leadership enters in where the field is ripe for the harvest, the results are extraordinary. The United Church is on the constant search for leaders, and when they are found is ready to equip them.

It is the philosophy of the United Church of Christ, as has been pointed out again and again, that the whole church should help all the parts and the parts the whole church, but neither should dominate the other, and so shut off free access to Christ, who is the inspiration at once of each part and of the whole; and nowhere is this more keenly felt than in the relations between the church and its colleges. In the United Church of Christ, a church-related college has a full guarantee of its own academic integrity: it elects its own board of trustees, appoints its own faculty, and devises its own curriculum. The church will aid it as it can, will depend upon it for trained men, but will not mother it; it will trust it to be itself and to do its best. Among the group of such institutions affiliated with the United Church of Christ are many in the front rank of privately supported colleges of the United States:

> Beloit College
> Carleton College
> Catawba College
> Cedar Crest College
> The Defiance College

Dillard University
Doane College
Drury College
Elmhurst College
Elon College
Fisk University
Franklin and Marshall College
Grinnell College
Heidelberg College
Hood College
Huston-Tillotson College
Illinois College
Lakeland College
LeMoyne College
Marietta College
Maunaolu College
New College
Northland College
Olivet College
Pacific University
Piedmont College
Ripon College
Rocky Mountain College
Southern Union College
Talladega College
Tougaloo Southern Christian College
Ursinus College
Westminster College
Yankton College

The affiliated academies are two:

Massanutten Academy
Mercersburg Academy

The United Church has relations with thirteen theological schools:

Andover Newton Theological School
Bangor Theological Seminary
Chicago Theological Seminary
Eden Theological Seminary
Hartford Seminary Foundation
Harvard Divinity School
Lancaster Theological Seminary
Oberlin Graduate School of Theology
Pacific School of Religion
Union Theological Seminary of New York
United Church of Christ Seminary at Minneapolis
Vanderbilt University Divinity School
Yale Divinity School

The United Church of Christ aims to give its ministers the best education the age can furnish. Many men, after being graduated from the theological seminary, stay on to take specialized work or go abroad to Britain or the Continent to do so.

A Healthy Race

The Constitution is likewise concerned for:

Health and Welfare
There shall be a Council for Health and Welfare Services with purposes and organization as described in the By-Laws of the United Church of Christ.

This Council, like that of the one for Higher Education, is composed of the executive heads of institutions operating in these fields which indicate their desire to be recognized as related to the United Church of Christ and which are accepted by the Council as conforming to its standards, together with the members of the board of directors of the Board for Homeland Ministries assigned to this Council. With the Board for Homeland Ministries, it devotes itself to the study and planning of the program of health and welfare ministries of the United Church. The need for communication among the promoters and administrators of these institutions being obvious, the Council and Board are called upon to furnish this—and in order that the institutions may not drift to the outside edge of the churches' attention, there is need also to maintain two-way lines of church-institution, institution-church concern. These also the Council and Board establish and cultivate.

The field of Health and Welfare services presents an interesting illustration of the kind of gain that can come from such a union as has been achieved in the United Church of Christ. The Congregational Christians, being in large part derived from old New England, had, generally speaking, no charitable institutions of their own. When the Pilgrims and Puritans came to Plymouth and Massachusetts Bay, they brought not merely a church with them: they brought a whole civilization. For them church and state were designed to serve each other, both being under the mandate of God, and in the division of responsibility between the two, worship and all that was immediately connected with it was assigned to the church, and all other services like schools and hospitals to the state. This precedent has made Congregational Christians (to the despair of some of the promoters of their denominational institutions) exceedingly sensitive to the needs of the community institutions in their neighborhood, and correspondingly oblivious of the needs of similar institutions under the banner of the church. The latter in Congregationalism were almost all of them on the foreign field, where the old New England pattern never held. The sense of responsibility for the institutions of the community is one of Puritanism's gifts to this country. It is not wholly a blessing, however; the division made by the Puritans tends to separate sacred and secular, and allow the church to feel that charities are not in its orbit. The background of the Evangelical and Reformed Church, on the other hand, was different. There the old European feeling that the church is the mother of all social good was to the fore. In consequence that church was able to bring into the United Church a great many institutions of the type that were consigned by the New England Fathers to the community as a whole—general hospitals, hospitals for the feeble-minded, settlement houses, and the like. These institutions have their own autonomy: they are the responsibility of self-perpetuating boards of directors, but the church at large also feels a concern for them. These institutions unite the church to the great and growing profession of social work, and the mutual reaction between the two is to the benefit of each: the church acquires that sense of need for high professional standards which animates the well-trained social worker, and the latter finds in the church a motivation for bettering the lot of humanity which has its roots not in the superficial ground of expediency but in eternity itself.

A new facility for the aging is established in the Washington-Baltimore area, which has the distinction of being the first project of its type to be planned by the United Church itself.

Programs of recruitment and scholarship will provide, it is hoped, an increased number of professionally competent administrators and caseworkers for the many various institutions. A call goes out constantly for nonprofessional helpers also. The concern of the United Church will presently be extended nationally to the field of the retarded child, the alcoholic, and others. That the Health and Welfare Council has a work to do is not questioned in the United Church of Christ.

Now the Constitution takes up

Pension and Relief Activities

All responsible denominations today have actuarially sound

systems of pensioning their superannuated ministers. These systems usually call for contributions from the denomination as a whole and, during their working years, from the ministers themselves and the churches which they serve. The United Church of Christ has such a system, based upon proved principles and skillfully administered; but there are always cropping up unusual situations which pensioning of the ordinary sort does not reach—cases where special grants are called for to meet special needs. Retired and active ministers and their families are included in this form of benevolence, and in it many individuals habitually participate by contributing specifically to a fund for such cases at Christmastime each year. Most of these needs are medical, for while general expenses were rising in the 1950's from 100 to 126 per cent, medical costs reached the figure of 156 per cent. The gifts have provided needed operations, removed cataracts, restored sight, provided hearing aids, taught Braille to men gone blind, trained young widows to become self-supporting. Such relief activities are referred to in the second paragraph quoted from the Constitution below.

For a denomination the size of the United Church of Christ, as will be understood, the millions of dollars involved in pension and relief activities call for highly skilled management and meticulous accounting. The Constitution affords the fundamental authorizations:

The pension activities of the United Church of Christ are administered by a non-profit membership corporation(s). The control of each such corporation lies in its members through a board of trustees chosen by the members from a list of persons whose names have been presented to and approved by the General Synod or by the Executive Council. Persons for this list may be proposed by any member of the corporation(s) or by the Trustees thereof. Such corporation(s) shall report its program and finances annually to its members and to the Executive Council, and to each regular meeting of the General Synod. The General Synod shall from time to time make examination of the practices and developments of such corporation(s).

The ministerial relief activities of the United Church of Christ, by whatever corporate bodies administered, are co-ordinated with the pension activities of the Church through the corporation(s) above described. The pension and relief corporation(s) shall submit to the Budget Committee of the General Synod a request for allocation of sufficient funds, from the budget to be recommended to the General Synod, for the payment of ministerial relief benefits and such other benefits as the General Synod may provide. Payment of such benefits shall be limited to the funds received for that purpose.

Chapter XVI

CHRISTIAN SOCIAL ACTION

The board for homeland ministries is not the only instrument used by the United Church to combat racial discrimination and other social ills in the United States. This work in the case of the Board is channeled largely through permanent institutions. Designed to be an instrument dealing more in the field of principles and to address itself to international as well as national social problems is the Council for Christian Social Action, which is authorized in the Constitution under the heading:

Social Education and Action

The General Synod shall establish a Council for Christian Social Action as the instrumentality of the United Church of Christ to study the content of the Gospel in its bearing on man in society, provide and publish information and literature on social issues, cooperate with instrumentalities of the United Church of Christ and with other appropriate bodies in making the implications of the Gospel effective in society, and formulate and promote a program of social education and action for the United Church of Christ.

The Council shall report its program and finances annually to the Executive Council and to each regular meeting of the General Synod. It shall submit to the Budget Committee of the General Synod a detailed request for support of its work through funds allocated from the budget to be recommended to the General Synod.

Like the Boards for World and for Homeland Ministries, this Council provides for the equitable representation of ministers, laymen, and laywomen in its membership. On matters of current social controversy, the Council for Christian Social Action calls together experts for discussion, seeks the advice and counsel of those whom it considers to be the most experienced and enlightened in the fields under discussion (many of them often outside the church) and after careful consultation with leaders and others in the United Church itself, publishes statements describing the issues and suggesting Christian solutions for study and action by the churches, the Conferences, and the General Synod itself. By this means the whole United Church is kept alive to the social questions of the day and to the necessity for solving them in accordance with the will of God.

In the area of the world of nations the Council has published papers on such themes as "Responsible Parenthood and the Population Problem," "Nuclear Weapons and the Arms Race," "National Responsibility and International Relations." It conducts seminars to introduce groups from the churches to the United Nations, where indeed it has an observer. International study tours have taken the members to many countries of the world and even around the world. These are more than mere tourist trips to see the sights. In every country visited, the members of the delegations— United Churchmen and -women paying their own way—wait upon heads of state or other governmental officials and leaders in education or church life to learn from them at firsthand what is being done in that country both domestically and in foreign relations to prepare those ways of peace and international harmony which accord with the standards of the Gospel. Now and then members of the staff study abroad in order to keep themselves *au courant* with foreign events in a personal way.

In the area of American life the Council makes films available, such as the one on the Christian meaning of daily work. It has produced literature on such subjects as "Ethical Issues in Industrial Relations," "The Churches and Migratory Agricultural Labor," "Medical Care for the Aging," "Gambling," "Obscene Literature," and "The Family and Rapid Social Change"—not to mention the ever highly charged theme of federal aid to public schools.

The Council for Christian Social Action has also grappled with the thorny problem of birth control in this country. Here, however, there is probably today overwhelming unanimity of opinion among the people of the United Church: they believe that there is theological and ethical justification for many of the voluntary controls which until recently have been condemned by more conservative churches.

In the area of race relations the Council for Christian Social Action has put out many a statement against the evil of segregation, and it has done more than put out statements. It has been active, for instance, in "The Greater Minneapolis Interfaith Housing Program." Minneapolis was chosen as the city in which to make this experiment because of its size, location, and ratio of white to nonwhite citizens. The program is a joint venture of the United Church Council with concerned citizens of that city who represent other Protestants, and Catholics and Jews as well. A full-time executive director works under a committee of citizens making surveys, engaging the aid of leading social scientists, sponsoring workshops, preparing housing bills for the legislature, and utilizing other co-operative means to settle families of different races in the same neighborhoods and help them live together in decency, instead of compelling the nonwhites, as is so often the rule, to live in neighborhoods unfit to rear children in.

The Council co-operates with the Board for Homeland Ministries in the program of community consultations in the Southland already described. It is also at the forefront of the movement against anti-Semitism. It has advice to give in the matter of interfaith and interracial marriage. American-Indian affairs are one of its concerns.

In the area of American politics, the Council has made studies on party platforms, the voting records of congressmen, the separation of church and state, and in many other fields. It provides leadership in programs designed to help the people of the churches to know and support the peace efforts of the government, and especially the United Nations itself. It tries to get the people of the churches, against the background of their Christian conscience, to think their way through such questions as cluster about the attitude of the administration to Communist China and the deplorable state of the Palestinian refugees. Although the complexity of such questions as these prevent arrival at any common opinion which might be known as the United Church attitude, the very thinking and studying lifts the people of the church out of the classification of those who read only the headlines and vote only with their party.

On the other hand, the Council does what it can to influence public policy on matters in which the judgment of the church is clear and unmistakable. Its representatives have appeared before Congressional committees to support measures protecting migratory farm workers, providing economic assistance in underdeveloped parts of the world, or serving some other obviously humanitarian purpose. It employs a staff member in the Washington office of the National Council of Churches (interdenominational), to keep his finger on the pulse of government and advise the churches. Through him it tries to keep the churches informed of government situations and actions, and the government informed of the Christian attitude on the great issues. This it does in the only possible way, by encouraging him to create all the bridges of communication possible between the leaders of government on the one hand and leaders of the church on the other. Often representatives of the two groups are called together in conferences, large or small.

The United Church of Christ is not, like the Society of Friends, a church which has generally regarded war as a sin in which none of its members should participate. Not a few of its members do, however, hold this view and hold it to the point of being willing to sacrifice even the esteem of their friends in order to sustain it. Being conscientious objectors in time of war they have suffered all the indignities that go with resisting popular opinion. The members of the United Church all regard war as an evil that should be exterminated from the earth, and though the majority believe that it is not the worst of all evils and must be balanced off against evils that nonresistance might permit, they unite with the minority wholeheartedly in seeking and sacrificing for a world of justice, in which peace ensues as a by-product. It is testimony to the influence of Christ that young men in the time of war departing from the same church, some to enter the army, some to enter a detention camp with other pacifists, have all retained with the church a strong bond of fellowship. So the United Church of Christ and the Christian Council for Social Action number among their supporters some who are willing to fight for peace in the ways of war, others who believe that participation in war is always unwarranted; they are convinced that in the long run followers of Jesus Christ, though at the moment they may appear to be moving in different ways, will eventually discover themselves to be converging on the same goal.

The Constitution now comes to a most important subject on which we have already written so many pages that no extended comment is necessary here:

Church and Ministry

The General Synod shall establish a Council for Church and Ministry as an instrumentality of the United Church of Christ. The Council shall study, plan and oversee the program of the Church in such areas of concern as pastoral relations, professional standards, education for church-related vocations, life enlistment, aid for students in care of Association, in-service training, religion and health, social and parish workers, military, industrial and institutional chaplaincies. It shall cooperate and counsel with Associations and Conferences in implementing the work and witness of the Church in these areas.

The Council shall report its program and finances annually to the Executive Council and to each regular meeting of the General Synod. It shall submit to the Budget Committee of the General Synod a detailed request for support of its work through funds allocated from the budget to be recommended to the General Synod.

Once more, it is provided that ministers, laymen, and lay-women shall be equitably represented on this Council.

The hundred and one tasks of the Council on Church and Ministry cannot be listed, and many of them are of the pastoral type which lift morale but defy description. It publishes the *Minister's Quarterly,* which is a link not only between the parish clergy but between them and the national agency chiefly concerned with their work. The Church Vocations Office, under the sponsorship of the Council, provides literature for churches, Associations, and Conferences to interest young men and women in church vocations, carries on extensive correspondence with young people who signify their interest in such professions, and provides leadership for institutes devoted to church vocations. The Council on Church and Ministry provides advice and such other aid as it can to students in care of Associations, co-operates with groups involved in psychological testing for the ministry, and serves as consultant at conferences of seniors at theological schools. This type of work brings the Council into closest touch with the divinity schools, and with the aid of their faculties the Council brings out from time to time manuals for ministers and for congregations. The Council is also in process of assembling in a repository of records such information about every minister of the church as may be of help to them in their professional life, if and when they move from one church to another. The Council encourages ministers to take the refresher schooling offered at La Foret and at Deering, and itself sponsors the summer schools for pastors on sabbatical leave held at Eden and at Lancaster Seminaries. It endorses, visits, and in every way supports the chaplains in the Armed Forces. It maintains several hospital chaplaincies, provides scholarships for ministers to study the relations of religion and mental health, and stands ready to advise ministers in local parishes in matters related to this field.

CHAPTER XVII

A CHURCH OF LAYMEN AND LAYWOMEN

THE NEXT CONSTITUTIONAL PROVISION IS ONE OF SUPREME MO-ment for the United Church of Christ for, as we have already shown, this is a church which from its earliest beginnings has regarded as an ecclesiastical disorder the belief that the hierarchy is the essential church; in its view a church is only half itself without full, rich, comprehensive, productive

Lay Life and Work

The General Synod shall establish a Council for Lay Life and Work as the instrumentality of the United Church of Christ responsible for increasing, developing and coordinating the activities and participation of laymen and laywomen in the Church as a means of witnessing effectively for Jesus Christ in all areas of life.

The Council shall report its program and finances annually to the Executive Council and to each regular meeting of the General Synod. It shall submit to the Budget Committee of the General Synod a detailed request for support of its work through funds allocated from the budget to be recommended to the General Synod.

Here it will be seen that the United Church of Christ makes a clean break with the dominant American tradition by putting its men's work and its women's work *together*. This is a lesson it has learned from Europe, where the churches look askance at the ecclesiastical practice of the United States, which builds up huge men's and women's organizations—especially the latter—apart from each other. They regard this as a form of segregation, not so evil as racial segregation, but nonetheless unnatural in the sight of God— and so does the United Church of Christ. Perhaps this separation is necessary in an early phase of social development when, emerging from an inferior status, women in company with men are denied positions of leadership commensurate with their equal abilities; but today the United Church of Christ believes itself—and indeed expects the rest of the American church soon to realize itself also—to be far beyond that stage. Nor is lay work to be completely separated from that which has to be done by and for ministers: on the Council for Lay Life and Work will sit an equal number of laymen, laywomen, and ministers, the latter minority to serve as liaison with the rest of the full-time leadership of the church.

Here it may be profitable to turn our attention back to the idea of the church as being held together by a Covenant—a Covenant altogether different from any other because it is given to us by God himself. By it he promises that he will impart life to each one of us and to all of us if we will only accept him in faith and let his life pass from each to all and all to each in a common communion. This involves each and every member of the church. The doctrine of the Covenant has as its unlimited corollary the belief in the priesthood of all believers. One may recall the wording of the Covenant with the Hebrews in one of its earliest forms: "Now therefore," says the Lord God, "if you will obey my voice and keep my covenant, you shall be my own possession among all peoples; for all the earth is mine, and you shall be to me a kingdom of priests and a holy nation." A good deal of nonsense has been talked about the priesthood of all believers in the misconception that it means that every man is his own priest, but the verse I have just quoted from Exodus indicates the contrary: every man, as a member of the priestly nation, is to be a priest to his fellow. A priest is one whose function it is to serve as an intermediary between God and man; and the doctrine of the priesthood of all believers is simply to the effect that it is not the office bearers of the church alone who witness to God in the world and serve him, but the entire church, corporately and individually. The New Testament (the New Covenant, remember), when it lists the gifts from God to man which make the latter serviceable in his kingdom, enumerates many which we commonly associate with the professional ministry, such as "prophecy," "exhortation," and the like, but it also includes some which seem to belong to laymen, such as "teaching" and "administration." For the sake of good order, there must be officers with given functions in the church, as there are in any organic society, but these men (and women) set apart are not *over* the church. They and the others are servants of each other because both are servants of Christ.

In the United Church, as in all other churches which follow the New Testament pattern, prospective ministers, before they are ordained, are examined by appointed bodies of the church including laymen. Laymen may occupy the highest honorary office in the gift of the United Church, that is, that of the Moderator of the General Synod. They take their place, on occasions, in liturgical and sacramental functions, and the whole movement of the church's contemporary history, based on its past and making toward its future, is in the direction of ever fuller lay participation.

Though the United Church is the child of a Western church which, through the Middle Ages, allowed the cleavage between priesthood and laity to widen to such an extent that the cup of communion was allowed to the former and denied to the latter, and the hierarchy was made virtually the only medium of Christ's spirit, it is also a child of a later age of the church when the laity were fully recognized as an indispensable part of it. For Protestants, a worshiping group itself is a medium of power: it becomes a symbol of the whole church throughout the world and in all generations; the two or three stand for the ten thousand times ten thousand. In them, in principle, are all the relationships of love in Christ which draw the members of the great church together. A Protestant, therefore, feels a critical diminution in spiritual significance when at a time of public worship the group is not present. Only when his brother is at his side in Christ's presence does he feel himself symbolically in touch with the church, for only then are to hand all the essentials of a strong and meaningful life—the divine source of loving power on the one hand, a brother man to love, and oneself, loving and being loved. This means that the church cannot be understood apart from its laity.

The lay members of the United Church have the same standing as the ministry vis-à-vis Christ, both having the same infinite need of the grace of God; but lay people are the special missionaries of the church to secular society. The layman is on the front line of economic, political, and social life, as a minister cannot possibly be. When a minister attempts to reform a secular group, he has first of all to overcome its feeling that he is an outsider—and in some cases he can never do this. He can never be to a group of insurance men what one who is an insurance man himself can be; a lawyer among lawyers; a saleswoman among saleswomen. He does not spend most of his waking hours in a nonecclesiastical occupation—but laymen do. They become expert where a minister does not even become a novice. They can speak the language of the particular segment of society in which they are *au fait*. Agriculture thinks in terms of the seasons, brokerage in terms of the market, and the lives of all revolve about the foci of their jobs. Only those who are familiar with the ways of a group from inside know where the spiritual stresses arise and how the Gospel can be best and most significantly applied. The natural channel for the Gospel to take to the workaday world lies in the persons of the Christian laymen and laywomen who live in that world.

The United Church of Christ is beginning to be aware, as the German churches became aware after the last war, that if the activity of the church is confined to the clergy, it is not fully alive. It is too late in the day for us to think that we can go back to the guilds as they were set up in the Middle Ages, each company of workers regarding itself as a kind of congregation within the church; but the principle of the guilds is a sound one. Every few years the laymen of the United Church hold a great national assembly, and there they have opportunity not only to compare notes as laymen, but to do so as members of their occupational groups—bankers and financial men, operators of factories, members of labor unions, teachers, homemakers, and others. Imagine the various groups returning to their occupational orbits. The thinking done together, the commitments made together, the recollections of fellowship not only with the total assembly but with the men and women of their own professional units, must obviously lend character to their business life and constitute them a leaven in the world to which they return. This is one of the ways the United Church of Christ constantly pours Christian idealism into the nation—through its laymen and laywomen. In this new combined venture, the laymen will certainly have much to learn from the laywomen, who have been cultivating the field of lay work for generations.

Some of the most useful people the church has ever given the world have been laymen and laywomen. The remarkable spread of the Gospel throughout the lands of the Mediterranean in the early days was due largely to laymen. Matthew was a tax collector, Mark was a secretary, Luke was a physician, John a fisherman. Many of the Christian writers of the next generations were unordained; indeed orders had not yet come to assume importance in the church. The vast development of the church through the centuries to the early Middle Ages would hardly have been possible without protagonists in the secular arena like Charlemagne himself. As we have already noted, John Calvin, through whom a major stream enters the tradition of the United Church of Christ, was never ordained. He provides the perfect illustration of the oceanic dimensions of the usefulness that a lawyer trained in the humanities can make available to the church.

The laymen and laywomen belong to the very essence of the United Church of Christ.

Last But Not Least

We have already spoken in passing, but now the Constitution itself makes mention of

Public Relations and Mass Communications

The General Synod shall establish an Office of Communication as the instrumentality of the United Church of Christ for public relations and mass communications, with responsibilities as defined in the By-Laws of the United Church of Christ.

The Office shall report its program and finances annually to the Executive Council and to each regular meeting of the General Synod. It shall submit to the Budget Committee of the General Synod a detailed request for support for its work through funds allocated from the budget to be recommended to the General Synod.

The work of this Office of Communication is to exercise leadership in establishing and maintaining public relations for the United Church of Christ and its instrumentalities; in conducting the denomination's ministry in television and radio; in producing audio-visual aids when requested to do so; in educational programing in the mass media for the benefit of the instrumentalities, regional bodies, and local churches; and in research in mass communication. The Office co-operates with similarly responsible offices of other denominations in the planning, production, distribution and utilization of mass media and audio-visual materials designed to promote and interpret the witness of ecumenical Christianity.

There is no more active office in the United Church than that of Communication. Its cardinal responsibility is to make the activities and concerns of the church available to the communication media of the land. For this its members must combine skills of news gathering and writing with a knowledge and understanding of the church. News stories are sent out, as are tape-recorded interviews and feature stories. The denomination, having from the start supported the policy of broadcasting religious matters on radio and television from an interdenominational rather than a sectarian base, works closely today in this field with other denominations and with the networks. "Off to Adventure," a series of children's television programs produced by the Office of Communication, has had unprecedented success.

This Office also is governed by a board of directors on which the distribution of seats is made equitably among laymen, laywomen, and ministers.

The last main paragraph in the eighth article of the Constitution is on

Stewardship

The General Synod shall establish a Stewardship Council as the instrumentality of the United Church of Christ to foster the principles and practice of Christian Stewardship and to discharge such other responsibilities as may be described in the By-Laws of the United Church of Christ or assigned to it by the General Synod.

The Council shall report its program and finances annually to the Executive Council and to each regular meeting of the General Synod. It shall submit to the Budget Committee of the General Synod a detailed request for support of its work through funds allocated from the budget to be recommended to the General Synod.

It is the duty of the Stewardship Council:

(a) To foster the principles of Christian stewardship;

(b) To co-operate with the Conferences and local churches in securing support for the United Church budget for *Our Christian World Mission* (which is the name for the annual giving of the churches to support all the benevolences we have been describing);

(c) To recommend to the Conferences suggested goals for meeting the United Church budget for *Our Christian World Mission;*

(d) To function as an informative and interpretive instrumentality in the development and distribution of information to assist in the reaching of these goals;

(e) To develop the policies and plans of the Stewardship Council and its Departments in close co-operation and consultation with the executive officers of the Conferences, who represent the interests of the Stewardship Council within their Conferences; and

(f) To be responsible for carrying out the general promotional policies of the instrumentalities of the United Church of Christ, and, in co-operation with the Conference officers, for promotion in the Conference.

To accomplish this herculean task the Council is divided into three departments:

The *Department of Stewardship Education* fosters the principles of Christian stewardship by means of a broad educational program interpreting the theological basis for the stewardship of all life at the heart of Christian faith and urging personal dedication to this faith.

The Department of Information and Interpretation develops literature and plans designed to evoke an interest in the growth and progress of the Christian faith throughout the whole world and thereby to attain the specific goals of *Our Christian World Mission.*

The Department of Promotion, in close co-operation with the other departments of the Stewardship Council, initiates and develops specific programs, methods, and techniques to assist conferences and local churches in attaining adequate financial support for the local church and for *Our Christian World Mission.*

Being a place where money is an immediate concern, the Stewardship Council could become, if bereft of Christian love, a source of pervasive discontent. It is made up of members representative of various instrumentalities of the church; each of whom might humanly strive for special favors.

Another point at which difficulty might be keenly felt is in the approach of the Council to the several Conferences in order to come to an agreement with them as to the amount that should be asked of their churches for the work and witness of the United Church at home and abroad. Here it would be easy for a mind without Christian imagination in any of the Conferences to set up the syllogism: there is only so much money to be given by the churches—the portion not given to the national and international needs will be left to meet needs within the Conference—*ergo:* we had better keep all we can within the Conference for our particular interests. Actually, however, this Council is what its name implies— a council of stewardship. Its continuous and extensive aim is stewardship. Its basic philosophy is that God has given us all we have, not so that we may own it in perpetuity and do with it according to our own selfish pleasure but so that we may use it as good stewards, always bearing in mind that it belongs ultimately to God and should be used to further his purposes. What loftier thought could control one's mind than that life gives one a chance to be a kind of junior partner to God, perfectly free within limits to do as one would with his own possessions, but morally committed to use them to the extent of one's power to advance the wonderful interests of the firm? At any rate this is the truth which animates the Stewardship Council and saves it from unseemly divisions within itself. Though each group connected with it will continue to hope that a high goal will be set for the giving to its particular project, it cannot, under the stewardship ideal, allow this hope to take on a selfish tinge.

The Constitution concludes with two articles commonly found in such documents. The first saves it from being a bar to progress and makes it instead the blueprint for orderly development that an instrument of its kind should be. This is:

Article IX. Amendments

The Constitution

Amendments to this Constitution may be proposed by a Conference, the General Synod or the Executive Council. Such proposed amendments shall be submitted in writing to the Secretary of the United Church of Christ at least three months prior to a meeting of the General Synod to which they are to be presented. At least two months prior to the meeting of the General Synod, the Secretary shall transmit such proposed amendments to the delegates, to the Conferences and to the local churches. Adoption of an amendment to the Constitution shall require a two-thirds affirmative vote of those present and voting in the General Synod and, before the next regular meeting of the General Synod, an affirmative vote of two-thirds of the Conferences. If so approved the General Synod, if in session, or the Executive Council, shall declare the amendment adopted and in force.

The By-Laws

Amendments to the By-Laws of the United Church of Christ may be proposed by an Association, a Conference, the General Synod or the Executive Council. Such proposed amendments shall be submitted in writing to the Secretary of the United Church of Christ at least three months prior to the meeting of the General Synod to which they are to be presented. At least two months prior to the meeting of the General Synod, the Secretary shall transmit such proposed amendments to the delegates, to the Conferences and to the local churches. Adoption of an amendment to the By-Laws shall require a two-thirds affirmative vote of those present and voting in the General Synod.

Last of all is the enabling

Article X. Effective Date

The General Synod shall declare this Constitution in force when it shall have been ratified or approved by not less than two-thirds of the Synods of the Evangelical and Reformed Church and by not less than two-thirds of the Congregational Christian churches voting, such voting to have been completed not later than June 1 immediately preceding the next regular meeting of the General Synod after the submission of the Constitution for the action of the Congregational Christian churches and the Synods of the Evangelical and Reformed Church.

The Constitution was declared to be in force at the meeting of the General Synod in Philadelphia on the fourth of July, 1961, in the same city in which the independence of the United States was declared, and on the same day of the month, one hundred and eighty-five years later.

CHAPTER XVIII

THE PAST IS PRELUDE

WHAT NOW OF THE FUTURE? THE SURVEY WE HAVE MADE OF the Constitution answers that question to a considerable degree, being studded with signs of preparation and direction, but it is also illuminating to note the kind of committees, authorized but not specifically mentioned by the Constitution, that the General Synod has actually set up. If a man's profession can be told by the tools he carries, it is not hard to judge, from the instruments which the United Church of Christ has provided for itself, what its future interests are likely to be.

In 1961 the Theological Commission was established, to serve the church by its counsel and studies on religious issues arising within the life of the communion or deriving from ecumenical sources. This Commission deals especially with the field of interest now commonly referred to as that of faith and order, including the doctrine of the church and the concept of the ministry. It assists the church in helping its members understand the Bible and in general think straight on religious matters, so that (as the resolution authorizing the commission says) ". . . the United Church of Christ may become ever more deeply rooted in the great Christian tradition and ever more sensitive to the need for understanding and proclaiming the faith in terms of contemporary life."

From this it may be learned that the United Church is determined not to go into the future as a company of people who are religious in their emotions but not in their minds. They desire completeness of Christian life: theirs is a faith that not only accepts questions but asks them; the whole man is involved. They know that the perseverance of the saints is made up of ever new beginnings—and for these beginnings thinking is demanded. When the human soul encounters God in Christ it receives from him a ring of keys, and then it is for the soul to proceed to open the doors of life about it. To that end the Holy Spirit will inspire the intellect—so the United Church of Christ believes.

More important than that: the United Church of Christ intends to be a worshiping church. The Commission on Worship was set up by the Executive Council in 1960 under the following mandate:

It shall be the responsibility of the Commission to pursue a scholarly study of worship and give leadership to the United Church ministers and churches in the conduct of worship, corporate and personal. It shall freely avail itself of literature, music, and the arts. While it will conserve the best in the traditions of worship which both constituencies bring into the United Church, it shall draw upon the treasures of the historic and universal Church, and from time to time shall prepare or propose for the General Synod's approval and commendation books of worship, hymnals, and other orders for the worship life of the United Church of Christ.

The United Church of Christ is aware that if God is forgotten in the church—and it recognizes from the history of the church that there are no better avenues of forgetfulness than forms of empty worship—the church becomes a mere social club. It is also aware, contrariwise, that forms of living worship normally provide the best avenues for the divine presence. So the Commission on Worship is brought into being. This Commission proposes not to provide worship forms selected from the literature of the past because they are pretty or even because they are old. It takes no stock in eclectic anthologies of any kind, but begins its work by asking the theological question, Why worship? and makes the answer to that question the organizing nucleus around which are grouped the forms which answer the question, How? It knows that forms are forms, and that all the aids to worship in the world cannot impart faith to a single soul—but to the soul that is thirsty for worship (and it is this thirst that shapes man in the image of God), a form that is relevant is one of the most grateful of all gifts. The only argument the soul has for its immortality is that divine things delight it and make it feel at home; the Commission regards itself as a maker of windows between the soul and those delights. Nothing is more momentous than worship, for it is the mother of all other forms in the church. The Benedictines never directly aimed at contributions to civilization; their idea was simply to stress and practice personal devotion in worship— but as a by-product their services to the church, to the world of learning, and to civilization in general were phenomenal. Like them, not knowing what results God will bring out of it, the United Church turns to worship.

It was in 1959 that the General Synod authorized another commission under the blanket powers given it by the Constitution—the Commission on Christian Unity and Ecumenical Study and Service. The importance which the church attaches to this Commission may be gathered from the specific vote by which it was authorized in the General Synod:

As an expression of the devotion of the United Church of Christ to the oneness of Christ's Church and of its steadfast purpose to be a uniting Church, the General Synod shall maintain a permament commission to be known as the Commission of Christian Unity and Ecumenical Study and Service.

It shall be the purpose and task of the Commission on Christian Unity and Ecumenical Study and Service to be alert constantly to evidences of Christian unity: To develop and nurture the ecumenical spirit within the United Church of Christ: To encourage responsible efforts being made anywhere to promote the unity of the Churches, to explore opportunities and initiate conversations toward the possibility of further union in which the United Church of Christ may be a participant, with formal procedures being subject to approval by the General Synod and to forward its labors by intercessory prayer, conferences, study of relevant issues, publication and distribution of pertinent literature, prophetic witness, and by exalting and aiding the achievement of love, fellowship, and service among the Churches.

It would be hard to imagine a stronger statement of direction and encouragement than that; in this field, as shown by the accomplishment it has already achieved and by the set of its mind as it looks toward the future, the United Church of Christ means business.

The Commission is helping the churches of the communion to appreciate the opportunities of the World and National Councils of Churches; it is pushing toward union with the Christian Churches (Disciples of Christ) and maintaining conversations with the Community Churches; and it is following with closest interest and warmest hospitality such proposals for union as that made by Dr. Eugene Carson Blake at a service in the Protestant Episcopal cathedral in San Francisco late in 1960.

An eighteenth-century atheist is said to have remarked that England was the country where Christianity did the least harm because it was divided into so many rivulets. Perhaps harm was to be expected from the actual Christianity of that day, but today many leaders of the Western world seem to realize that the one force that will hold it together and save it from destroying itself is real Christianity—of which actual Christianity is always only the sacrament. And

today in America, where the stream of the Gospel is divided
into more than two hundred and fifty denominational rivulets,
how can one expect to see real Christianity? All that one can
say is that many churches are beginning to look in the direction of unity. An adumbration of full-orbed ecumenical
Christianity is made in the United Church of Christ and
other such unions; anticipations of it are surely found in the
World Council and National Council and state councils of
churches; but we must regretfully admit that to the ordinary community the work of these councils might as well be
in the stratosphere. The One, Holy, Catholic, and Apostolic
Church is not easy to discern, one fears, in the ordinary
American town or city. Nonetheless the United Church of
Christ, working with other like-minded communions, will try
to make it discernible.

The three commissions mentioned prove the desire of the
United Church of Christ to be a thinking church, a worshiping church, and an ecumenical church. One other committee
not mentioned in the Constitution but authorized in the By-
Laws gives occasion for a further characterization: the United
Church of Christ is a forward-looking church, for surely no
church to which the past is all and the future nothing would
appoint a Long-Range Planning Committee. This Committee
at the time of its appointment was, I believe, unique in American ecclesiastical organization, though since that time others
have recognized the potential usefulness of its functions and
appointed similar bodies for their branches of the church.
The functions in general are to protect the church from
senescence—a condition to which all institutions have an
inveterate tendency. The Long-Range Planning Committee
consists of people chosen for their objectivity, their sense of
churchmanship, and above all their knowledge of the world.
They are asked to make a continuous study of the needs of
people at home and abroad, and in the light of the conclu-
sions to which they come, develop long-range plans with the

boards to keep the church and its agencies not merely busy on the unfinished tasks of yesterday but also alive to the new duties of tomorrow.

The Long-Range Planning Committee, looking into the future, proposes to make enquiry about many of the matters we have treated in this book—about the role of lay people in the church, for instance; about the proper training for the ordained ministry; about the responsibilities which devolve upon a "uniting church"; about the better stewardship of the church's resources; about higher education viewed from a Christian standpoint. The background of the enquiry will be the changing contemporary culture. How can the church penetrate this effectively? Is the church listening sufficiently to, sufficiently aware of, the vast movements of our time which are molding the minds and souls of men? New disciplines like sociology and demography are contributing knowledge about such matters as the depersonalization of human beings in the population explosion: is the church prepared to apply this knowledge? New nationalisms are appearing around the world, and non-Christian religions are resurgent: is the Gospel being cast in a framework which is intelligible and available to modern man? The United States is becoming, along its eastern seaboard, one vast city; the church has flourished in the suburbs but perished in the inner cities; do we need to develop a new urban churchmanship?

These questions being asked by the United Church through its Long-Range Planning Committee indicate something of the character of the church. The answers to the questions are, to be sure, in the hands of God alone, but the United Church, believing that he is likeliest to impart his answer to those who study and enquire, looks toward the future with an open and eager mind which combines, paradoxically, uncertainty and confidence.

CHAPTER XIX

AND SO, GOOD READER . . .

W<small>E HAVE COME TO THE END OF OUR JOURNEY TOGETHER, NOT,</small>
I hope, without profit. I have been discussing why I am a
United Churchman, and in order to do so I have given you
a great many facts about the United Church with some hint
at the belief and spirit which inform the facts. I am a United
Churchman because, in general, I like the facts, but most
especially because I like the belief and spirit—and, after all,
it is by its belief and spirit that a church must be judged.
George Tyrrell said before he died, "God will not ask us,
What sort of Church have you lived in? but, What sort of
Church have you longed for?" This is also the question he will
ask of each church: What sort of church have you yearned
to be? I think I am a United Churchman not so much because
of what the United Church is—for heaven knows that it is full
of us human beings with unlovely traits—as because of what,
in its best, its most clairvoyant moments, it desires to be.

It desires no salvation for itself apart from the rest of the
world: it seeks no exclusive future; it does not believe that
the universe is tilted in its favor—and none of its forms point
that way. The United Church realizes that it is continually
being dragged down by its human contacts to the status of
an ordinary society, but this it is determined not to be, since

278

it works under the blistering light of the mandate: Be ye perfect, even as your heavenly father is perfect.

The United Church prays that its statistics may show that it is alive and growing but that they may never become its idol. Statistics may even expand like an inflamed appendix while the patient dies. It seeks not proud numbers nor bulging church buildings but rather a full and gorgeous faith.

A member of one of the congregations of the United Church, William Ernest Hocking, asked a set of questions a number of years ago which the United Church does not cease to ask of itself:

Which religion, in its account of the need and lostness of the human heart, can get farthest beyond platitudes and mere general lament, into the region of the literal struggle of human life with evil, sordidness, and that blight of meaninglessness which besets human success no less than human failure?

Which religion does in fact most verifiably save men from greed, lust, and hatred, and without destroying their virility and effectiveness as members of race and social order?

Which religion is most fertile?

Which religion is most fertile in men?

And which religion, while thus serving the public life of its time can best retain its own proud authority?

The United Church believes that this religion is Christianity at its best, and seeks to cultivate it.

The United Church is no devotee of the indecisive. It knows where it intends to go, but all the while it realizes that the final decision as to its destiny will always be God's. As the Chinese proverb has it: a thousand poles to push the boat and two thousand oars to row it are not as good as a tattered sail. The two thousand times a thousand members of the United Church of Christ try to keep it on its way, but they also lift a sail toward God and pray that he will fill it with his gracious wind.

BIBLIOGRAPHY

ABBA, RAYMOND. *Principles of Christian Worship.* New York, Oxford University Press, 1957. This book sets forth the standards of public worship in Reformed Churchmanship, especially in the Congregational tradition.

ARNDT, ELMER J. F. *The Faith We Proclaim.* Philadelphia, Christian Education Press, 1960. A most readable presentation of the theology of the Evangelical and Reformed Church.

ATKINS, GAIUS GLENN. *An Adventure in Liberty.* Boston, Pilgrim Press, 1961. A very brief history of the Congregational Christian Churches.

BOARDS AND COUNCILS OF THE UNITED CHURCH OF CHRIST. *Annual Reports.* United Church of Christ, 297 Park Avenue South, New York 10. Invaluable for description of contemporary activities.

Book of Worship. St. Louis, Eden Publishing House, 1947. The services commonly used in the Evangelical and Reformed Church.

COMMUNICATION, OFFICE OF. *Releases.* Office of Communication, 289 Park Avenue South, New York 10. For all stop-press news of the United Church of Christ.

Constitution and By-Laws of the Evangelical and Reformed Church. 1959. Evangelical and Reformed Church, 1505 Race Street, Philadelphia 2. The practices and procedures of one of the communions forming the United Church of Christ.

Constitution and By-Laws of the United Church of Christ. 1961. United Church of Christ, 297 Park Avenue South, New York 10. Available in brochure form.

DOUGLASS, TRUMAN B. *Mission to America.* New York, Friendship Press, 1951. Excellent background for Christian work in our own country.

DUNN, DAVID, ED. *History of the Evangelical and Reformed Church,* Philadelphia, Christian Education Press, 1961. The definitive volume on the subject.

281

GOODSELL, FRED FIELD. *You Shall Be My Witnesses*. Boston, American Board of Commissioners of Foreign Missions, 1959. An interpretation of the history of the oldest foreign missionary board in the country.

HALLER, WILLIAM. *The Rise of Puritanism*. New York, Harper & Bros., 1957. A historical account by an expert.

HINKE, WILLIAM J. *Ministers of the German Reformed Congregations in Pennsylvania and Other Colonies in the Eighteenth Century*. Lancaster, Pa., Historical Commission of the Evangelical and Reformed Church, 1951. A historical approach—to be had from the Evangelical and Reformed Church, 1505 Race Street, Philadelphia 2.

JENKINS, DANIEL. *Strangeness of the Church*. Garden City, N.Y., Doubleday, 1955. A view of the Christian Church by a Congregational thinker at home in both Britain and America.

MAURER, OSCAR E. *Manual of the Congregational Christian Churches*. Boston, Pilgrim Press, 1951. The nearest these churches, which also had part in forming the United Church of Christ, came to a Constitution and By-Laws.

NIEBUHR, H. R. *The Purpose of the Church and its Ministry*. New York, Harper, 1956. Reflections on the aims of theological education.

NORTON, JOHN. *The Answer*. Translated from the Latin by D. Horton. Cambridge, Harvard University Press, 1958. A goldmine of information on the principles and practices of the New England churches of the first generation.

RICHARDS, GEORGE W. *History of the Theological Seminary in Lancaster*. Lancaster, Pa., Theological Seminary of the Evangelical and Reformed Church. An excellent history of the Reformed part of the Evangelical and Reformed Church.

ROUNER, ARTHUR A., JR. *The Congregational Way of Life*. Englewood Cliffs, N.J., Prentice-Hall, Inc., 1960. An intimate view of the gathered church by a parish minister familiar with the history and principles of Congregationalism.

SAYRES, A. N., AND STANGER, R. C. *March on with Strength*. Philadelphia, Christian Education Press, 1953. Vignettes from the history of the Evangelical and Reformed Church.

SPIKE, ROBERT W. *In But Not of the World*. New York, Association Press, 1957. *Safe in Bondage*. New York, Friendship Press, 1960. Two most readable books on the life and outlook of the churches seen by an observant and scholarly officer of the Board for World Ministries.

STEWARDSHIP COUNCIL. *Publications*. Stewardship Council of the United Church of Christ, 1505 Race Street, Philadelphia 2. These materials, chiefly in brochure form, are unexcelled in their understanding of the purposes and ongoing enterprises of the church.

INDEX

academies, 248

Africa, 218ff

Alexandrian custom, 143

Alliance of Reformed Churches, 183

amendments, 270

American Bible Society, 183

American Board of Commissioners for Foreign Missions, 196, 222

American Home Missionary Society, 35

American Missionary Association, 38, 227

Anabaptist Movement, 100f

ancestry of United Church of Christ, 13ff, 17, 22, 33ff, 72, 125ff, 144

Anderson, Leila, 231

Angola, 220

Antichrist, 45

Apostles' Creed, 58, 64f, 93

apostolic succession, 115f, 118

Article I of Constitution, 108, 112

Article II of Constitution, 112

Article III of Constitution, 113

Article IV of Constitution, 117, 120, 123, 125, 131ff

Article V of Constitution, 138f, 146, 151, 158, 164ff

Article VI of Constitution, 177ff, 183

Article VII of Constitution, 177ff, 183

Article VIII of Constitution, 193, 226, 242, 255, 259, 261, 266ff

Article IX of Constitution, 270

Article X of Constitution, 271

arts, fine, 243f

Associations, 98, 103f, 112, 116, 132f, 136, 139ff, 143f, 163f, 166ff, 170ff, 179, 190, 259, 271

Associations, Congregational Christian, 14, 169

Athanasian Creed, 58

Augsburg Confession, 36, 59

Augustine, St., 12, 28, 96, 150

Auler, H. N. Jr., 221

Bainton, Roland Herbert, 83

baptism, 87, 89f, 123f

Baptist Churches, 36f, 89

Basis of Union and Interpretations, 18, 30, 65, 67

Beecher, Lyman, 83

Bellamy, Joseph, 83

Bennett, John Coleman, 83

Bible, 46ff, 51f, 59, 76, 93, 125, 145, 149, 263

Boards,—see under several names

Boehm, John Philip, 34, 96

burial, 156
Bushnell, Horace, 83
Business Management, Board of, 227
By-Laws of United Church of Christ,
132, 164f, 171, 175, 192, 194,
246, 267, 271, 276

Calhoun, Robert Lowry, 83
Calvin, John, 34, 59, 92, 96, 127,
138, 266
Calvinism, 14, 22, 34, 37, 60, 189
Cambridge Platform, 14
Cambridge Synod, 14, 23
Charlemagne, 266
China, 214
Christian Church, 15, 36f, 60, 181
Christian Education and Publication,
Board of, 227
Christian Social Action, Council for,
254ff
Christian Unity and Ecumenical
Study and Service, Commission
on, 274f
Church and Ministry, Council for,
259f
Church Building Society, Congre-
gational, 227
church extension, 229ff
Church Finance Advisory Service,
236f
church meetings, 122f
Church of England, 21, 37, 39, 93,
104, 126, 129f, 159, 186
Church of South India, 11
Church of Sweden, 21, 93
church union negotiations, promise
and pitfalls, 17
city work, 232ff
Clement VII, 185
colleges, 247
commissioned workers, 139, 166
Commission on World Service, 196,
222, 253
Communication, Office of, 84, 266f
Community Churches, 184, 275
Conferences, 98, 103f, 112, 132f,
136, 141, 143, 165ff, 168ff, 190,
231, 255, 259, 268f, 270f
Conferences, Congregational Christian, 13f, 25, 133, 169
confession of sin, 157f
confirmation, 64, 123f, 152
Congregational Christian Churches,
13, 15ff, 20, 22ff, 26f, 29f, 32f,
36, 38, 40, 114, 121, 125, 131,
133f, 152, 168, 181, 183, 246,
250, 271
Congregational Churches, 14ff, 22,
36ff, 62, 119f, 142, 144, 154,
159, 181
Congregational element, 142, 190
Congregationalism, 17, 20, 31, 37,
60, 74, 130, 173, 183, 186
Congregational Methodist Churches,
38
congregations, 69f, 73, 104, 117ff,
120f, 123, 135f, 161
Constitution, 13ff, 19, 42, *passim*
Constitution of the United States, 13,
16, 25
Councils—see under several names
counseling, pastoral, 154, 157ff
covenant, church, 119
Covenant of Grace, 52ff, 90f, 94, 102,
115, 118f, 126f, 130, 135, 154,
262f
Convention, 169
creeds, 58, 60ff
Cromwell, Oliver, 57
Cyprian, St., 125

Date, effective, 271
Decius, Nicolaus, 74
Disciples of Christ, 37, 184, 275
Dort, Synod of, 24
Dwight, Timothy, 83

Eastern Orthodox Church, 39, 46, 87,
126, 129, 152f, 157
ecumenical movement, 35, 39, 181,
183ff, 193

Eden Theological Seminary, 36
education, 193, 241f, 246
Education Society, Congregational, 227
Edwards, Jonathan, 82
Eliot, John, 38
Elmhurst College, 36
Emmonds, Nathaniel, 83
Episcopal element, 114ff, 190
Episcopalianism, 17, 20
Europe, missions in, 224f
Evangelical Protestant Church, 38
Evangelical and Reformed Church, 13, 15ff, 20ff, 26f, 29f, 32f, 35f, 38, 40, 59, 114, 120f, 125, 131, 133, 152, 154, 168, 181, 183, 246, 251 271
Evangelical and Reformed Synods, 25
Evangelical Synod of North America, 24, 34f, 59
evangelism, 227ff
Executive Council, 179f, 197, 252, 254, 259, 261, 266, 268, 270f
extreme unction, 157

faith of the historic church, 23, 50, 68, 86
Falkner Swamp, 34, 90
Ferré, Nels Fredrik Solomon, 83
Fisher, G. F., 191
Franck, César, 74
Franklin and Marshall College, 35
Free Christian Churches, 181
Friends, Society of, 89, 109, 258

General Council, Congregational Christian, 14, 17, 26, 30, 33, 133
General Synod, 24, 65, 98, 100, 102ff, 112, 133, 136, 140, 168f, 171f, 177ff, 187, 194, 196f, 226, 243, 245, 174ff, 252ff, 259, 261, 266ff, 270ff
Ghana, 219f
gradualness, 28
Grant, Robert, 74

Greece, 222
Greene, Oramel, 239

Harner, Nevin, 213
Harvard University, 38, 247
headquarters, 181
health and welfare, 249f, 251
Hebrews, 40, 53ff, 57, 128, 130
Heidelberg Catechism, 34, 36, 59f
Henry VIII, 185
Herald of Gospel Liberty, The, 181
Herbster, Ben. M., 27
Hocking, William Ernest, 279
Holy Spirit, 46, 51, 65, 125, 148, 273
Homberg, Synod of, 24
Homeland Ministries, Board for, 134, 180, 226ff, 242ff, 246, 255
Home Missionary Society, Congregational, 227
Home Missions of the Reformed Church in the United States, Board of, 227
Honduras, 221
Hopkins, Samuel, 83
Horton, Walter Marshall, 83

Ignatius, St., 113
India, 216f
Indonesia, 215
Instrumentalities, 193ff
International Congregational Council, 183
International Missions, Board of, 196, 222

Japan, 210f
Jones, Abner, 181

Kethe, William, 74
Korea, 216

laity, 142f, 261ff
Lancaster Theological Seminary, 35
language, ecclesiastical, 23
Laud, William, 22
law, 30f, 33

Lay Life and Work, Council for, 261f
Lay Ministers, 166f
laying on of hands, 143
learned ministry, 148f
Lebanon, 223
Licentiates, 140
litigation, 26f, 31
Long-Range Planning Committee, 276f
Lord's Supper, 87, 89, 91, 94ff, 182
loyalties, 21
Luther, Martin, 35, 59, 91f, 96, 127, 138, 185
Lutheran Church, 159
Lutheranism, 35, 60, 74, 93, 127, 185, 189
Luther's Catechism, 36, 59f

marriage, 153ff
Melanchthon, Philipp, 59
Mercersberg Academy, 35
Mercersberg Movement, 78, 95, 245
Methodism, 36f, 127, 189, 191
Mexico, 221
Micronesia, 213f
Minear, Paul Sevier, 83
Minister's Quarterly, 259
Ministry, 75ff, 138ff, 146, 159ff, 164f, 259
missionary theology, 197ff
Morikasa, Isamu, 213
music, 73

name: United Church of Christ, 11, 108ff
National Council of the Churches of Christ in the United States, 11, 39, 181, 183, 275f
National Missions, Board of, 227
Nevin, John Williamson, 78, 95
New England Theology, 83
Nicene Creed, 58, 64, 67, 93
Niebuhr, Helmut Richard, 83f
Nollau, Louis, 96
Norton, John, 75

office bearers of the United Church, 28, 113ff, 153, 178f
O'Kelly, Thomas, 36
Okinawa, 216
Olevianus, Caspar, 60
ordination, 63f, 139f, 142, 144, 153
ordination of women, 144ff
Owen, John, 75

Pauck, Wilhelm, 83
Peace Corps, 203
penance, 157f
pension and relief activities, 251
Pentecostalism, 189
Philippine Islands, 213
Pilgrim Fathers, 37, 96, 250
Plan of Union, 15
Plymouth, 37, 250
politics, 19f
Pope, Liston, 83
prayers, 75f
preaching, 77
Preamble of Constitution, 17, 42, 45f, 50, 58, 67, 85, 98
Presbyterian elements, 33, 133, 142, 190
Presbyterianism, 17, 20, 22, 31, 36f, 74, 127, 173, 183, 186, 189
Press, United Church, 240
privilege of call, 166
Protestant Episcopal Church, 114, 189, 275
Publishing Society, Congregational, 227
Puritans, 37, 72f, 75, 104, 154, 185, 243f, 250
purposes of the United Church, 42ff

race relations, 162f, 170, 173, 237ff
Rauch, Frederick Augustus, 78
reading, public, 76
Reformation, 34f, 40, 63, 70, 91, 95, 152
Reformatusok Lapja, 180
Reformed Churches of Europe, 34f, 60, 72, 74, 83, 93, 159, 173, 185

Reformed Church in the United States, 24, 34, 78
Renaissance, 80, 185
Rhodesia, 219
rites, 151f
Roman Catholic Church, 39, 45f, 60, 84, 87, 93, 126, 129, 182, 185
Rome, Synod of, 23f

sacraments, 87, 91, 93, 97, 152
Salem, 119
Saybrook Synod, 23
Schaff, Philip, 78, 95
Schroer, Gilbert W., 213
science, 79f
Servetus, 23
Service Committee, Congregational Christian, 196, 222
Smith, Elias, 181
social action, 255f
Söderblom, Nathan, 20
Statement of Faith, 65ff
stewardship, 267f
Stewardship Council, 267f
Stone, Barton W., 37
Students in Care of Association, 139
Sunday School Extension Society, Congregational, 227
Synods, Evangelical and Reformed, 169
Syria, 223

Talmage, T. DeWitt, 150
Temple, William, 39, 197
Tersteegen, Gerhardt, 74
Theological Commission, 272
theological schools, 248f, 260
thought, Christian, 78ff, 84, 147ff
Tillich, Paul, 84

town and country work, 231f
treasury, 181
Turkey, 223
Tyrrell, George, 278

United Church of Canada, 11
United Church Herald, 180f
United Nations Educational, Scientific, and Cultural Organization, 203
unity and diversity, 99ff, 132, 141, 177, 187f
Ursinus, Zacharias, 60

Watts, Isaac, 74
Wesley, John, 104, 127, 186
Western Church, 40, 83, 89, 104, 129, 152f, 157, 159
Westminster Assembly, 60
Westminster Confession, 60
Wilder, Amos Niven, 84
Williams, Philip E., 213
Williams, Roger, 101
Wise, John, 14
Woman's Home Missionary Federation, Congregational, 227
Word of God, 46ff, 187
world confessional bodies, 181f
World Council of Churches, 20, 42, 145, 181, 183, 188, 275f
World Ministries, Board for, 134, 196, 198, 243, 255
Worship, 64, 67ff, 120, 158, 241
Worship, Commission on, 273f

Yale University, 38, 247

Zwingli, Ulrich, 59, 92, 96

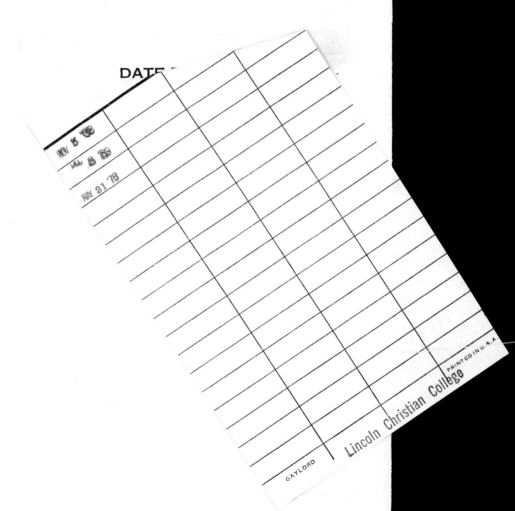